The Baptist Missionary Handbook
A Biblical, Historical, and Practical Guide

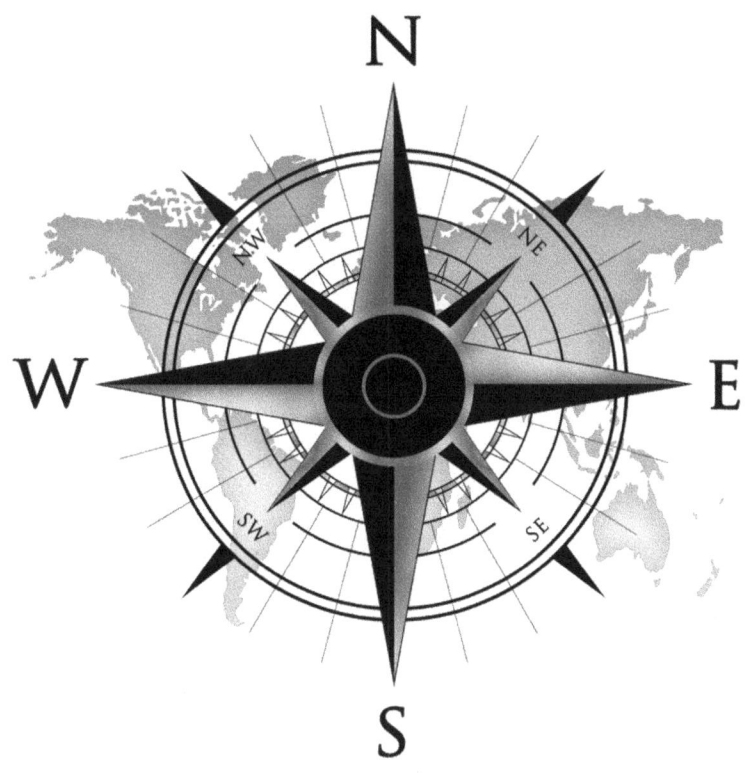

The Baptist Missionary Handbook
A Biblical, Historical, and Practical Guide

Danny S. Jones, Th.D.

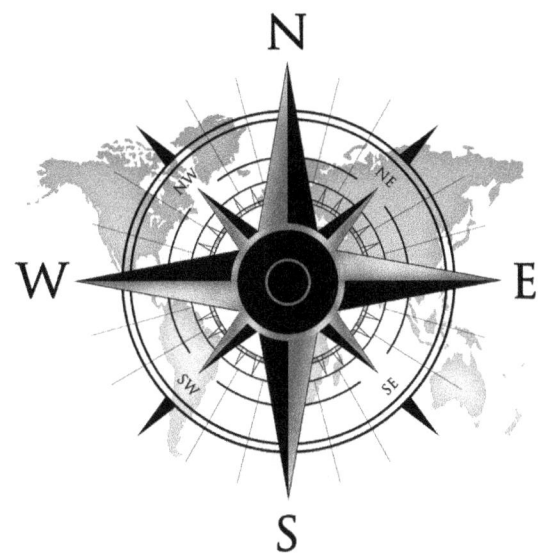

BAPTIST TRAINING CENTER PUBLICATIONS
WINTER HAVEN, FLORIDA

Copyright © 2017 by Danny S. Jones
All rights reserved. No part of this publication may be reproduced, distributed, or transmitted in any form or by any means without the express written permission of the publisher except in the case of brief quotations embodied in critical reviews and certain other noncommercial uses permitted by copyright law.

First Edition: 2017
Printed in the United States of America

Baptist Training Center Publications
A ministry of:
Westwood Missionary Baptist Church
3210 Ave. G NW
Winter Haven, FL
www.baptisttrainingcenter.org

Library of Congress Control Number 2017911219
Jones, Danny S., 1976 –
The Baptist Missionary Handbook: A Biblical, Historical, and Practical Guide / Danny S. Jones
ISBN: 978-1-947598-00-3 (paperback)
ISBN: 978-1-947598-04-1 (hardcover)
ISBN: 978-1-947598-03-4 (e-book)

All Scripture quotations are taken from the King James Version

Cover photo courtesy of Frank A. Gutierrez, taken in a dugout canoe on the Orinoco River, Puerto Inirida, Colombia.

CONTENTS

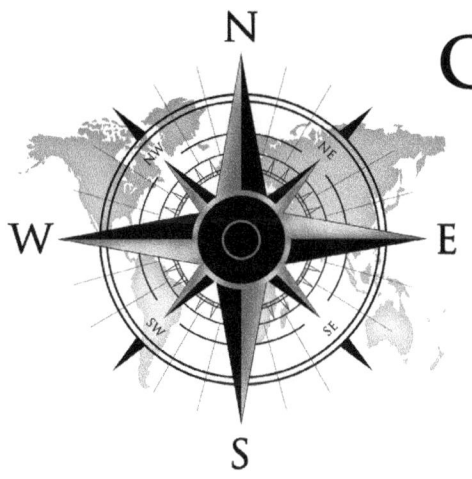

DEDICATION 13

PREFACE 15

INTRODUCTION 19

1 MISSIOLOGY 27
    Definition of Missiology 27
    The Necessity of the Study of Mission Work 29
    Surrendering Our All to the Lord 30
    The Need for Mission Work 32
    Mission: The Lifeblood of the Local Church 35

2 WHAT IS A MISSIONARY? 37
    The Definition of the Word "Missionary" 37
    The Biblical Pattern of the Missionary 41
    Is Everyone a Missionary? 45
    Are There Other Types of Missionaries? 45

3 THEOLOGY OF MISSION WORK 47
    The Theological Discipline of Missiology 47
    Missio Dei: The Mission of God 48
    Theological Considerations of Mission Work 50
    Mission or Missions? 52

4   Ecclesiology of Mission Work.............................55
    The History of "Church"..55
    Basic Tenants of Scriptural Church Doctrine.....................57
    Biblical Church Authority.......................................59
    The Source of Church Authority..................................60
    God's Executor..63
    Delegation of Church Authority..................................63
    Corporate Authority...64
    Biblical Church Mission Work....................................67
    The Responsibility of the Church to the Missionary..............67
        Spiritual Support..68
        Physical Support...69
        Emotional Support..70
        Financial Support..73
    The Responsibility of the Missionary to the Church..............77
        Subjection...77
        Communication..79
        Representation...80

5   Biblical Basis of Mission Work................................83
    Survey of Mission Work in the Old Testament.....................83
        Mission Through the Preaching of Noah......................84
        Abraham: The First Cross-cultural Missionary...............85
        Mission Through the Biblical Type of the Exodus............87
        Joshua: The Missionary Conqueror...........................87
        David: The Missionary King.................................88
        Mission Through the Testimony of Solomon...................89
        Mission Through the Symbolism of the Tabernacle............90
        Psalms: The Missionary Hymnbook............................92
        Jonah: The Reluctant Missionary............................94
        Israel: The Light to the Gentile Nations...................95
    Survey of Mission Work in the Gospels...........................96
        The Seeking of that which was Lost.........................97
        The Saving of that which was Lost..........................97
    The Gospel Message and the Sin Curse............................99
    The Missionary Heart of Christ..................................99
    The Great Commission of the Church.............................101
    Missionary Methods in the Book of Acts.........................103

    Establish the Calling *104*
    Be Sent Through a Local Church *104*
    Work as a Team *106*
    Work with Known Contacts *107*
    Begin in Large Population Centers *108*
    Be Bold yet Wise to Opposition *109*
    Work with Those Who are Responsive *110*
    Plant Churches as People are Converted *112*
    Confirm the Souls of the Disciples *114*
    Ordain Leaders in Every Church *114*
    Teach Principles of Autonomy *115*
    Return for Furlough *117*
    Continue Discipleship with Believers *118*

6   Mission Work in the First Century A.D. 123
    Apostolic Mission Work 123
    Andrew 124
    Philip 124
    The Brethren of the Lord 127
    James the Less 130
    Matthew 131
    Thomas 131
    Bartholomew 132
    Thaddaeus 132
    Simon the Zealot 133
    John the Beloved 133
    Paul 134
    Peter 136

7   Post Apostolic Mission Work 139
    Early Mission Work to the Rise of Catholicism 139
    The Rise of the Roman Catholic Church 142
    Eastern Churches Reject Roman Rule 144
    Persecution as a Stimulus for Mission Work 145
        Persecution of Nero *145*
        Flavian Persecution *146*
        Trajanic Persecution *147*
        Hadrianic Persecution *147*

8 THE BAPTIST MISSIONARY HANDBOOK

Persecution of Marcus Aurelius 147
Persecution of Maximinus 148
Persecution of Decius 148
Persecution of Valerian 148
Diocletianic Persecution 149
Persecution of Galerius 149

8 CHURCH PERPETUITY THROUGH MISSION WORK 151
The Spread of Christianity Throughout the East 151
The Novatians 154
The Donatists 154
The Paulicians 155
The Petrobrussians, Arnoldists, and Henricians 156
The Waldenses 157
Other Names given to True Churches 158

9 MODERN BAPTIST MISSION WORK 163
The Father of Modern Mission Work 164
The First Baptist Missionary from America 166
The Organization of Baptists in America 169
The Southern Baptist Convention 171
Landmarkism: A Return to Biblical Mission Work 171
Associations of Landmark Baptist Churches 175
Independent Baptist Churches 177

10 ESTABLISHING THE CALL OF A MISSIONARY 181
The Commission Verses the Call 181
Principles of the Calling of God 182
The Principle of the Faithful Servant 182
The Principle of the Seeking Servant 183
The Principle of the Sacrificial Servant 184
The Principle of the Willing Servant 186
The Desire to Do Mission Work 188
Confirmation of a Specific Calling 189
Ability Versus Availability 190
Assessing the Character of the Missionary 191
A Personal Walk with God 192
Spiritual Discipline 193

   Self-Discipline 194
   Personal and Spiritual Maturity 195
   Moral Purity 196
   Personal and Family Wholeness 197
   A Servant's Attitude 198
   Teachability 199
   Adaptability 199
   Compassion for Others 200
   Identifying and Implementing Spiritual Gifts 201
 Knowledge and Skill Assessment 203
   Biblical and Theological Knowledge 203
   Culture, Geography and Demographics 203
   Communication 204
   Ministry Experience 205
   Leadership, Servanthood, and Discipleship 206
   The Faith Aspect of Mission Work 207
 Four Principles of Faith 208
   The Principle of God's Presence 208
   The Principle of God's Provision 209
   The Principle of God's Protection 210
   The Principle of God's Power 212

11 DEPUTATION AND FUND RAISING 215
 Ministry Presentation and Fund Raising 215
 Missionary Reports and Letter Writing 217
   The Title 217
   The Masthead 218
   Grammar and Spelling 218
   Section Breaks 220
   Font (Type Style) 220
   Headlines 220
   Graphics and Photographs 220
   Captions 221
   Design 221
   Simplicity 221
   Readability 222
   Consistency 222
 Prayer Cards, Bookmarks, Magnets, etc. 222

10 THE BAPTIST MISSIONARY HANDBOOK

    Public Speaking Techniques of Deputation 223
    The Missionary Display 226
    Deputation Logistics 227
    Missionary Video Production 228
    Missionary Website Production 229
    Online Media Strategies 229

12 THE CROSS-CULTURAL MISSIONARY 231
    Culture and Worldview 231
    Cultural Bias and Acculturation 232
        Assimilation 233
        Separation 234
        Marginalization 234
        Integration 235
    Hot Climate Versus Cold Climate Cultures 235
    Direct vs Indirect Communication 237
    Individualism vs. Collectivism 238
    Inclusive vs Exclusive Cultures 239
    Cultural Concepts of Hospitality 241
    Monochronic vs. Polychronic Cultures 242
    Past, Present or Future Oriented Cultures 243
    High vs Low Context Cultures 244
    Cultural Contextualization vs Religious Syncretism 246
    Culture shock and Cultural Stress 248

13 MISSIONARY PRACTICALITIES 251
    The Missionary Field Survey 251
    Shipping and Shopping Overseas 252
    Field Survey Checklist 253
    Housing and Living Conditions 254
    Teaching English as a Second Language 256
    Missionary Kids on the Foreign Field 257
    Hospitals, Medication and Diseases 257
    Mental and Emotional Health 258
        Compassion Fatigue 260
        Intervention Strategies 262
    Furlough and Reverse Culture Shock 263

Evangelistic Strategies in Mission Work 264
Autonomous, Reproducible Churches 267

BIBLIOGRAPHY 271

INDEX 287

List of Figures

Figure 1. Missionary Insights: Surrendering Our All to the Lord 30

Figure 2. Statistics of world evangelism in 2017 33

Figure 3. Missionary Insights: Keeping Focus 39

Figure 4. Missionary Insights: Discovering the True Meaning
of Mission Work 58

Figure 5. Missionary Insights: Pray for Your Missionaries! 71

Figure 6. An example of receipt and distribution of a
missionary's financial support 75

Figure 7. Missionary Insights: A Special Care Package 76

Figure 8. Missionary Insights: The Lord Changed His Heart 81

Figure 9. Missionary Insights: Truth Hurts 86

Figure 10. Missionary Insights: Which Way Are You Walking? 93

Figure 11. Biblical Steps of Mission Work in the Book of Acts 105

Figure 12. The First Christian Martyrs 125

Figure 13. Map of the evangelization of Western Europe in
the first century AD 126

Figure 14. Missionary journeys of the apostles in the Middle East. 129

Figure 15. Dates from historical records showing the spread of Christianity
in Northern Africa, Gaul, Hispania, and Bithynia 141

Figure 16. Map listing the dates of a significant Christian
population in the selected areas 143

Figure 17. A list of Roman persecution of Christianity by date and the
emperor under which the persecution occurred 146

Figure 18.	An antoninianus (double denarius) coin of emperor Diocletian	149
Figure 19.	A map charting the spread of Christianity in the Far East during the early centuries of mission work	153
Figure 20.	Names given to Baptist groups throughout Europe, Asia, and Africa	159
Figure 21.	A list of early Baptist churches in America	170
Figure 22.	Missionary Insights: Obedience and Willingness	187
Figure 23.	Missionary Insights: Examining my Spiritual Condition	194
Figure 24.	Missionary Insights: I Shall Not Slide	202
Figure 25.	The Four Principles of Faith	208
Figure 26.	A sample newsletter showing the basic essential design segments in a typical layout.	219
Figure 27.	Deputation Tips	225
Figure 28.	Missionary Insights: Politely Refuse Before Accepting	238
Figure 29.	Missionary Insights: Inclusive Means Never Alone	240
Figure 30.	Missionary Insights: Don't Split the Check	242
Figure 31.	Field Survey Checklist	253
Figure 32.	Missionary Insights: The Importance of a Survey Trip	255
Figure 33.	Personality Assessment Tests	259
Figure 34.	Disorders assessed in mental health screening	259
Figure 35.	Missionary Insights: Finding a Love for Souls	261
Figure 36.	Six Methods of Missionary Evangelism	265
Figure 37.	Missionary Insights: A Lesson Learned	266
Figure 38.	Missionary Insights: Depend on the Lord, Not the Missionary	268

Dedication

Dedicated to the men who have given their lives to the propagation of the gospel of Jesus Christ, the faithful women who have sacrificed so much to stand beside them, and the families of those who go. May God bless you on your journey!

Danny S. Jones

Preface

The work of the mission of God, to seek and to save that which is lost, is the subject of this book, and has been my passion over the course of the past sixteen years that I have labored both on the foreign mission field and in the field of missionary training. I have found few other works spanning the scope of Biblical, historical and practical principles of mission work as it should be conducted through local churches, and have written this book to fill that void. In undertaking this monumental task, I, no doubt, will fail in touching on every pertinent subject that a missionary ought to know. Having served on the foreign mission field, I can certainly say that many lessons that must be learned and much of the knowledge that is required of a missionary can only be obtained by experience. Ink on a page may be able to tell a missionary that he must have faith and reliance in God, but only experience can teach it.

The theme of this book is to present a comprehensive work on the topic of mission work and missionary training through Biblical foundations, theological insights, historical context, and practical implementation of scripturally sound principles. This subject was chosen for several reasons. First, there is a lack of comprehensive, Biblically sound material on the subject, and because of that deficiency in material, many Baptist seminaries have elected not to teach missiology as a part of their curriculum. As a missionary, and having spoken to many other veteran missionaries, a consensus has been formed desiring that the principles of mission work be taught in a structured and comprehensive format. This plea from missionaries has come from the desire to fill that void in education. The wish of each veteran missionary is that new missionaries might not have to make the same mistakes in learning these principles, but that they may be taught before moving to the field. Because of the immense scope of the subject, this book is limited to the most rudimentary of topics on mission work. If all the research that has been put into this book were to be written on paper, it would no doubt be ten times the length. However, to present the subject matter in an ordered fashion as it should be taught in a missionary training school, the subjects appear in the following three sections:

1. A Biblical and Theological Survey of Mission Work

2. A Historical Survey of Mission Work Throughout the Ages

3. A Practical Guide to Modern Mission Work

In the pages that follow, I have sometimes digressed, to occasionally include personal anecdotes related to the topic of missionary training and preparation. This is quite necessary because the topic of this book includes material that must be mentioned from personal experience and practical research which can only be found outside of the bounds of the written page. Much of the practical information presented here is not found in any work of literature. My hope is that this work will add to the body of knowledge of the study of missiology, and will expand the material available to schools, missionaries, and churches who are actively carrying out the Great Commission of Jesus Christ.

Over the course of my research over the past several years, this work has taken shape in a way that has not only opened my own eyes to the scope of the mission of God, but also transformed my life, my ministry, and my knowledge of the work of the Lord. It is my prayer that these pages will be a blessing to all who read it, will instill a greater respect for the missionaries who came before us, and will ignite a flame of passion for the lost world around us. Whether a prospective missionary, a veteran missionary, a pastor, minister or church member, every Christian has a part to play in the global drama of God's plan: to go, to send, to support and to pray. May we all do our part.

Danny S. Jones, Th.D.
Missionary to Thailand

Introduction

As I stepped onto the foreign field for the first time, the daunting task in front of me seemed almost insurmountable. I knew it would take a lot of hard work, but I wasn't sure where to begin. My prayer is that this handbook will be a helpful study in your personal journey in mission work and a head start in the right direction for those headed to the field.

The goal of mission work is for all the world to call upon the name of the one true Lord and God of the universe. Right now, most of the world is calling upon somebody or something else for their needs, for their comfort, and for their salvation. Some call on Buddha. Some call on Allah. Some call on evil spirits. Some call on money. Some call on themselves. But the One the world needs to call upon is the one true God.

Who is the One that the world needs? Who is this Savior that the gospel proclaims? He's the one who created earth, the moon, and the stars. He's the One who put the fish in the sea, the birds in the air, and the animals in the forest. He's the One who breathed life into the nostrils of man and made him a living soul. He's the One who called out to a lost humanity and promised a Redeemer.

He's the One that Abraham followed to the promised land. He's the One that Isaac trusted to take his place on the altar. He's the One that Jacob wrestled with until dawn. He's the One that spoke to Moses in the burning bush; the One that brought the plagues down upon the Pharaoh of Egypt; the One that helped Joshua conquer the land of Canaan; the One that David praised in the Book of Psalms; the One that gave wisdom to Solomon; the One that Daniel prayed to in the den of lions; the One that walked in the fire with the Hebrew children; the One that came down in human flesh from His throne in glory; the One that was born of a virgin under a miraculous star in a little village called Bethlehem. He's the One who lived a sinless life. He's the One who performed miracles, turned water into wine, healed the lame, gave hearing to the deaf, restored sight to the blind, fed the multitudes, brought the dead back to life, and calmed the sea. He's the One who went to the cross for your sin and mine. He's the One who was beaten, spat upon, mocked, crowned with thorns, and crucified. He's the One who bore the sin of the world and died to set us free. He's the One who went to the tomb and the one who rose again from the dead - conquering death, hell and the grave. He's the One who's coming again! He's the one called Jesus, upon whom, if any person places their trust, they will be saved.

The world needs to call on Him - on Jesus. Not on Buddha; not on Allah; not on Mohammed; not on spirits; not on religion; not on material wealth; and certainly not on self. A Christian's desire should be for the world to call upon Christ because God's desire is for the world to call upon Christ. The mission of the local church: to evangelize the world with the gospel, baptize converts, and indoctrinate them through the planting of churches – all stem from the basic heart's desire of the Lord Himself. God wishes to redeem mankind to Himself so that He can have a relationship with His creation. In essence, the mission of the church is the mission of God. Mission work extends from the heart of the Divine.

In Romans 10:13-18, Paul writes of five simple steps that are necessary in mission work (and it's also a great synopsis of this book): Send, Preach, Hear, Believe, and Call.

> *For whosoever shall call upon the name of the Lord shall be saved. How then shall they call on him in whom they have not believed? and how shall they believe in him of whom they have not heard? and how shall they hear without a preacher? And how shall they preach, except they be sent? as it is written, How beautiful are the feet of them that preach the gospel of peace, and bring glad tidings of good things! But they have not all obeyed the gospel. For Esaias saith, Lord, who hath believed our report? So then faith cometh by hearing, and hearing by the word of God. But I say, Have they not heard? Yes verily, their sound went into all the earth, and their words unto the ends of the world.*

- **The lost can't call upon Jesus until they believe in Jesus**
- **The lost can't believe in Jesus until they hear about Jesus**
- **The lost can't hear about Jesus until someone preaches about Jesus**
- **And someone can't preach about Jesus unless churches are sending them out to preach about Jesus**

SEND

Local churches need to be sending. It is the duty, obligation and purpose of the local church. Mission work is the lifeblood of a church. Without it, churches are dead. The Bible commands churches to "Go... into all the world, and preach the gospel to every creature" (Mark 16:15). Preben Vang put it this way, "The church is not an add-on to the Christian life. Rather, individual Christians live their lives through the church as vital parts of a body. It simply violates the language of Scripture to speak of the church as an organization designed to be a filling station for individual Christians who have need of special encouragement and support." The church is not a social club for Christians, but rather the outlet through which believers may find and carry out the will of God.

PREACH

Preachers need to preach the Word of God. Most of what is preached across the world is all fluff and feathers: feel-good messages with a few stories and some humanistic psychobabble. Preachers of the Word of God need to be just that: preachers of the Word of God. Faith cometh by hearing, and hearing by the Word of God, not some fluffy, feel-good stuff meant to scratch the itching ears of unrepentant sinners. Churches need to get back to the Word of God, preaching it as it is to men as they are, or better yet, preaching it as it is, to show men who they are, and tell them how they ought to be.

HEAR

Preachers can't preach if a church doesn't send them, and people can't hear the word of God unless someone preaches the Word of God. The fact of the matter is, there *is* preaching going on – in churches, over the airwaves, and all around the world. There's preaching all around you. But are you listening to the preaching? Whether you are searching for God or are a seasoned servant of the Lord, do you hear the preaching? When you come to church, do you actively participate, hanging onto the Words of Life that are being given to you from the pulpit? Do you hear? Have you heard that Jesus died for you? Have you heard that He rose from the grave and conquered death? Have you heard that you can believe on Him, confess that He is Lord and have eternal life? Are you listening? Your life, your destiny, your very soul depends on your answer! Are you listening to the most important thing you will ever hear in your life?

Believe

So if you hear, do you believe? Do you believe that Christ is not only the Son of God, but God the Son? Do you believe that you are a sinner on your way to hell without Christ? Do you believe that Jesus is the only way, and that no other god, no other religion, no other sacrifice, no other act of service, nothing, no, nothing else can save you apart from trusting in the finished work of Jesus Christ on the cross? You've got to believe! There's no other way. But, how do you believe? You can't see Him. You can't touch Him. You can't feel Him. There are no means of scientific measurement to prove His existence. How do you believe? Faith is the key. And once you take that step of faith, He starts showing you all kinds of proof; all kinds of evidence. The faith of a Christian has substance. The faith of a Christian has evidence.

Call

After the churches send, after the preachers preach, after the sinners hear the message of the gospel and believe, only then will they call upon His name. Maybe you need to call out to Him to save you today. Maybe you're saved but haven't called on him in a long time. All the missionary effort throughout all the world is focused on this one thing: introducing people to Jesus so that they might call on Him.

The message of the gospel has been preached boldly throughout every generation. Every generation from Christ until now has not only had access to the truth, but have held the true, preserved Word of God and had true, local New Testament churches. The Mormons believe that the world was void of the truth for centuries until Joseph Smith came on the scene in the 1800s. The Protestants believe that the world had only the corrupt Catholic church until they showed up in the 1500s. A lot of Baptists have even bought into that alternative history, thinking that true Baptist churches are just another Johnny-come-lately denomination. Baptists have been around since Jesus started His first church on the seashores of Galilee. (And Christ started that church with disciples who were baptized by a Baptist preacher.) When those disciples went out into all the world, they started more Baptist churches. Now they weren't all called Baptists, that name was given to us by our enemies. They had many names: Christians in Syria, Novatians in Phrygia, Donatists in Africa, Waldenses in the valleys of the Piedmont, Paulicians in Armenia, Petrobrussians and Henricians in France, Albigenses in southern France, Lollards in England, Bogamils in Bulgaria, Cathari in southern Europe, Paterines in Italy, the Chaignards in Dauphine, Tramontani in the Swiss Alps, the Turlepins in Belgium, and all were called Anabaptists by their enemies. But all held to Baptist doctrine.

What did these men have that they could evangelize the whole world in their generation? The answer is simple. They had a personal experience with Jesus Christ. When you have a personal experience with Jesus, you will never be the same. When you have a personal relationship with Jesus, you will begin to think, act, and wish the same things that Christ wants. And what is His most pressing desire for the world? It is that they might call upon Him. So, may churches SEND! May preachers PREACH! May the world HEAR! May the sinner BELIEVE! May each soul CALL upon the name of JESUS CHRIST!

And may YOU (if the Lord is calling) GO! Go, to the ends of the earth to reach the desperate sinner in need of a Savior. Go, to tell them of Jesus. Go, to teach them His Word. Go, to play *your* part in the worldwide mission of God!

PART I

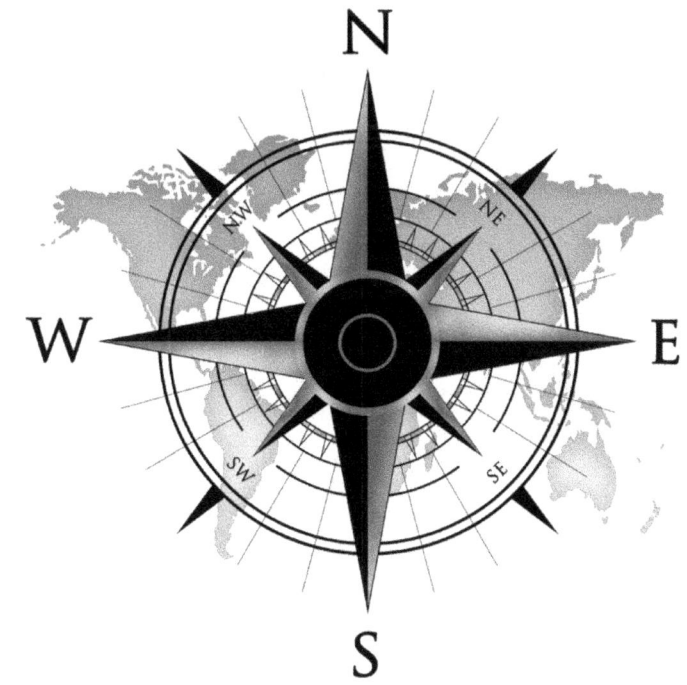

A BIBLICAL AND THEOLOGICAL SURVEY OF MISSION WORK

Chapter One

MISSIOLOGY

Definition of Missiology

Missiology is the study of the practical and theological aspects of Christ's commission to the church to spread the gospel throughout the world. The study of missiology is a study of the meaning of mission work, the message of mission work, the mandate for mission work, the mode of mission work, the means of mission work, and the methodology of mission work.

Success in mission endeavors must begin with a clear understanding of the meaning of mission work. According to Merriam Webster, *mission* is "a specific task with which a person or a group is charged." *Mission* must be properly considered as what is done; an action. *Mission* does not refer to an organization, an assembly, a building, or a person or group of persons. *Mission*, in

> *Missiology is the study of the practical and theological aspects of Christ's commission to the church to spread the gospel throughout the world.*

the strict sense of the term refers to the work of Christ's churches in carrying out the great commission (Dearmore 302).

The message that is carried to the world in the name of Christian mission work is that of the gospel of Jesus Christ. Much humanitarian and social help is done in the name of Christian mission work. Yet no act, no matter how well intended, can be considered mission work apart from the message of the gospel (M. Barnett 166). This message is a simple one that transcends all cultural and political boundaries. The great God of the universe has come to earth to save humanity from sin. God came in the person of Jesus Christ, was born of a virgin, lived a sinless life, and sacrificed His life upon a cross to pay our sin debt. After three days, He conquered death and rose again from the grave. The message of the gospel, or the good news of Jesus Christ, is that anyone who will place their faith in Christ will be saved, forgiven of their sins, placed in the family of God, and given eternal life in heaven with the Lord.

The Great Commission of Christ is the church's mandate for mission work. Given in all four gospels and also in the book of Acts, Matthew 28:19,20 sums up the three main commands of the commission: evangelization (disseminating the gospel message), baptizing the saved (which infers public identification and assembly of local churches), and indoctrination (which is discipleship of believers in the Word of God). An in-depth analysis of the Great Commission is given in chapter four on the Biblical basis of mission work in the Old and New Testament.

Mission work must be done in the proper mode. Paul told Timothy that if a man "strive for masteries, yet is he not crowned except he strive lawfully" (2 Tim. 2:15). In any ordered program, there are rules. Christian mission work is no exception. God has laid down several ground rules in the New Testament for doing mission work that churches must abide. According to Scripture, the proper mode of all ministry and work for the Lord is through the body of Christ, which is a local New Testament church. (Terry, 641).

James Hudson Taylor stated, "God's work done in God's way will never lack God's supplies" (Lyall 37). Worldwide mission work is a faith based enterprise that must rely upon the provision of the Lord. No matter what channel the supply may come from, whether it be individual supporters, local church offerings or "tent making" income through self-employment, all needs of a missionary are met through the providence of God. When a missionary relies upon himself or others to take care of his needs rather than relying on the Lord, the focus is taken from God and faith is left out of the picture. The mission then becomes the enterprise of man and not the work of the Lord.

> *"God's work done in God's way will never lack God's supplies"*
> *- Hudson Taylor*

Biblical mission work can only be correct by using Biblical methodology. Acts chapter thirteen outlines the basic Biblical method of mission work: God called missionaries who are ordained and sent out by a local church, are then led by the Holy Spirit to evangelize, plant churches, and disciple believers (Hesselgrave 97). There are undeniably many other principles and examples in the New Testament that should be followed in conducting mission work according to Biblical methodology which is addressed in chapters four and five.

The Necessity of the Study of Mission Work

At its heart, mission work is the conversion of the lost and education of those new converts into the doctrine of Christianity through the planting of churches. However, many new church plants bear little resemblance to the churches of prior generations either in practice or doctrine (Terry, 639). This had led to thousands of schisms, denominations and even various world religions which have formed over the centuries by mission work which has been guided by the

Surrendering Our All to the Lord

Hebrews 12:2-3 "Looking unto Jesus the author and finisher of our faith; who for the joy that was set before him endured the cross, despising the shame, and is set down at the right hand of the throne of God. For consider him that endured such contradiction of sinners against himself, lest ye be wearied and faint in your minds."

Oswald Chambers boldly chided, "How dare we talk of making a sacrifice for the Son of God! We are saved from hell and total destruction, and then we talk about making sacrifices!" Christ made the ultimate sacrifice for us. He died for you and me. All our efforts, struggles, pain and trials pale in comparison. Even our righteousness is as filthy rags. We live in a day where freedom of religion is enjoyed and even taken for granted. We have not yet "resisted unto blood, striving against sin." We may face a harsh word here and there and cry "persecution!" The fact of the matter is that we all have many miles to go to be in that perfect place where God wants us to be in our lives. None of us have yet attained the goal to which we strive. Each day is a constant battle, and each day we must decide to follow Jesus. Surrendering your life to follow Christ is not something that you do one time and then forget about. It is a daily affair. Do not compare yourself to any other person than Christ Himself. Only then will you see that you have such a long way to go. Look to Christ, the author and finisher of your faith. Then, make Him Lord of your life. Make Him number one in your life today! Is there anything in your heart or life that is keeping you from total surrender to the Lord right now? If so, what? Write them down. Then pray about those things, handing them over to the Lord. Hold nothing back, and you will experience peace and blessing like you've never known!

Figure 1. *Missionary Insights: Surrendering Our All to the Lord*

maxim of every man doing that which was right in his own eyes (Judges 17:6). Without the study and implementation of correct missiological principles and Biblical doctrine, schism, division, and syncretism with existing pagan religions is an inescapable inevitability (M. Barnett 424).

When recruiting missionaries, many preachers often say that God does not care about one's ability, only their availability. This is taken from a quote by the Mormon "Apostle" Neal Maxwell who said, "God does not begin by asking us about our ability, but only about our availability, and if we then prove our dependability, he will increase our capability!" (Wright 212). Despite being a Mormon concept, many Baptist preachers herald that concept from the pulpit. That standard cannot be applied to any other profession such as a mechanic or a surgeon. Ability, experience, and knowledge is much more important for the most important job on earth. A missionary is a teacher and mentor to pastors, church leaders, new Christians and converts from other religions. He is there to train a whole society about God and Scripture. To send a person who is untrained in Scripture, ministry experience, cross-cultural understanding, and church planting methodology can be disastrous (Dearmore 299).

Another reason for the necessity of the study of mission work is the fact of missionary attrition (Hoke 269). According to a study by the World Evangelical Alliance, called Reducing Missionary Attrition Project (ReMAP), the average attrition rate of missionary personnel is astounding. Forty-seven percent of missionaries leave the field within the first five years (Taylor 13). Statistics show that the number is much higher for independent missionaries or those who do not work through large denominational agencies (Ibid). The study determined that there was a high correlation in missionary retention and the following factors: college education, prior ministry experience, proper screening, and psychological wellness (Ibid). A proper training program coupled with Biblical education and ministry experience was shown to reduce the number of missionaries leaving the field (Taylor 26).

The Need for Mission Work

According to the statistics of the Joshua Project, there are over 7.3 billion people on earth and more than 3 billion of them live within people groups with little to no gospel witness (joshuaproject.net). Despite the missionary efforts being made today, there are still 4,087 unreached people groups in the world. There are 2,643 people groups that do not have a Bible in their primary language (Ibid). Less than twenty percent (19.6%) of the world's population has been significantly reached by evangelical Christianity (Ibid). The numbers are staggering, yet even in the absence of these statistics, the Biblical commands of Christ obligate His churches to the task of mission work.

> *But when he saw the multitudes, he was moved with compassion on them, because they fainted, and were scattered abroad, as sheep having no shepherd. Then saith he unto his disciples, The harvest truly is plenteous, but the labourers are few; Pray ye therefore the Lord of the harvest, that he will send forth labourers into his harvest. (Matthew 9:36-38)*

As the Scriptures relate the mission of God to sinful man, it also relates the progressive process of lust and sin. To understand the necessity of the mission of God to the lost, we must understand the reason for man's lostness. In Genesis 3:6 Eve was tempted in the garden by the serpent. In this passage, the Bible relates the pattern for sin.

The first step of temptation is seeing evil as good. Verse six states, that Eve "saw that the tree was good for food." God had clearly commanded that the tree was off limits. However, the serpent tempted Eve to change her perspective of the situation and look upon what was certainly sinful as good rather than evil. Isaiah speaks of this same evil and condemns it in Isaiah 5:20, "Woe unto them that call evil good, and good evil; that put darkness for light, and light for darkness; that put bitter for sweet, and sweet for bitter!"

> ▶ **WORLD POPULATION: ALMOST 7½ BILLION**
>
> ▶ **TOTAL PEOPLE GROUPS: 10,112**
>
> ▶ **UNREACHED PEOPLE GROUPS: 4,334**
>
> ▶ **PEOPLE GROUPS WITHOUT A BIBLE IN THEIR PRIMARY LANGUAGE: 2,643**
>
> ▶ **PERCENT OF THE WORLD SIGNIFICANTLY REACHED BY CHRISTIANITY: 19.6%**
>
> SOURCE: JOSHUAPROJECT.NET

Figure 2. *Statistics of world evangelism in 2017*

The second step in temptation is a longing desire to sin. Eve looked at the fruit and saw that it was "pleasant to the eyes." This phrase literally means "a longing desire or lustful appetite as she continually stares." There is aesthetic beauty to sin, but the end result is always death. There is always a drawing to every sin. James 1:15 states, "Then when lust hath conceived, it bringeth forth sin: and sin, when it is finished, bringeth forth death."

The third step of temptation is belief that sin will bring benefit. Eve saw that it was "a tree to be desired to make one wise." Sinful temptation causes irrational thinking. To say there is no benefit to sin is untrue, but the benefit is a fleeting pleasure. The irrational thinking is that the fleeting momentary pleasure of sin is greater than the consequences.

The fourth step of temptation is bringing sin close. The Scriptures states that "she took of the fruit thereof" (Genesis 3:6) This phrase is often passed over in Biblical exposition, but it is important. Before a person sins, they must be positioned to do it. She picked the fruit and had it in her hand. Had she not picked it, she would not have eaten it.

David should have been on the battlefield with his men, but instead chose to stay home, when he fell into sin with Bathsheba (2 Samuel 11:1-2). Had he been where he should have been, he would not have fallen into sin. Before Lot moved to Sodom, he looked longingly towards the green fields, pitched his tent in that direction, then he moved in completely (Genesis 13:10-12). If a person is not in the presence of sin, temptation will be easier to resist.

The fifth step is the actual act of disobedience. The Bible states that Eve "did eat" (Genesis 3:6). The act of sin is itself just another step in the temptation/sin process. However, you may step away and stop this process at any time before the act of sin actually happens. Unfortunately, neither Eve nor her husband resisted the temptation; Eve fell by deception, Adam fell by a willful and voluntary act of sin. The sixth and final step in this process that follows the act of sin is the malignant contagion of it. What sin does to one, it also does to many. For this reason, the curse of Adam fell to all mankind. Genesis 3:6 states that Eve "gave also unto her husband with her; and he did eat." Sin is never a solitary act; it always affects others. Many times, a person's sin is the agent of temptation that causes others to fall into sin.

Reading between the lines of the cause of man's original sin and God's subsequent response will enlighten the view of the love of God - even as He cursed the world and all mankind. As Eve approached Adam with the prospect of eating the forbidden fruit, Adam made a conscious choice. Even though Eve had been deceived (1 Timothy 2:14), the commandment had still been broken, and the penalty still had to be paid. Adam knew the consequences, and effectively had to choose between living with his creator or dying with his wife (Genesis 2:17). Just imagine the sorrow that Adam felt in that moment, knowing the coming destruction that his wife had brought upon herself. His heart torn in anguish between God and Eve, he had a decision to make with lasting consequences. Of course, Adam chose to eat of the fruit. His sin was not because of deception; it was both a willful and cognizant choice to disobey. This disobedience brought the entire world under the curse of sin, and with it, Adam's sin brought death (Romans 5:12). Though the Lord in His justice condemned the world, He made a way of salvation. Through the sacrifice of blood, God clothed the disobedient sinners to cover their sinful shame and nakedness, and thereby educated the first family in the way of redemption. The Lord prophesied of the coming Messiah which would once and for all bruise the head of the evil one and bring salvation to all who would believe (Genesis 3:15). *Missio Dei*, the Mission of God, is a necessity in the world today because of the sin curse (Ashford 18).

Mission: The Lifeblood of the Local Church

"In a real sense mission is the very lifeblood of the church" (Van Rheenen 31). The Great Commission of the church is a commission to mission work. Apart from mission work, there is little purpose for the church or reason for existence. We may argue that the church is meant for worship, however, proper worship will always include three things:

1) *A revelation of God's holiness*
2) *An innate sense of one's own worthlessness in comparison*
3) *A proper desire to serve the Lord and His purpose (Isaiah 6:1-8).*

The purpose of the Lord for this world is redemption, and the purpose of the Lord for the church is to spread the gospel of salvation, propagate new believers and churches through baptism and church replication, and disciple those who come to know the Lord as their Savior (Moreau 84). We may also argue that the church exists to teach God's Word through corporate Bible study and the preaching of the Word. However, it may be countered that within the teaching of Scripture, which is not only necessary but an

> **The church is not a social club for Christians, but rather the outlet through which believers may find and carry out the will of God.**

integral part of the Great Commission, is the teaching of mission work. Furthermore, a Biblical education is worthless if there is no application of the principles that are taught. "But be ye doers of the word, and not hearers only, deceiving your own selves" (James 1:22). In other words, the Bible teaches us to "Go… into all the world, and preach the gospel to every creature" (Mark 16:15). Preben Vang put it this way, "The church is not an add-on to the Christian life. Rather, individual Christians live their lives through the church as vital parts of a body. It simply violates the language of Scripture to speak of the church as an organization designed to be a filling station for individual Christians who have need of special encouragement and support" (M. Barnett 152). The church is not a social club for Christians, but rather the outlet through which believers may find and carry out the will of God.

Chapter Two

WHAT IS A MISSIONARY?

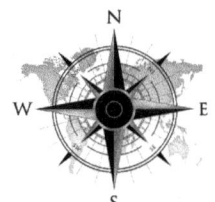

The Definition of the Word "Missionary"

To properly define and execute the mission of the Lord, the term missionary must be defined, and theological questions with serious practical implications must be answered. What is the job of a missionary, according to the Bible? Is a missionary an ordained position? Can those doing other "helps" ministries be considered missionaries? So, what exactly is a missionary? The modern term *missionary* is never found in Scripture, yet there are many missionaries that are spoken of in the Bible. In the New Testament, there are three Greek words that are used meaning "to send." Those words are: ἀποστέλλω *apostellō* (Strong's G649) meaning to formally commission by authority or send on a mission to carry out the wishes of that authority; πέμπω *pempō* (Strong's G3992) simply meaning, "to send out or dispatch;" used interchangeably in the New Testament with *apostolos* and ἀπολύω *apoluō* (Strong's G630) meaning "to loose, to set at liberty, to send away and set free." The Biblical word *apostle* is used as a transliteration of the word *apostolos*, meaning "sent one" (Bromiley 192). In this sense of the word, an apostle is a missionary, or one who is sent. The book of Romans also mentions an important principle in mission work, namely, a man cannot be a Biblical missionary without being sent out with authority to preach. This principle is clearly given in Romans 10:15, "And how shall they preach, except they be sent? as it is written, How beautiful are the feet of them that preach the gospel of peace, and bring glad tidings of good things!" The answer to the rhetorical question posed here is that they cannot preach unless they are sent. The word here for sent is actually *apostello*, meaning to send out by one with the authority to send. Only God's local New Testament churches have the authority to send out a missionary.

There are two different types of apostles mentioned in the New Testament. The first type of apostle found in the New Testament is that of "sent ones" of Jesus Christ. The twelve disciples who were called by Jesus Christ in the gospels were known as apostles. By definition, these men were "sent ones," or those who were sent out by Christ Himself, during His ministry upon the earth. Acts 1:20 describes the office of these twelve men as a "bishoprick," from the word ἐπισκοπή *episkopē* (Strong's G1984) in Greek, meaning "overseership." In the following verses, the criteria for being one of the twelve apostles is given in the search for a replacement for Judas Iscariot. Verse twenty-one states that the replacement must be "of these men." The word used for *men* is ἀνήρ *anēr* (Strong's G435). According to Thayer, this term is not speaking of mankind, but specifically of the male gender (Thayer). An apostle must be a man. The second condition was that he must have "companied with us all the time that the Lord Jesus went in and out among us, beginning from the baptism of John, unto that same day that he was taken up from us" (Acts 1:21,22). The apostles were men who were disciples of John the Baptist, having been baptized by him, and then called out by Christ. They would then have followed Christ throughout His earthly ministry. The last qualification is found in verse twenty-two which states that they must be, "a witness with us of his resurrection." The twelve original apostles

> ## KEEPING FOCUS
>
> ***Philippians 3:20 "For our conversation is in heaven; from whence also we look for the Savior, the Lord Jesus Christ"***
>
> If we are living our lives according to our own thoughts, feelings and opinions, then we are not following Christ. Truly being a Christian, or "Christ-like" involves total abandonment of ourselves along with complete reliance upon the Lord. Our conversation (literally, our "citizenship") is in heaven, given to us by God and enacted in our hearts by the Holy Spirit. Our conduct should be becoming of a citizen of heaven and fitting of a child of God. Our thoughts and feelings, our opinions and personality should no longer be our own, but that of Jesus Christ living in us. When others look at you do they see Christ shining through or do they see the sin nature seeping out? As we struggle and strive on a daily basis to be more like our Lord, we must leave behind not only the things of the world, but also our own selves so that we can become more like Him. Our focus should be on the Savior. When we keep our eyes on the Lord, He is able to guide our lives. When our hearts are distracted by the world and disillusioned by sin, that sin will take over as the controlling influence in our lives. Mission work starts in the heart, and your own heart is the first on the list of ones to be reached.

Figure 3. *Missionary Insights: Keeping Focus*

must also have seen the resurrection of Christ, having been an eye witness of the risen Savior. Doubtless, there were many who fit the qualifications, yet two were nominated, and one was chosen to take the place of Judas Iscariot.

There is no mention of the succession of this office after Acts chapter one. There were, however, several others mentioned in the

New Testament that were known as apostles. Since Scripture must line up with Scripture, and others who were called apostles do not line up with the definition of apostle found in Acts chapter one, it can only be deduced that there was a second type of apostle found in the Bible. Paul was referred to as an apostle, though not one of the twelve. So too were others in the New Testament that might not meet the criteria of apostles of Jesus Christ. Paul was not a disciple of John the Baptist. Paul was neither baptized by John nor the original apostles of Jesus Christ, but of Ananias of Damascus. Paul did not company Christ through His earthly ministry, though it can be argued that He did see the risen Lord, and possibly spent time in Arabia being discipled by Christ himself. Nevertheless, this does not change the fact that Paul does not meet the former criteria. So, what type of apostle, or "sent one" was Paul? We must conclude that there is a second type of apostle, a second type of "sent one" mentioned in Scripture. Barnabas is called an apostle in Acts 14:14. Andronicus and Junia are mentioned as noted among the apostles in Romans 16:7. Paul includes both Silas and Timothy as fellow apostles in First Thessalonians 2:6, and mentions Apollos as an apostle in First Corinthians 4:6,9. In Galatians 1:19, James, the Lord's brother is called an apostle, though he was not one of the twelve. In Philippians 2:25, Epaphroditus is called an *apostolos* (translated "messenger") of the church of Philippi (M. Barnett 361). This second definition of apostle is what would today be termed a "missionary" (Bromiley 192). This is found in Acts chapter thirteen, in which the second type of "sent one" was sent out, not by Christ personally, but through the means of that which the Lord left upon the earth to carry out His purpose. They were sent out by a local church, namely, the church at Antioch. Though the Greek root is *apostelló*, (Strong's G649) the common

> ***Missionary: one who is sent out by the authority of a local church to further the mission given to the church in the Great Commission.***

term used today would not be a transliteration of that word, but rather, to prevent confusion of terminology, the one sent out by the church is today called a "missionary," and the original men sent out personally by Christ are termed "apostles."

With these facts in mind, the Biblically based definition of a missionary is: one who is sent out by the authority of a local church to further the mission given to the church in the Great Commission.

The Biblical Pattern of the Missionary

The pattern of mission work is found in Acts chapter thirteen, namely: God called, church sent, Spirit led missionaries. At the church in Antioch, Acts 13:1 mentions the name of several prophets and teachers. Mentioned at the top of the list was Barnabas. The prominence given to Barnabas suggests that he may have been the head pastor of the church at Antioch at the time (Gavila). In reference to the Biblical pattern which is laid out in this chapter, the Holy Spirit of God speaks to this faithful church which is hard at work in His service. Verse two states that "they ministered to the Lord, and fasted" (Acts 13:2). A very important principle is found in these words. God calls upon those who are already busy in the service of the Lord. "Let a man so account of us, as of the ministers of Christ, and stewards of the mysteries of God. Moreover it is required in stewards, that a man be found faithful" (1 Corinthians 4:1-2). A person who is not witnessing where he is will probably not witness on the mission field. A person who is not faithfully studying God's Word now will find it no easier to study when he is on the mission field. If he does not have a constant and earnest prayer life at home, the mission field will not miraculously transform him into a spiritual giant. God calls those who are already working. He uses those who are faithful in what they should be doing now to do greater things in the future. In Acts 13:2, the Lord called the church at Antioch to set two faithful men aside for a specific ministry in mission work. This call did not come to Paul and Barnabas alone, but to their whole church. The word

> **Biblical Pattern of Mission Work in Acts 13:**
> - *God calls*
> - *Church sends*
> - *Spirit leads*

"they," mentioned in verse two, is speaking of those who were in the church that was at Antioch. God's chosen plan to carry out His commands and commission in this present age is through the means of His local New Testament churches. The Great Commission was specifically given to the church, and not to individual Christians nor any other organization, association, fellowship or otherwise (Cross, Landmarkism: An Update 26). Just as the commission was given to the church, so too was the call. This does not, however, preclude the fact that a missionary also experiences a personal call upon his life (Sills 47). There is evidence in the book of Acts that an individual call upon a missionary, given by God to a single person, effected the entire group of missionaries who embraced it as a corporate calling of the missionary team. In the narrative of the call of Paul to Macedonia, the Holy Spirit had appeared to Paul in a vision. The words of Luke, the physician and fellow missionary laborer of Paul, in Acts 16:10 are of special note, "and after *he* had seen the vision, immediately *we* endeavored to go into Macedonia, assuredly gathering that *the Lord had called us* for to preach the gospel unto them." (author's emphasis) The vision was given to Paul, but the calling was inclusive of the missionary team. Luke states that the "Lord had called us" and not just Paul. It is then seen that the Scriptures give reference to individual callings (Paul's vision), corporate callings through discernment of leadership (Luke's assurance that they all were called through Paul's pronouncement of the Lord's leading), and church-wide callings (The Holy Spirit's calling of Paul and Barnabas revealed to the church at Antioch). The Bible clearly indicates a principle here that ought to be followed today; that principle is that mission work must be done through the auspices of a local New Testament church (Ibid). No room is given in Scripture for a mission board system. There is no mention nor allowance for para-church missionary societies (Brooks). No system of denominational hierarchy is mentioned in the Bible, nor can we find even a hint of a scriptural basis for one. Ephesians 3:21 states, "Unto Him be glory in the church." As Paul writes in the second epistle to Timothy, chapter two verse five, "And if a man also strive for masteries, yet is he not crowned, except he strive lawfully." God's will must be done God's way, and God's way is to serve Him through a scriptural, local church (Dearmore 322).

> *God's will must be done God's way, and God's way is to serve Him through a scriptural, local church.*

The Holy Spirit said, "Separate me Barnabas and Saul for the work whereunto I have called them" (Acts 13:2). According to the meaning of this phrase, they were to be set apart for a specific ministry by the church of their membership, according to the call of the Lord revealed to the church. In Acts 13:3, the church at Antioch did three things before sending out the missionaries: they fasted, they prayed, and they laid hands on them. To signify the seriousness of this God-called ministry effort, the church fasted. Putting away the fleshly desires of the world and abstaining from bodily nourishment, the church focused upon the spiritual matters at hand. In doing so, they gave themselves over to prayer and personal conversation with the Lord, certainly offering up supplication for the missionaries: their safety, their success, and their wellbeing.

Lastly, the church at Antioch laid their hands upon their missionary team, signifying that they were setting them apart to the work of the mission of the Lord to which He had called them to. There is much speculation as to what the laying on of hands in this verse actually was, whether an ordination to the office of missionary, an ordaining of these men to the gospel ministry, or simply an act of approval by the church, commending them to the ministry of the Lord's mission. Paul speaks of two offices of the church, pastors and deacons, in the epistles to Timothy and Titus. So, the first possibility of the position of a missionary being an ordained church office is nowhere else elaborated upon in Scripture. It is also known that both Barnabas and Paul had been preaching the gospel and serving in churches for many years. According to the time line of Acts, a period of over twelve years had elapsed in the ministry of Paul from his conversion in AD 34 until his first missionary journey in AD 47. Throughout that time, Paul was busy preaching the gospel, so it may be determined that this was not an ordination to the ministry. The third possibility, that of the church laying on of hands as an act of approval and commendation is the most probable one, according to the context of the rest of the New Testament (Dearmore 318).

The next point of the Acts 13 plan for Biblical mission work is that the missionaries were sent out by their local church. In verse three, it states that "they," speaking directly of the church at Antioch "sent them away." The word used here for "sent away" is the Greek word ἀπολύω *apoluō*, (Strong's G630) meaning sent by, sent from, or sent out of that particular church. It cannot be overemphasized that the Biblical pattern for mission work is through the efforts and by the authority of local, scriptural churches, and none else. Much mission work is done today by mission boards, private agencies, para-church organizations or denominational establishments (Reed 79). Mission work by these types of organizations cannot be justified Biblically, and must be considered as deviating from the plan of God laid out in the New Testament. No other type of missionary activity can be considered as scriptural missionary activity other than that of local churches carrying out the commands and commission of our Lord and Savior Jesus Christ (Graves 35).

Finally, in Acts 13:4, Paul and Barnabas were "sent forth" by the Holy Ghost. Here, a third Greek term is used, ἐκπέμπω *ekpempō* (Strong's G1599) meaning to send forth or dispatch on a temporary errand. Not only were the missionaries sent forth by the authority and commendation of their church, but they were also sent forth on their errand by the Lord, being guided and led by the Holy Spirit. This is no minor point, for if a missionary is not carried through his mission by the presence and guidance of the Holy Spirit, failure, disappointment and spiritual calamity will certainly follow (Dearmore 327).

Is Everyone a Missionary?

The Biblical role of a missionary may be summarized as follows: being called specifically by God for a special purpose of spreading the gospel in a geographically different area than that of his church; being set apart specifically by his church for that purpose; being sent out by the church of his membership on the mission which God has called him (and his sending church) to do; and being guided, directed and dispatched upon that mission by the working of the Holy Spirit in his life. In light of these qualifications, the commonly held saying that "everyone is a missionary" is just not true (Hoke 21-22). Certainly, every child of God should be a witness and testimony to those around them, but to say that everyone is a missionary not only cheapens the position and qualifications of true Biblical missionaries, but also teaches something that does not line up with Scripture nor can be defensible in the light of Biblical testimony.

Are There Other Types of Missionaries?

The question arises of the other ministers and ministries which go by the name of "missionary." Are there other types of missionaries, such as those doing "helps" ministries? First Corinthians 12:28 speaks of those in the church whom God has set for a ministry of "helps." This word in the Greek is only found in this verse, ἀντιλήμψεις *antilēmpseis*, (Strong's G484) meaning to help or take hold of in the stead or place of another. Certainly, there is a place for many diverse types of ministries in God's service. Some are called to teach, others might be called to help with children, while still others might do physical labors or use their specific talents for the Lord. Some of these ministries might even be to encourage and strengthen believers away from their own local congregation, such as ministering to other churches of like faith. In the sense of the phrase, "sent one" they might be called a missionary. Today there are many of these ministries with names such as: "missionary counselors," "gospel music missionaries," "missionary builders," "sports missionaries," etc. However, the Biblical based pattern of the New Testament, must restrict our use of the term missionary to a God called, church sent, Spirit led preacher of the gospel who has been set apart for the ministry and sent out into a separate geographical location with church authority to evangelize, baptize, organize churches, disciple converts, train leaders, edify believers, and return to his sending church to report and strengthen the brethren back home (Hesselgrave 93 ff).

Chapter Three

THEOLOGY OF MISSION WORK

The Theological Discipline of Missiology

Missiology is simply the study of Christian mission work, its theological foundations, and practical applications (Moreau 17). Within missiological training schools, the study of mission work includes aspects of missionary training in areas such as: cross-cultural adaptation, historical missionary foundations, language acquisition, mission work in the Old and New Testament, the Pauline example of mission work, deputation and fund raising, missionary psychology, evangelism and church planting techniques, practical living on the mission field, marriage and family living on the mission field, strategic planning for mission work, and practical on-the-field training with veteran missionaries (Jones 10 ff). The study of missiology is of the utmost importance to those who plan on serving the Lord on the mission field. Getting the training that is necessary for foreign mission work can be compared to basic training, or "boot camp" for soldiers. Serving the Lord on the foreign field is certainly comparable to being on the front lines of battle in a war raged not with tanks and guns, but a spiritual battle for the very souls of the lost world. A missionary must be prepared and capable of facing the battles that he will endure on the field (Moreau 173). Sending an unprepared soldier into battle will almost certainly result in unfortunate casualties, whether it be the missionary or those around him. Not only is the study of mission work important to a missionary candidate, it is also useful to those in churches who support missionaries on the field. Correct theology in relation to mission work could rectify the majority of harmful and doctrinally unsound practices that are being disseminated among missionaries today. Every member of every church should be schooled in the principles and practices of the commission of Christ, for it is the very reason for the existence of the institution of the church, the job of every church and the foundation for the propagation of the gospel message of Jesus Christ throughout the world.

Missio Dei: The Mission of God

The mission of the local church: to evangelize the entire world with the gospel of Jesus Christ, baptize converts and indoctrinate them through the proliferation of new churches – all stem from the basic heart's desire of the Lord Himself: that is, God wishes to redeem mankind to Himself so that He may have a relationship with His creation (Ashford 18). In essence, the mission of the church is the mission of God (M. Barnett 19). Mission work extends from the heart of the Divine. Local churches, missionaries and evangelists are but tools in the hands of the Lord. We are His workmanship, but the work is His. Christians would do well to remember that the first missionary was the Lord Himself, who sought out lost mankind in the garden of Eden. *Missio Dei* is the Latin form of the phrase, "The Mission of God," or the "sending" of God (Moreau 17). The Hebrew word שׁלח shâlach is translated in the King James Version "to send" 848 times (Strong's H7971). The same word in the Septuagint in Greek is ἀποστέλλω apostellō.

All throughout Scripture, God is seen as a God who sends. The Father sent the Son, who sent the Spirit, who sent the church, who sent missionaries throughout the world. Mission is much more than an act of ecclesiology or an act of soteriology. Mission is an attribute of the character and nature of God (Bosch 389 f). Plainly stated, the doctrine of mission is the doctrine of God the Father sending God the Son into the world to save lost humanity, and the Father and the Son sending the Spirit into the world to convict, to guide, to seal and to make intercession for us. Mission is the Father, Son, and Holy Spirit sending the institution of the church into the world to carry out God's Great Commission (Ashford 18). Through local churches, the missionary is sent into the world to continue the cycle. According to David J. Bosch, "mission is not primarily an activity of the church, but an attribute of God. God is a missionary God." (Bosch 389-390).

Jurgen Moltmann says, "It is not the church that has a mission of salvation to fulfill in the world; it is the mission of the Son and the Spirit through the Father that includes the church" (Moltmann 64).

> **Doctrine of Mission:**
> *The Father sent the Son.*
> *The Father and Son sent the Spirit.*
> *The Father, Son, and Spirit sent the church.*
> *The church sends the missionary.*

More than six thousand years have passed since the day that God asked the most pressing, the most thought provoking, the most piercing, and the saddest question in human history. Eve had been deceived by the serpent in the garden. Adam had made a willful choice to throw away his relationship with a Holy Creator and die with his wife. He chose sin and death over perfection and life. He deliberately disobeyed God and did the one thing that the Lord told him not to do. He had sinned. He was ashamed. They covered themselves in fig leaves, and when they heard the voice of the Lord walking in the garden in the cool of the day, they tried to hide from Him. The Lord called out, and some may wonder why the Lord had to ask where they were, as if He did not know. It was not for God's benefit that the Lord asked where Adam was. It was for the benefit of humanity. It was so that people would see that it was God Himself who first sought after the lost. It was God himself who first called out for man to come back to Him. It was God Himself that could be called the first gospel evangelist, the first soul winner, the first missionary. Through the process of worldwide mission outreach, God still calls out those three heart piercing words to the lost, "Where art thou?" The question is not asked because God does not know the location, the position, or the spiritual condition of the lost. The question is asked so that the lost soul may evaluate where he or she is, where they are headed, what their positional standing is with their Creator, and where they stand in their spiritual condition. God, through the person of the Holy Spirit, is still asking the same question to people today… "Where art thou?"

Theological Considerations of Mission Work

A theological truth exists in the realm of mission work that must be expounded upon. This theological truth is the fact that everyone, everywhere and throughout all ages has had access to the plan of salvation through Jesus Christ. This truth is attested in Titus 2:11, "For the grace of God that bringeth salvation hath appeared to all men." This comes as a surprise to many, and is in direct opposition to the heresy that Christ's coming will only take place after the world has been reached with the gospel. In Second Peter 3:9, the Bible states, "The Lord is not slack concerning his promise, as some men count slackness; but is longsuffering to us-ward, not willing that any should perish, but that all should come to repentance." Salvation is universally offered to all because Christ died for every person, holding the sin curse of everyone upon Himself while He was crucified upon the cross. Isaiah 53:6 states that upon Christ, God laid the iniquity of the sin curse of all mankind. First Timothy 2:6 states that Christ gave himself as a ransom for all. Hebrews 2:9 states that Christ "tasted death for every man." Again, in First John 2:2, Christ has become that propitiation for the sins of the whole world.

Establishing the fact that salvation is universal in its execution, it must therefore also be universal in its offer. This does not mean that salvation is universal in its efficacy, i.e., not all will accept the plan of salvation. However, all will be offered the plan of salvation (it "hath appeared to all men"). In First Timothy 4:10, the Bible states, "we trust in the living God, who is the Saviour of all men, specially of those that believe." No man, woman or child shall be able to accuse the Savior of not allowing them the chance to accept salvation. The book of Romans illustrates this point beautifully,

> *For the wrath of God is revealed from heaven against all ungodliness and unrighteousness of men, who hold the truth in unrighteousness; Because that which may be known of God is manifest in them; for God hath shewed it unto them. For the invisible things of him from the creation of the world are clearly seen, being understood by the things that are made, even his eternal power and Godhead; so that they are without excuse. (Romans 1:18-20)*

A doctrinal heresy has emerged in recent times that teaches that Christians must reach the world with the gospel before Christ can return. This heresy comes from a misinterpretation of verse fourteen of Matthew chapter twenty-four, "And this gospel of the kingdom shall be preached in all the world for a witness unto all nations; and then shall the end come." Proper exegesis of this passage in Matthew will reveal that this is speaking of the tribulation period, and not of this present dispensation of time. It is absurd to think that the Lord Jesus Christ is waiting on his disobedient servants to evangelize every person in the world before He can return. Another version of this heresy is that of amillennialist doctrine which propagates that view that Christians will usher in the kingdom of God by winning the world to Christ (Hodges 22), and that this kingdom is not a physical presence of Jesus Christ upon the earth for a thousand years, but rather a spiritual kingdom in the hearts of mankind as the entire world is converted (Slick). Both of these heretical views rely on the assumption that the world does not yet have universal access to the gospel message. Scripture reveals several truths that destroy this assumption. First, the knowledge of the Lord is universal (atheists notwithstanding) as seen in passages such as Psalm nineteen and Romans chapter one. Second, the plan of salvation is universally offered as seen in passages such as John 3:16 and Hebrews 2:9. Third, the Holy Spirit's conviction of the sinner, and by extension the offer of the choice to accept or reject God's plan of salvation is universal, as written in John 16:8, "And when he is come, he will reprove the world of sin, and of righteousness, and of judgment." Lastly, the gospel message has most assuredly already been preached throughout all the earth, even in the first generation of churches after the ascension of Jesus Christ. This fact is attested to in Romans 10:18, "But I say, Have they not heard? Yes verily, their sound went into all the earth, and their words unto the ends of the world." This worldwide evangelistic effort of early church mission work is discussed further in chapter eight: Church Perpetuity as Evidence of Mission Work. Does that mean that every person has heard the gospel? Does that mean that we ourselves should not go? The apostles reached the world in their generation. Our mission today is the same. We need to reach the world in our generation.

Mission or Missions?

Many twentieth century theologians have replaced the commonly used term *missions*, referring to mission work, with the singular form, *mission*. The singular is certainly more theologically correct. The common use of the word *missions* in the plural rather than the singular *mission* has led to many bad doctrines and practices. There is only one mission, the mission of God. That mission is to redeem a lost humanity to a holy God. By the authority of Jesus Christ, that mission was given to the local New Testament church, as enumerated in the Great Commission of Matthew 28:18-20. Regardless of the number of missionaries, ministries, or outreaches, there are not multiple missions. Each true missionary, each true ministry, each true outreach is striving for the same mission, and that mission is the mission of God to seek and save the lost. The Catholic church, which teaches that there is but one universal church, popularized the use of *missions*, referring to individual points of outreach by its missionaries, since they could not rectify the use of the word *church* with their universalist teachings. It is theologically incorrect to refer to a building, an assembly, or any other group or object as a *mission*. Whether one is inclined to use the theologically accurate term *mission*, or the commonly used term *missions*, the word should always refer to the work of carrying out the Great Commission of Jesus Christ by the efforts of a local church. For the sake of clarity and consistency, you will find the term "mission work" rather than *missions* used throughout this text.

Chapter Four

Ecclesiology of Mission Work

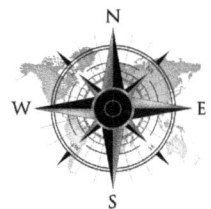

The History of "Church"

The roots of the word ecclesiology come from the Greek ἐκκλησία, *ekklēsiā* (Strong's G1577) meaning *congregation* or *church*; and -λογία, -logia, (Strong's G3056) meaning *word, knowledge,* or *study.* The English word church comes from the old English word *circe*, meaning a *circle*. In pre-Christian times, places of worship were in the form of a circle, such as that of Stonehenge. It is cognate with the word circus, which also means ring or circle and was used to describe large stadia or amphitheaters which were places of assembly (Harper).

> *A scriptural New Testament church is a local, visible, called out assembly of scripturally baptized believers that have covenanted together to carry out the work of the great commission.*

The word church is a late invention, and was first used in the English language by the Protestant scholar Theodore Beza. Through his work in preparing his edition of the Textus Receptus Greek New Testament, he convinced the English translators of the Geneva Bible to discontinue the common usage of the translation of *ekklēsiā* as *congregation* or *assembly*. Instead, they would use the newly coined word **church** to fit the Anglican doctrine of a universal, invisible incorporation of all believers. Previous English versions, including Tyndale's New Testament (1526), the Matthew's Bible (1537), and the Great Bible (1539) all used the term congregation. The Bishop's Bible, and the 1611 translation of the King James Bible continued the use of the word church, bringing it into common English vernacular (Abrams III).

From the fourth century, Christians used the Greek word *kyriakon*, meaning "of the Lord" to describe houses of Christian worship from about AD 300, but more often used the word *ekklēsiā*, referring to the church body

> *Ekklesia always referred to an assembly in a specific location, existing within definable geographical limits.*

or *basilica*, referring to the building. The word *ekklēsiā* is used 115 times in the New Testament (Strong's G1577). It is translated 113 times as church and two times as assembly. In classical Greek, the word *ekklēsiā* meant "an assembly of citizens summoned by the crier, the legislative assembly" (Liddell, 206). *Ekklēsiā* comes from two root words meaning *to call* and *out*. It was used commonly as early as the fifth century BC to refer to a congregation or assembly of people who were called out for a specific meeting or purpose.

> *It is attested from Euripides and Herodotus onwards (5th cent. BC), and denotes an assembly of competent full citizens of the polis, city. It reached its greatest importance in the 5th century BC, and met at regular intervals (in Athens about 30--40 times a year, elsewhere less frequently) and also in cases of urgency as an extra-ordinary ekklesia. Its sphere of competence included decisions on suggested changes in the law*

> *(which could only be effected by the council of the 400), on appointments to official positions and -- at least in its heyday -- on every important question of internal and external policy (contracts, treaties, war and peace, finance). To these was added in special cases (e.g. treason) the task of sitting in judgment, which as a rule fell to regular courts. The ekklesia opened with prayers and sacrifices to the gods of the city. (Brown 291)*

Ekklēsiā always referred to an assembly in a specific location, existing within definable geographical limits. There is no biblical basis for the belief in a universal assembly. This belief cannot logically stand. It is a contradiction of terms.

Basic Tenants of Scriptural Church Doctrine

The Lord Jesus Christ founded His church during His personal ministry and commissioned it to evangelize, baptize, and teach all nations. A scriptural New Testament church is a local, visible, called out assembly of scripturally baptized believers that have covenanted together to carry out the work of the great commission given by its founder, Jesus Christ. (Terry, 114) According to the book *Missiology*, there are

> *at least four essential truths which characterize a New Testament church. One as to its nature, a New Testament church is a visible body. Two, a church is composed of believers, baptized in the Lord Jesus Christ. Three, organizationally a New Testament church consists of baptized followers of Jesus Christ who have come together voluntarily... Four, the above definition suggests that a New Testament church's function is the promotion of Christ's redemptive purpose for all humans. (Terry, 115)*

Jesus Christ gave the authority to carry out the commission exclusively to the church (Reed 78). No other person, organization, association, fellowship, etc. has scriptural authority to carry out that commission.

> ## DISCOVERING THE TRUE MEANING OF MISSION WORK
>
> *Matthew 28:19-20 "Go ye therefore, and teach all nations, baptizing them in the name of the Father, and of the Son, and of the Holy Ghost: Teaching them to observe all things whatsoever I have commanded you: and, lo, I am with you alway, even unto the end of the world. Amen."*
>
> The Lord commanded us to go into all the world and preach the gospel to all people. When we arrive on the field, it is easy to forget the one true goal of our mission – to make disciples. The physical needs of the people are great, and it is easy to want to focus on those needs rather than their greatest need of all: salvation. Our goal is not to save souls (that is the work of the Lord Himself). We are commanded to go and tell them the good news of salvation, and once they have accepted that message and placed their trust in Christ, we are to continue to teach and disciple them to follow the Lord. Yet, we can never disciple another if we ourselves are not disciples of the Lord. How is your walk with God? Are you following Him as you ought to? The Great Commission was a commandment of Christ to the church. What can you do personally to help fulfill this commandment through your church?

Figure 4. *Missionary Insights: Discovering the True Meaning of Mission Work*

Others may assist in the ministry of the church, but the authority lies within the church alone. That authority is non-transferable and cannot be delegated to anyone or anything outside the local, New Testament church. To allow any person or group of persons a voting voice in the affairs of the church and its ministries undermines the authority of that church and is the root of the formation of an inter-church ecclesiastical organization. Such is the result of the doctrine of a universal church in practice. Churches cannot scripturally combine or jointly sponsor a ministry without giving up church sovereignty.

Association among churches is strictly for the fellowship and cooperation among individual churches to advance the gospel through individual church ministries. An association cannot scripturally possess any ecclesiastical power or authority, nor can it scripturally own, operate or control a ministry that should otherwise be under the authority of a local, New Testament church. Biblical mission work result from God-called, church sent, spirit-led men, foreign or national, under the authority of a local church.

Biblical Church Authority

Jesus Christ walked along the seashores of Galilee two millennia ago, and as He called those first fishermen to follow Him, He called out His assembly – His church. All authority to carry out the Great Commission has been vested in the local church alone. Founded and commissioned by Christ, the institution of the local, New Testament church has withstood the evils of twenty centuries of trials, holding on to the promise that Christ would be there always, even unto the end of the world. Many pastors today teach that it is all right to change methods as long as the message is not changed. However, actions speak volumes as to what one believes. When the methods alter the divine, Biblical plan of the Lord, those methods are in direct conflict with the cause of Christ.

The Greek term translated church is ἐκκλησία (*Ekklēsiā*) (Strong's G1577), meaning called out. The word was used to carry the sense of an organized assembly called out to enact business of some kind. The Catholics have perverted the word to mean a universal hierarchy of clergy and laity. To refute the Catholics, Protestants have prostituted the meaning of church even further, saying that it is a universal, invisible conglomeration of all the saved. Yet, it is evident that the only true meaning of church can be a local, visible assembly of believers with the authority to carry on business for the Lord. Anything else could not possibly fit the bill. "We speak of the church as a local group because the missionary purpose admits of no abstract sense, but only can be defined and explained in the concrete terms of local, visible, organized bodies of believers in Jesus Christ" (Terry, 116).

The Source of Church Authority

To have proper authority, a church must be authorized from the correct source – the source with the power to authorize. Only the Lord Jesus Christ carries this power. The word *power* in Matthew 28:18 is translated from the Greek word

> *Christ is the founder of His church, and all authority comes from Him.*

ἐξουσία *exousia* meaning "authoritative right" (Strong's G1849). There have been many other institutions founded by various people, but they all lack the one necessary ingredient that makes them scripturally authorized. That one ingredient is power from the Lord. Second Timothy 2:5 states, "And if a man strive for masteries, yet is he not crowned, except he strive lawfully." The Word of God teaches that we must serve Him according to His divine plan. There is no place in God's service for an individual to take matters into his own hands and simply ignore God's will and way of doing things.

Church authority is of Christ and from Christ because the church was founded by Christ. Jesus promised that He would build His church upon the Rock. That Rock was Jesus. To the church He gave the authority – the keys. "And I say also unto thee, That thou art Peter, and upon this rock I will build my church; and the gates of hell shall not prevail against it. And I will give unto thee the keys of the kingdom of heaven: and whatsoever thou shalt bind on earth shall be bound in heaven: and whatsoever thou shalt loose on earth shall be loosed in heaven" (Matt. 16:18,19). The keys represented the authority of the church to carry on kingdom business until Christ's return. Christ is the founder of His church, and all authority comes from Him, for it was given to Him by the Father.

> *And he is before all things, and by him all things consist. And he is the head of the body, the church: who is the beginning, the firstborn from the dead; that in all things he might have the preeminence. For it pleased the Father that in him should all fulness dwell. (Col. 1:17-19)*

To recognize this fact is to recognize that Jesus Christ started His church, and it was already in existence before the day of Pentecost. Church action was taken when Matthias was voted to fill the office of Judas Iscariot as prophesied in the Old Testament (Psalm 109:8). If the church was not started until the day of Pentecost, then this vote would have been void and not of the Lord. Yet, the church was already in place, assembled together, waiting on the empowering of the Holy Spirit to carry out the charge given to the church by Christ. It should be noted that "there is no power but of God: the powers that be are ordained of God. Whosoever therefore resisteth the power, resisteth the ordinance of God: and they that resist shall receive to themselves damnation" (Rom. 13:1,2). Therefore, if the authority did not come from God, there is no authority and there is no power. The source of church authority comes from God through Christ Jesus His Son.

In the last verses of the book of Matthew is found what is known as the Great Commission of Jesus Christ to His church (The singular form is used because there was only one church in existence at the time.) It must again be emphasized here that the Great Commission was not given to individual Christians nor was it given to the apostles. The Great Commission was given to the church.

All saints, including the apostles, must serve the Lord within the confines of a scriptural church. Even Paul was sent out by the church at Antioch. There was no usurping that authority. The apostles possessed power from God and carried out their duties, yet it must be noted that even they were members of and submitted to the authority of the church of their membership. Christ's orders to His church can be broken into three distinct parts:

1. Evangelize. Jesus told the church that while you go, teach all nations the Gospel of Christ.

2. Baptize. After salvation, immerse them for public identification with Christ. The duty to baptize those who have accepted Christ as their Savior solely rests in the local church. No other person nor organization has the right to baptize. If baptism is not administered in its scriptural mode (total immersion) by a scriptural authority (a local, New Testament church) then the baptism can be considered neither scriptural nor pleasing to God. Therefore, the baptism that does not meet these requirements cannot be considered true baptism at all.

3. Indoctrinate. Then, after they are saved, baptized and have covenanted together in full fellowship with a scriptural church, teach them the ways of Christianity. It is the responsibility of the local church to indoctrinate new believers by teaching them the Word of God. It is this area that many churches have failed miserably. It is because of the lack of sound, Biblical teaching that heresies arise and schisms occur. Because of this woeful lack of Biblical education, churches have relied upon para-church organizations to take up the slack. Young preachers are sent to schools abroad to learn the Bible because churches have neglected the mandate to indoctrinate. Many times, they attend schools that are knowingly not of like faith and practice. There is nothing unbiblical with a Bible school as long as it is operated under the authority of a scriptural church, for it is the duty of the church to educate men and women in the Word of God, not that of an extra-church organization.

God's Executor

An executor is one that is appointed by a testator to carry out the terms of a will. The Lord's churches are His executors. God has given His commands to His church and expects those commands to be carried out. Though our Lord is very much alive, He has left His will with His churches to be executed until He returns. His will is fully contained in His Holy Word. As executors, God's churches have only the power to carry out or execute the commands already given by God, the Great Testator, in His Will and Testament.

> *Churches have no power beyond the role of executor. They cannot change God's will or commands to suit themselves. They cannot add to God's commandments nor take away from them. To do so a church would be in violation of what God had established her to do. She has no authority to legislate. She only has authority to execute law already made in heaven. That is all – and any church going beyond this is in trouble with God. Those who constitute her membership may not know it. They may not admit it. But one day when all are called into account, those involved shall be made acutely aware of it and shall be judged for the misuse of power. (Brooks 4)*

Delegation of Church Authority

Our sovereign Lord has chosen His churches to be the administrators of His work on earth. Christ exclaimed, "All power is given unto me in heaven and in earth" (Matt. 28:18). He then delegated that power or authority to the church. The church is now the sole executor of God's divine will and re-delegation of that authority can only be done by Him who first gave that authority. Churches have no such power to give up or turn over their authority to others. J.M. Pendleton writes,

> *The church at Corinth could not transfer her power to the church at Philippi, nor could the church at Antioch convey her power to the church at Ephesus. Neither could all the apostolic churches combined delegate their power to an association or synod or convention. That church power is inalienable results from the foundational principle of Congregationalism – that this power is in the hands of the people, the membership. And if the power of a church cannot be transferred, church action is final. That there is no tribunal higher than a church is evident from Matthew 18:15-17. (J. Pendleton 165)*

Corporate Authority

Since there can be no re-delegation of church authority, there can neither be any union of authority. Corporate authority is the basic premise of the convention system as well as the Roman Catholic hierarchy. Corporate authority leads to the practice of universalism. Today, there are numerous organizations, schools, associations, etc. that have been built upon the premise of "co-sponsorship" and boardism (Ashcraft 5).

Scarboro states, "That while Baptists have a New Testament form of local church organization and government, they are trying to build up an Episcopal form of missionary organization and management, borrowed from the Roman genius for organization, and the two things are in immediate and irrepressible conflict" (Scarboro).

Association is scriptural. It is the work that is shared, not the authority. The late Ben M. Bogard put it most clearly when he said, "There is no scriptural way by which churches may combine, but they may associate as equals. This associating does not consist in meeting at a given place, but the churches associate in the work" (Bogard, Associations Are Scriptural). It is Biblical for local churches to help other churches for the cause of Christ. Churches do not combine in a corporate union to

ECCLESIOLOGY OF MISSION WORK 65

form a power greater than the local church, because the local church is the final authority left upon this earth for executing God's will. When a church turns over its power to another governing body, whether it be a convention or a board of trustees, it loses its sovereignty. If a person were to give up his right to vote, he would be giving up his freedom and his voice. Likewise, churches who hand over the right and responsibility of enacting the will of God to any other body abdicate their sovereignty and authority as a church of God. Dr. Ray O. Brooks illustrates this point in the following quote:

> *"What must be guarded against is for any church to involve herself in a situation whereby her sovereignty could be violated. A union of authority would most certainly establish such a condition. For if two or more churches should determine to elect a board through which they would execute Great Commission work, they would have established a system through which the sovereignty of any one of the churches could be violated. For instance, if three churches should decide to operate a Bible school, how could they do it? Each of three churches could elect three trustees and then the three churches could elect a trustee-at-large. The responsibility of managing the school could be given to this Board of Trustees. The actions of the Board of Trustees would of course be amendable to the three churches. This may sound good, but what if churches number one and two vote to uphold some action of the Board of Trustees, and church number three votes against the same action. What happens to the sovereignty of church number three? It is violated. Thus, it has been shown that the association of these three churches in executing the Great Commission work is unscriptural. Church sovereignty has been violated. Let it also be noted, if it is scriptural to execute the third point of the Great Commission as a Union effort of the authority of three churches, then it would certainly be scriptural to execute the other two*

> *points by the same union of authority. Stated another way, this simply means that if it is scriptural to teach 'all things whatsoever I have commanded you' by the joint authority of three churches, then it would be scriptural to send out missionaries by joint authority and it would be scriptural to baptize by joint authority. It is the principle that is wrong, not what point of the Great Commission is being executed.*
>
> *It should also be noted, that if it is scriptural for three churches to join their authority in executing the Great Commission, then it is scriptural for three hundred or three thousand churches to do the same. It is the principle that is wrong, not the number.*
>
> *Two conclusions can be drawn from all this: 1) When any principle of local church authority is compromised, the stage has been set for wholesale violations; 2) When any church enters into any area of associating that can compromise her sovereignty, she is associating in an unscriptural way." (Brooks)*

"When men assume unscriptural powers and depart from God, substituting their own plans for his, He leaves them to their own devices and they perish in the wreck of their own labors" (Scarboro). There is no other man that could so eloquently state the matter of church authority as could our Lord. Never was Christ in favor of a hierarchy of church authority, nor did He want His disciples lording over one another.

> *But Jesus called them unto him, and said, Ye know that the princes of the Gentiles exercise dominion over them, and they that are great exercise authority upon them. But it shall not be so among you: but whosoever will be great among you, let him be your minister; And whosoever will be chief among you, let him be your servant: Even as the Son of man came not to be ministered unto, but to minister, and to give his life a ransom for many (Matt. 20:25-28).*

If corporate authority exists between churches, one will inevitably lord over another. One will certainly be violated. Union cannot exist in an inter-church relationship. "It is clear to this writer that for church association to be scriptural, there can be no union of authority of the churches; no combining of authority; no co-sponsoring in the strict sense of the term" (Brooks).

Biblical Church Mission Work

The Bible clearly states how mission work is to be conducted. Acts Chapter 13 gives the pattern of God called, church sent, Spirit led missionaries. Acts 13:2 ends in the words, "I have called them." If the Lord actually called Paul and Barnabas (and He did), it must be agreed that God not only approved of the mission endeavor, He initiated it. Acts 13:3 states that the church "sent them away." If the church sent the missionaries, (and she did) it must be agreed that they were following the teachings and commandments of Christ and the apostles that the local church carries the authority to evangelize, baptize and indoctrinate. Acts 13:4 states "So they, being sent forth by the Holy Ghost" cannot make the subject matter any clearer of the fact that Paul and Barnabas were under the direction and leadership of the Spirit of God. Therefore, this chapter is not only an account of an early church sending out missionaries, it is also an account of mission work as it should be done according to God's divine will.

The Responsibility of the Church to the Missionary

It is the responsibility of the sending church to take care of the needs of their missionary. The authority conferred to the local church by Jesus Christ gives that church the right to perform mission work and send out missionaries. Yet, with every right comes a responsibility. The responsibility of the church to her missionary is to make sure that both he, his family and the needs of the work are all provided for. This includes spiritual support, physical support, emotional support, and financial support. Though other churches may help in providing these needs, ultimately the obligation falls squarely on the shoulders of his sending church.

Spiritual Support

Mission work, though a work of physical labor, is first and foremost a spiritual task. The local church and the missionary are instruments of the mission, yet they are but tools in the hands of the One who truly enacts and completes the mission. Without the Lord, any action, no matter how noble or sincere, is vain. It is the responsibility of the church to provide her missionary with the weaponry and resources to fight the spiritual battle that rages on the mission field. This spiritual support must come in the form of constant, earnest prayer. Saints on their knees keep missionaries on their feet. Too much talk is given about finances of mission work and not enough about prayer for mission work. The true power of mission work lies not in how much money is given, but in how many effectual fervent prayers are offered. Churches would be wise in learning from the humble sinner bowed in prayer in the corner of the temple, rather than boasting like the proud Pharisee of how much money they give. E.M. Bounds stated it beautifully,

> *The key of all missionary success is prayer. That key is in the hands of the home churches. The trophies won by our Lord in heathen lands will be won by praying missionaries, not by professional workers in foreign lands. More especially will this success be won by saintly praying in the churches at home. The home church on her knees fasting and praying, is the great base of spiritual supplies, the sinews of war, and the pledge of victory in this dire and final*

> *Saints on their knees keep missionaries on their feet.*

> *conflict. Financial resources are not the real sinews of war in this fight. Machinery in itself carries no power to break down heathen walls, open effectual doors and win heathen hearts to Christ. Prayer alone can do the deed. (Bounds)*

The Biblical example of mission work in Acts 13 starts with a church which is fasting and praying as the Spirit calls out the missionaries. In Acts 13:2, the mission work commences with fasting and prayer. The power of a missionary to succeed or fail in the mission endeavor lies firmly upon the spiritual stores that he receives through the prayers of the saints on his behalf. A person might argue that God alone holds spiritual power. However, prayer is the key to unlock that power from the Lord. James Chapter four teaches an important principle that states, "ye have not because ye ask not." The Lord is ready and willing to answer the prayer of faith offered to Him for the furtherance of His mission.

Not only should there be constant earnest prayer, but there should also be constant mission education. Every member of a church should know the mission and be personally involved in the mission work of their church. Churches should educate their members on the Biblical teachings of mission work, the personal work and struggles of their missionaries, and the importance of support and involvement in mission work. Experience is the best teacher to excite and involve the congregation in the mission endeavors of the church. A church whose membership is actively involved with their missionaries by going on mission trips is a church that is growing both spiritually and numerically.

Physical Support

A missionary must be supported physically as well as spiritually. There are physical tasks and struggles that a missionary cannot (and by right should not have to) do alone. It is nice to tell the missionary that the church cares for and prays for him, yet to show him physically and personally by visiting him on the mission field is a blessing that not only helps the missionary, but also the church. Short term mission trips to help teach, to preach, to witness, to pass out fliers and tracts, to hold vacation Bible school, or to simply encourage a missionary and his family are all means of physical support.

Building construction on the mission field is another means of physical support. Building trips can be combined with evangelistic or teaching teams to help strengthen the work on the field. Some would decry the money spent on airfare and expenses as a waste that could better be spent on other things. I once had the same thought when 25 people came to help me finish a church building in Thailand. When I calculated the amount of money that the group spent to come to Thailand, it added up to over $35,000. What I could do on the mission field with that amount of money! They could have stayed home and just sent the money, I thought. One day I voiced my opinion out loud to another missionary, who quickly chastised me for thinking such a thing. "That IS mission work," he said. "Now 25 lives have been changed. So much more will be done for the Lord than you could ever have done with that money."

Emotional Support

The importance of emotional support for a missionary and his family is evidenced in the rate of missionary attrition. Often times, missionaries feel alone on the field and completely cut off from the life and country they have left behind. In years past, it was very difficult to keep in constant communication overseas. However, in this present day, there is no excuse for a lack of communication between churches and missionaries. For instance, when I first went to the mission field, there were no cell phones. I was on a ten-year waiting list for a land line. Mail was slow and unreliable, sometimes taking months. To contact the States, we had to go into town to the phone company office. There, they had three phone booths that could call the United States. I brought lots of change and paid close to six dollars a minute for a very

> ### PRAY FOR YOUR MISSIONARIES!
>
> **Psalm 5:3 "My voice shalt thou hear in the morning, O LORD; in the morning will I direct my prayer unto thee, and will look up."**
>
> Our lives took a drastic turn when we stepped on that plane headed for the mission field, and it's been an eventful journey. We've climbed high mountains and walked through deep valleys. Our first year on the field proved to be a very rocky start for the mission work in Thailand. We had constant problems with our visas, trouble from non-believers, and we were harassed constantly by those of other "Christian" denominations. Satan's fiery darts began to weigh heavily on my soul. We've had our lives threatened, we've had to leave the country, and we've even had our church building set on fire. The isolation from other Christians added to the stress of the many problems and trials that we faced on the field. One day, I was at a particularly low point and I thought I couldn't go on. An entire congregation walked out on a sermon, renouncing Christ as the only way to heaven. By the next day, I was ready to quit when the postman dropped by with a letter. It was from a supporting church telling me that they had prayed for me on a Wednesday night. Everyone that prayed signed their names to the letter. I turned the envelope over and noticed that the letter had been sent six weeks before. Even though those prayers had been uttered many weeks ago, the Lord knew just when I needed an answer. Even though that letter had been sent a month and a half prior, it got there right on time!

Figure 5. *Missionary Insights: Pray for Your Missionaries!*

bad connection. Over the years, things changed. The rice patties and fields of water buffalo around our home turned into housing developments. Our unstable power that was on about 8 hours a day became 24-hour, stable electricity. After nine years, we even got running water to our house! Communication changed also. We got cell phones and dial-up internet. Then came DSL and high-speed internet, along with video chats and free VOIP calls to the U.S. Even in the most remote areas, missionaries can carry satellite phones or some type of communication base to the outside world. With these tools, churches should regularly contact their missionaries. Pastors should stay in touch and be involved in the lives of their missionaries. Many churches assign an individual or family to act as a personal liaison between the missionary and the church. When there are personal needs or matters of importance, this individual or family acts on their behalf.

Several other ways that churches can provide emotional support to their missionaries is by mailing cards, letters, and care packages to the missionary and their families. One of the greatest joys a missionary has on the field is receiving some form of special communication or contact from his friends, family, and sending church. Special communication does not include hitting the "Like" button on a Facebook post or forwarding an email that was written by another person. In this electronic age, it may be a lost art, but a person who would take the time to write a hand-written letter will show that they value their missionary enough to contact him in a special way.

A birthday, anniversary, or get-well card signed by members of the sending church shows a missionary that his church cares about him personally, and has not forgotten him and his family. A care package filled with items that cannot be obtained on the mission field turns grown men into children opening Christmas presents. A jar of peanut butter, bottle of Dr. Pepper, special scented candles or lotion for the missionary wife, or favorite candy for the missionary kids can brighten up a missionary's emotional well-being in an extraordinary way.

Financial Support

Financially, many sending churches may elect to pay a certain percentage of the missionary's salary, requiring the rest to be raised by other supporters. However, if a missionary has an urgent need or other churches fail to help their missionary, the sending church has no right to shirk their responsibility. They must provide for their own. Many families have left their homes to serve God on the foreign field, living destitute, without the basic necessities of life or even the money to provide food for their children: all because their sending church would not hold up their responsibility to provide financially for their missionary. Recently, a Baptist missionary died in a foreign hospital, being refused care because he did not have the money to pay. There have been missionaries who needed to return home, but their sending church refused to allow it. There have been sending churches who have arbitrarily cut off all support of a missionary while serving on the field, leaving him with no means of support whatsoever. These things ought not to be so. The sending church has a duty, a commitment, a responsibility, and furthermore, a moral obligation to support its missionary in every way.

Missionaries receive funds from three channels: the sending church, other supporting churches, and individual donations. However, the source of all mission finances is ultimately the Lord. Once the missionary and the sending church understands this concept, and by faith realizes that God will provide for everything necessary to accomplish His work, there will be less apprehension, frustration, and worry about the financial aspect of mission work.

While on deputation amongst the churches, a missionary will also receive gifts and offerings that can help pay for the added expense of traveling on the road. Those travels are sometimes tens of thousands of miles over the course of just a few months. When a newly commissioned missionary first starts to raise support, the sending church may want to pay him a full salary until he can raise the support needed. There are pros and cons to this. One positive aspect is that a missionary and his family is fully taken care of by his church. He can feel confident that in times of need, his church is there to fully support him and the mission work that he has set out to accomplish. However, there are also some negative aspects of paying a full salary to a missionary while on deputation. The missionary could use the salary as a crutch, providing little motivation to quickly raise support. The missionary could also become a financial burden to the sending church for an extended period of time. Most importantly, the process of deputation is a faith building exercise for a missionary, for him to fully comprehend the concept of absolute faith in the providence, protection, and power of God in his life and ministry. Deputation is the proving ground of faith for a soldier of God before he is thrust onto the front lines of battle on the mission field. By providing a full salary, the missionary completely misses this important aspect of deputation.

The local church is the singularly authorized agent of mission work on earth. Many churches have elected to send their missionaries through boards, associations, or clearing houses because they feel as if they do not have the capability nor the manpower to handle this enormous task. There is, however, no other authorized nor more capable body to accomplish the task of the Lord's work than that which is ordained of God to do it: the local church.

Biblically, the local church is the sending agency of the missionary. Therefore, it must consider the requirements to fulfill the financial aspects of the ministry: a mission treasurer to receive and disburse funds, equipment and supplies for proper bookkeeping, means of conveying monies to the missionary overseas, and financial reporting to both the body of the sending church and other supporters. The church treasurer, or perhaps a separate person designated "mission treasurer" should be appointed by the sending church to receive and disburse funds. Bank accounts should be opened by the church, and the personal account of the missionary should always be kept separate from the mission account, for ethical accountability and ease of bookkeeping. A salary for the missionary should be established by the sending church that is taken from the mission account and paid to the missionary on a regular basis. Keeping mission funds (which are under the control and distributed by the sending church) separate from the missionary's personal salary will simplify matters when the missionary files his taxes. Most churches pay their missionaries as contract labor for tax purposes, and as such must give them an annual 1099 form for filing as a "self-employed" worker. Churches and missionaries should consult the IRS or bookkeeping agency on the current tax code and how an overseas worker should file.

There are several ethical considerations concerning finances that must be addressed. Churches should be blameless and transparent to the world in their financial dealings, not only because of the legal implications of civil and criminal liability for inappropriate use of funds (and increasing scrutiny of the IRS in recent years), but also for the general testimony of the church in its community and the prospect of bringing a reproach upon the mission and

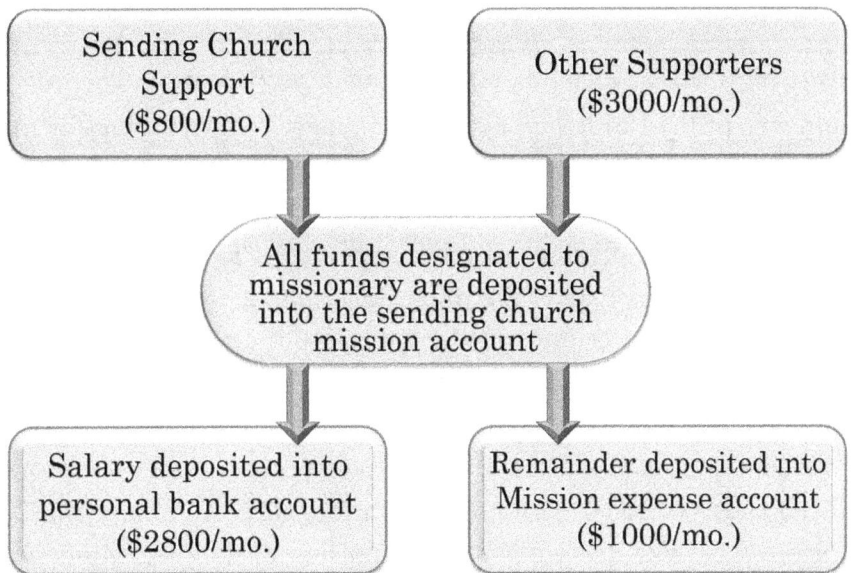

Figure 6. *An example of receipt and distribution of a missionary's financial support*

> ### A Special Care Package
>
> Here's a story that may sound silly to some, but special to missionaries. I remember a box that came from home that had a can of Dr. Pepper, which is my favorite soda. There was no Dr. Pepper to be found on the field where we worked. My kids also loved it, as well as two other missionaries who came to work with me. The can sat for months on a shelf, waiting for some special celebration to open it. I don't remember the event, but the day finally came that we decided to drink it. I had some tiny ketchup cups like you can find in a fast food restaurant. I got out six of them and carefully poured just a few drops of Dr. Pepper in each one. We all looked at the cups and had a good laugh, but were all eager to taste just a sip of home. We savored the taste slowly, watching the bubbles rise. It wasn't about the soda. It was special because it reminded us of home. It reminded us of how much our church and folks back in the States cared about us.

Figure 7. *Missionary Insights: A Special Care Package*

ministry of the Lord. The overhead expenses of providing for the financial needs of the missionary should fall squarely upon the shoulders of the sending church, rather than expensing these costs to the incoming offerings of other supporters. The reason for this is that supporters expect that their donations to a missionary will be going to that missionary. Many non-profit organizations spend just a tiny fraction of all donations on the work that they present publicly, while most of the money is funneled into overhead costs of administrative salaries, office expenses, etc. Because of this fact a large portion of potential supporters are leery of any church (or other organization) who takes a portion of their donations for overhead costs. Furthermore, it is completely unethical to take funds that have been donated and specifically designated for a certain purpose and use them for a different purpose. For instance, if a check is received that is designated for "Building Fund," yet the church, treasurer or missionary decides to use these funds for a separate purpose without consulting the giver, this is unethical behavior. All funds given to a missionary or mission project should be given to the missionary or project to which it was designated.

The Responsibility of the Missionary to the Church

There are three primary responsibilities that a missionary has to his sending church: subjection, communication, and representation.

Subjection

A missionary should subject himself to the authority of the Lord, his church, and his pastor. A missionary's first loyalty and commitment must be to the Lord. As an ambassador for Christ in foreign lands, the missionary is representative of what a Christian should be. His life may be the very first impression of Christianity upon a lost soul. The purity (or contamination) of his testimony can affect the lost on a personal basis and also the community at large. Every action, every word, and even the thoughts of the missionary must first be weighed by the measure of God's standard. He must remember that he is a follower of Christ, and by following Christ's example, he should place himself under the subjection of the Father in heaven. Far from the prying eyes of his sending church and supporters, he may be tempted to do things which are not moral, Biblical, or ethical. However, the Lord is always watching, and he will give account of himself and his actions one day. The Lord will hold a missionary to a higher standard than others because of the responsibility which is placed upon him.

A missionary is a member of and is subservient to the authority of his sending church. As a member, a missionary is obligated to obey what the church asks him to do. With that in mind, the church should choose a man in whom they trust implicitly. A missionary works hundreds, if not thousands of miles away from the sending church, and will for the majority of the time act without the direct and personal oversight of the pastor or sending church. For this reason, a missionary must be a man of upstanding and unquestionable moral character who can be trusted to carry out the wishes of the sending church regardless of the lack of personal oversight on the field. Over time, the independent actions of a missionary may contribute to an attitude in which he feels that he is not subject to the authority and control of his church. He may question the wisdom of the pastor or church body who is not present on the mission field to realize the struggles and day to day realities of his life. To some extent, these are valid concerns, however, they do not lessen the fact that the sending church holds the authority from the Lord, and a missionary must be in subjection to it.

> *The missionary is a member of and is subservient to the authority of his sending church.*

Also, as a member of his sending church, a missionary should, while he is home with them, partake of the Lord's Supper with the church of his membership. Landmark Baptists who hold to local church doctrine must come to the conclusion that the Lord's Supper is a local church ordinance and should be restricted to the members of that local church. Many missionaries, though admitting belief in the practice of restricted communion, will allow for a missionary exception on the mission field. This is, in essence, the practice of catholic (universal) church doctrine. There is no better illustration to teach a new church the scriptural principles of ecclesiology than for a missionary to abstain and show through his example that he will only partake of the Lord's Supper in the church of his own membership.

Not only is a missionary under the subjection to the Lord and his sending church, he should also be in subjection to the leadership of his pastor. The Lord has placed the pastor at the helm of the local church and has ordained him as the under-shepherd of the flock. A missionary must realize that the Lord will work through the office of the pastor to share special spiritual insights and direction to the membership of the local church. Each staff member of the church should be in subjection to the man entrusted by the Lord to be the spiritual leader of the church. This includes missionaries on the mission field.

Communication

A missionary is obligated to report his work to the sending church, not only as a matter of accountability, but also of Biblical principle and precedence. In the book of Acts, Paul returned from his missionary journey to his sending church in Antioch, and there reported to them of all that the Lord had done.

> *"And thence sailed to Antioch, from whence they had been recommended to the grace of God for the work which they fulfilled. And when they were come, and had gathered the church together, they rehearsed all that God had done with them, and how he had opened the door of faith unto the Gentiles" (Acts 14:26-27).*

He should keep regularly scheduled contact with his pastor and his sending church, keeping them fully informed of the happenings of the mission field. It is just as important for a missionary to keep in contact with his church as it is for the church to keep in contact with its missionary. Communication is a two-way street. He should initiate contact with his church by making phone calls, writing letters, sending cards and thank-you notes, sending emails, and even sending regular video updates to the church. Whatever the means of communication, a missionary must not forget this important responsibility.

A missionary must also never forget to send out regular mission reports or prayer letters to his church and other supporters. There is an old adage that is quoted by many pastors, "No report, no support!" Many supporting churches live by this creed, and the wise missionary will take this warning to heart. With the ease of the internet today, sending reports to supporters is simple, fast, and inexpensive. There are many other ways to reach supporters besides printed reports such as email, online bulletin boards, Facebook, and blogs just to name a few.

Representation

A missionary is a representative for Christ, an ambassador of the Most High God, a witness to the redemption of the Lamb of God, and a shining light in a world of darkness. A missionary must remember that he represents the Lord in his testimony. Many people on the mission field have no concept of what a Christian should be. A missionary will represent Christ and Christianity as possibly their only example. He will be a pastor to pastors, a guide to the lost, a counselor to the needy, a teacher to hungry souls and an example for new believers to pattern their lives and ministries after. A missionary does not go to the field representing himself. His mission is much larger than himself. A missionary goes to the field representing Jesus Christ.

Not only is he a representative of Christ, but a missionary is also a representative of his sending church. As a missionary visits other churches on deputation, he acts as the emissary of his church, a delegate representing the mission of his church to others. He must properly conduct himself, in and out of the pulpit. Just as the actions of children reflect upon their parents, the actions of a missionary reflect upon his sending church. Yet, a missionary's representation of his church does not stop there. His actions, speech and personal conduct represents his sending church on the field as well. A backslidden missionary who has fallen into sin can ruin his life, his personal ministry, the mission work on the field, and the good name of his sending church.

THE LORD CHANGED HIS HEART

Ezekiel 36:26 A new heart also will I give you, and a new spirit will I put within you: and I will take away the stony heart out of your flesh, and I will give you an heart of flesh.

When I joined my church over twenty years ago, I met Bro. John, an elderly deacon and church treasurer, who was always excited about going on the next mission trip. When a financial need came up for one of the missionaries, he was the first to give and the first to incite other to do the same for the cause of Christ. The pastor told me that Bro. John wasn't always like that. Actually, as the treasurer, he would often speak out against spending church funds on mission work. Then something happened that changed his heart, his life, and his outlook on just about everything. What changed him? He went on a mission trip. He saw with his own eyes the great spiritual need of the world and the battles that the missionaries faced. The Lord changed his heart and started a fire that kept spreading throughout the church with missionary zeal. When church members get actively involved in mission work, lives are changed and churches grow. Whether an established church at home or a new church plant on the mission field, there is no better way to stimulate church growth than getting the membership actively involved in mission work.

Figure 8. *Missionary Insights: The Lord Changed His Heart*

Chapter Five

BIBLICAL BASIS OF MISSION WORK

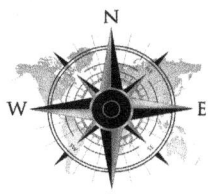

Survey of Mission Work in the Old Testament

All throughout Scripture, God is seen as a God who sends. "The Bible is the record of the missionary activity of God" (Terry, 10). The Father sent the Son, who sent the Spirit, who sent the church, who now sends missionaries throughout the world. The first mission-centric verse in Scripture in Genesis 1:1. To what extent? Revelation 14:6-7 explains, "And I saw another angel fly in the midst of heaven, having the everlasting gospel to preach unto them that dwell on the earth, and to every nation, and kindred, and tongue, and people, Saying with a loud voice, Fear God, and give glory to him; for the hour of his judgment is come: and worship him that made heaven, and earth, and the sea, and the fountains of waters." According to Scripture, the everlasting gospel which is to be preached throughout eternity is not the gospel of salvation. The gospel of salvation is limited in scope to the dispensation of human history which shall end when the sin curse is finally and forever eradicated. However, from the beginning, and throughout all eternity there is and ever shall be proclaimed the "everlasting gospel" for all of creation to fear, give glory to, and worship the Creator of all things. (Revelation 14:6-7) The gospel of salvation which is now preached under the constraints of the sin curse is certainly included under the overarching scope of this gospel of creation, however it is only a part - one that shall end when the curse is lifted and there shall be no more sin nor yet any sinner to be saved.

Every page of God's Word is replete with the idea of mission work. Dr. Nina Gunter states, "If you take missions out of the Bible, you won't have anything left but the covers" (Culbertson, 2013). The Great Commission is to go into "all the world" (Matt. 28:19). This command of universal evangelism is significant because we serve a universal God. Howard Culbertson writes,

> *...when God commands us to evangelize the whole world, He is not telling us to barge into places where He has little or no right to be. God loves the whole world precisely because He created it all. Therefore, shouldn't we call those at 'the ends of the earth' to offer 'glory and honor' to the One who brought the universe into existence and who has reached out to all in the person of Jesus Christ? (Culbertson, 2013)*

Mission Through the Preaching of Noah

Tradition states that Noah spent 100 years building the ark, and preached judgment upon the world for those 100 years, yet everyone mocked him and no one was saved. The Bible does not plainly state that it took 100 years to build the ark, nor does it say that Noah was mocked as he brought the message of doom upon the earth during those years. However, II Peter 2:5 does say that Noah was a preacher of righteousness, explaining a most difficult passage in First Peter.

> *"For Christ also hath once suffered for sins, the just for the unjust, that he might bring us to God, being put*

> *to death in the flesh, but quickened by the Spirit: By which also he went and preached unto the spirits in prison; Which sometime were disobedient, when once the longsuffering of God waited in the days of Noah, while the ark was a preparing, wherein few, that is, eight souls were saved by water"* (1 Peter 3:18-20).

Christ, through Noah, preached righteousness to the people of the antediluvian era (Kaiser Jr. 6). Unfortunately, none but Noah and seven others in his immediate family were saved from destruction. Peter states that those who heard the message of righteousness by Christ through the preaching of Noah were now in prison, a euphemism for the bounds of hell. Nevertheless, Noah's missionary efforts were not in vain. In contrast to Lot, who had been disobedient in leading his own family to the knowledge of righteousness, Noah's wife, three sons and their wives were saved from destruction. Despite the fact the only eight souls were saved Noah's missionary effort was most certainly successful. Noah was faithful to the Lord and obeyed His commandments. Success is mentioned but one time in Scripture, in Joshua 1:8 "This book of the law shall not depart out of thy mouth; but thou shalt meditate therein day and night, that thou mayest observe to do according to all that is written therein: for then thou shalt make thy way prosperous, and then thou shalt have good success." Success in God's eyes is not measured by the number of souls that are saved or baptisms that are performed, nor even churches that are planted. Success is following the Word of the Lord and obeying it. If a Christian does what he knows he ought to do according to God's will, then that Christian is successful.

Abraham: The First Cross-cultural Missionary

In the book of Genesis, God sends Abraham into a new land, from his home in Ur of the Chaldees to Canaan, making him the first cross-cultural missionary mentioned in the Scriptures. Through the obedience and testimony of Abraham, the one true God came to be known in this foreign land. God blessed Abraham's obedience

> ### TRUTH HURTS
>
> **"Am I therefore become your enemy, because I tell you the truth?"**
>
> Paul asks the Galatians a pungent question after delivering a dissertation of sharp rebuke for their swift departure from the gospel of grace. The fact remained... Paul loved these people. That is why he told them the truth, just as a mother when she points out the unkempt appearance of her child - not because she is critical of the child, but because she loves him. We must endeavor to "speak the truth in love." On the mission field, it is easy to get caught up in a "social gospel" of trying to help the needy and emotionally wounded, while forgetting about the true spiritual needs of the people. We try so hard in so many ways to get people just to come, that it is easy to water down our preaching, our witnessing, our religious fervor and even our beliefs to try to win some. A wise man once said, "What you win them with is what you win them to." Our duty is to propagate truth. When the truth rubs us the wrong way, it's not the truth that needs to turn around - we do. Above all, never water down the truth of God's Word. No matter what the consequences, we as God's children must stand fast, grounded in the truth of God's Word.

Figure 9. *Missionary Insights: Truth Hurts*

by giving him the promise that all nations through him would be blessed. Abraham is a perfect Biblical example of an Old Testament cross-cultural missionary. Abraham heard the call of God and was obedient to the Lord's command. The call upon Abraham's life was a call to mission work. He was to leave his home, travel to a foreign land, and there serve the Lord. Lastly "Abraham is the means, he is not the goal. It is through him that others will be blessed by blessing, but the purpose goes beyond Abraham: 'all the peoples on earth will be blessed.'" (Moreau, 31)

Mission Through the Biblical Type of the Exodus

Moses was sent to Egypt, a Biblical type of the world, to rescue and lead God's people into the promised land. There can be no question as to the symbolism here. Moses was sent on a mission by God, and therefore qualifies for the position of an Old Testament missionary. However, it was not just for the nation of Israel that Moses was sent. Exodus 9:16 is a key verse in understanding the full scope of the mission of Moses, "And in very deed for this cause have I raised thee up, for to shew in thee my power; and that my name may be declared throughout all the earth." Here, as in many other verses in the Old Testament, it is evident that the mission of God, though centered around a chosen people, was a universal mission for all mankind. Not willing that any should perish even in the dispensation before the new covenant, we find in Exodus 12:38 that the sojourn of the nation of Israel out of Egypt includes those of other races (Kaiser Jr. 16). "And a mixed multitude went up also with them." The nation of Israel, and more importantly, God Himself, was willing to accept all those who would follow the Lord.

Joshua: The Missionary Conqueror

Joshua, whose name in Hebrew is the same as the name *Jesus*, meaning "savior," was the missionary conqueror (Kaiser Jr. 20). Over 400 years of longsuffering grace had been given to the nations of the Canaanites to repent and turn to the one true God while the nation of Israel was held in Egyptian bondage. The Canaanites were not without a witness to the truth. There was righteous Abraham, who, no doubt, was not secret in his worship of the Lord God. There was Melchezidek, the priest of the most high God who lived in Salem, later known as Jebus, and then Jerusalem (Kaiser Jr. 38). There was Isaac, the son of promise, who served the Lord and was counted faithful in Hebrews 11, sharing his faith with his two sons, Jacob and Esau. After four centuries, the people of Canaan had turned their backs upon God and served idols. God now raised up a man in Moses' place to lead the nation of Israel into the promised land. Though it may be argued that the conquering of the land was in judgment, God also had an alternate purpose. Both the presence of the nation of Israel in the land and the miracles of the Lord performed in the taking of the land were to show God's mighty hand to all the earth, so that they would know that Lord God of Israel was the one true God.

> *"For the LORD your God dried up the waters of Jordan from before you, until ye were passed over, as the LORD your God did to the Red sea, which he dried up from before us, until we were gone over: That all the people of the earth might know the hand of the LORD, that it is mighty: that ye might fear the LORD your God for ever" (Joshua 4:23-24).*

David: The Missionary King

King David has a special place among the pages of God's Word. He also holds a special place in the missionary plan of the Lord (Kaiser Jr. 21). The Lord extended the promise of Abraham in a more specific way to David. It would be through his line, through his seed, that the Messiah would come. The Lord promised that through Christ the throne of David would endure forever. It was to David that God would order the building of the temple in Jerusalem, where all nations would one day come to worship. It was through the words of this royal psalter that the Lord's missionary heart would be revealed. Even from an early age, God showed His power through David for the express purpose of a missionary message to the world: "that all the earth may know that there is a God in Israel." As God won the battle over Goliath through young David, he spoke openly that the salvation of the Lord did not come by the works of man, but by the power of God.

> *Then said David to the Philistine, Thou comest to me with a sword, and with a spear, and with a shield: but I come to thee in the name of the LORD of hosts, the God of the armies of Israel, whom thou hast defied. This day will the LORD deliver thee into mine hand; and I*

> *will smite thee, and take thine head from thee; and I will give the carcases of the host of the Philistines this day unto the fowls of the air, and to the wild beasts of the earth;* <u>*that all the earth may know that there is a God in Israel.*</u> *And all this assembly shall know that the LORD saveth not with sword and spear: for the battle is the LORD's, and he will give you into our hands. (1 Samuel 17:45-47)*

Later, David went on to rejoice, as he did many times in song, "Sing unto the LORD, all the earth; shew forth from day to day his salvation. Declare his glory among the heathen; his marvelous works among all nations" (1 Chronicles 16:23-24). David plainly declared not only his personal missionary heart, but that the very heart of God was that of a missionary God. All throughout the pages of the Old Testament, we find verse after verse of God's missionary zeal to bring not only Israel, but the entire world to the saving knowledge of the Lord. It is God's desire to redeem His lost creation back to personal fellowship, back to righteousness, and back to holiness in Christ.

Mission Through the Testimony of Solomon

> *Moreover concerning a stranger, that is not of thy people Israel, but cometh out of a far country for thy name's sake; (For they shall hear of thy great name, and of thy strong hand, and of thy stretched out arm;) when he shall come and pray toward this house; Hear thou in heaven thy dwelling place, and do according to all that the stranger calleth to thee for:* <u>*that all people of the earth may know thy name, to fear thee, as do thy people Israel*</u>*; and that they may know that this house, which I have builded, is called by thy name. (1 Kings 8:41-43)*

Solomon, the wisest man who ever lived, gained his spiritual insight from God Himself. It was with this knowledge that he called upon the Lord during the dedication of the temple of Jerusalem. During

Solomon's day, there were those who came from all over the world to worship the one true God, and did so at the newly constructed temple. By reading Solomon's words, it is not too difficult to deduce the fact that there were many people of the gentile nations who called upon the name of the Lord. The people of Israel were to be a light to the Gentiles, and the temple and all its symbolism was a testament to both the presence and salvation of the Lord.

Mission Through the Symbolism of the Tabernacle

God gave very specific instructions for the building of the tabernacle. Galatians 3:24 explains that the symbolism found in the Old Testament was in every way to point to Christ and salvation through Him. "Wherefore the law was our schoolmaster to bring us unto Christ, that we might be justified by faith." Each part of that divine plan for the tabernacle was significant and symbolic of God's plan of salvation for not only the people of Israel, but the entire world (Levy 5). It is not the purpose of this work to go into an in-depth treatise of the symbolism of the tabernacle, however several main points will be considered. First, the Brazen Altar was a testament of the sacrifice for sin, pointing to the substitutionary sacrifice of Christ on the cross. Secondly, the Brazen Laver symbolizes the Word of God, whoso looking into it may not only see himself and his own condition, but will find that which washes clean. The Golden Lampstand was to light the holy place of the tabernacle, symbolic of Him who not only brings light, but is the true light of the world - Jesus Christ. John states in his gospel in John 1:9, "That was the true Light, which lighteth every man that cometh into the world." The Table of Shewbread is most certainly a symbol pointing to Jesus, who taught His disciples that He was the Bread of Life. John 6:51 states, "I am the living bread which came down from heaven: if any man eat of this bread, he shall live for ever: and the bread that I will give is my flesh, which I will give for the life of the world." The Altar of Incense represented prayer and intercession, as the burning savor of incense rose up, so too would the prayers of the saints to the Lord. The Veil of the Temple, though beautiful in its handiwork, represented a terrible fact of the sin curse: that mankind was separated from God by their sin. However, through the mediatorial sacrifice of Jesus Christ, the veil was not only symbolically removed, but actually ripped in two from top to bottom. Matthew 27:51 states, "And, behold, the veil of the temple was rent in twain from the top to the bottom; and the earth did quake, and the rocks rent." Within the Holy of Holies lay the Ark of the Covenant and the Mercy Seat. The Ark of the Covenant was representative of the presence of God with mankind. As God's glory rested upon the ark in the Old Testament, so too did Emmanuel, "God with us" come to show His presence with mankind in the New Testament. Even still today, the Holy Spirit of God dwells in the believer. First Corinthians 3:16 states, "Know ye not that ye are the temple of God, and that the Spirit of God dwelleth in you?" The final item of the Tabernacle, the Mercy Seat is a symbol of the propitiation of Jesus Christ.

> *"The cover of the ark on which rested the cloud or visible symbol of the divine presence. It was called Mercy Seat, or propitiatory from ἱλαστήριον hilastērion (Strong's G2435) - because it was this which was sprinkled over with the blood of atonement or propitiation, and because it was from this place, on which the symbol of the deity rested, that God manifested himself as propitious to sinners. The blood of the atonement was that through or by means of which he declared his mercy to the guilty"* (Barnes, p.188).

The shed blood of Jesus Christ provides the atonement for sin. David Levy writes, "In the New Testament, propitiation has the idea of satisfying the righteous demands of a holy God, making it possible for the removal of sin that stands between God and mankind" (Levy 94).

Psalms: The Missionary Hymnbook

The book of Psalms is the inspired hymnal of the believer. The Psalms could also be called a missionary hymnal, as numerous verses declare the glory of God to the heathen (Kaiser Jr. 27 ff). Of the multitude of verses in the Psalms about reaching the world, the following are considered here:

Psalm 18:49 is quoted by Paul in Romans 15:9 as an Old Testament proof that the Lord extended His call to salvation to the Gentiles, "Therefore will I give thanks unto thee, O LORD, among the heathen, and sing praises unto thy name." Romans chapter 15 provides a Biblical exposition of Old Testament mission work to the Gentiles.

The twenty-second Psalm is both Messianic and prophetic in nature. It was the first verse of Psalm 22 that Christ quoted upon the cross when He exclaimed, "My God! My God! Why hast thou forsaken me?" Toward the end of the Psalm, the words, "the great congregation" are found.

> *My praise shall be of thee in the great congregation: I will pay my vows before them that fear him. The meek shall eat and be satisfied: they shall praise the LORD that seek him: your heart shall live for ever. All the ends of the world shall remember and turn unto the LORD: and all the kindreds of the nations shall worship before thee. For the kingdom is the LORD's: and he is the governor among the nations. (Psalm 22:25-28)*

This "great congregation" is referring to the congregation of the righteous who worship the Lord. Within this congregation are found not only the tribes of Israel, nor is it confined simply to the children of Abraham, but to "all the kindreds of the nations." David here declares that God is not merely God of the nation of Israel, but His kingdom is universal in nature. The Lord is both God and King over all nations.

Also, it is found in Psalm 86:9 that "All nations whom thou hast made shall come and worship before thee, O LORD; and shall glorify thy name." The Lord's universal governorship is also here declared to be the Maker of all nations, and because the Lord made all nations of men upon the earth, it is the eventual destiny of those nations to return to the Lord, worship the Lord, and glorify the Lord. Of course, not all men will turn to God. Yet this verse which is missionary at heart is also a prophetic vision of the future when Christ will reign supreme upon the earth. In that day, all nations will come to worship Him and glorify His name.

Psalm 96:1-3 is a joyful commandment to all mankind to not only praise God, but to be a witness into all the earth. These verses might very well be the Old Testament version of the Great Commission. "O sing unto the LORD a new song: sing unto the LORD, all the earth. Sing unto the

---

WHICH WAY ARE YOU WALKING?

"Look unto me, and be ye saved, all the ends of the earth: for I am God, and there is none else" (Isaiah 45:22).

I have noticed that most people visiting a foreign mission field will come away with either an exceptionally positive experience or an extremely negative attitude. Our walk with the Lord is very much the same. In our spiritual lives, we are either walking closer to the Lord or walking further away from Him. There seems to be no middle ground. One thing is for sure: there is no standing still. You are either becoming more like Him or you are backsliding. The trials faced on the mission field can help a missionary grow closer to the Lord. Many, however, become angry at God and the people to whom they were sent to minister. When we find ourselves having an angry spirit and a cynical attitude, it is then that we must realize that we have taken our eyes off the Lord, and are focused on the world. If we "turn our eyes upon Jesus, the things of earth will grow strangely dim." Our outlook and attitude will change!

Figure 10. *Missionary Insights: Which Way Are You Walking?*

LORD, bless his name; shew forth his salvation from day to day. Declare his glory among the heathen, his wonders among all people." Israel had failed greatly in their missionary effort to reach the gentile nations for God. However, the command to Israel to reach the world was clearly given, again and again. Moreau states, "In Exodus 19:4-6 God tells Moses to announce to Israel that because he himself brought Israel out of Egypt, they will be his special possession, his kingdom of priests, his holy nation. By designating them as his "special possession" God shows that he places a high value on people. As his "kingly priests," "the whole nation was to function on behalf of the kingdom of God in a mediatorial role in relation to the nations" (Kaiser 13). As a "holy nation," they were wholly God's, set apart for his service, not for their own ends" (Moreau, 36).

In the New Testament, a great mystery was revealed. That mystery was of God's plan for His church, not of salvation. The redemptive plan of God was clearly revealed in the Old Testament. The plan of redemption has always been the same, from the time of Adam until today. From the first symbolic sacrifice until the final sacrifice of Jesus Christ upon the cross of Calvary, the message of salvation is this: God saves by sacrifice. God used Israel, both through the mighty works performed in the sight of the nations and through the sacrificial symbolism of the temple service, to be an example to the rest of the world of the salvation of the Lord. Psalm 98:2-3 states that the salvation of the Lord was never hidden. It has always been clearly shown throughout every corner of the earth. "The LORD hath made known his salvation: his righteousness hath he openly shewed in the sight of the heathen. He hath remembered his mercy and his truth toward the house of Israel: all the ends of the earth have seen the salvation of our God." Truly, these passages and many others show that the book of Psalms is a missionary hymn book, declaring God's redemptive plan not only to the nation of Israel, but to the ends of the world.

Jonah: The Reluctant Missionary

God sent Jonah to preach to the sworn enemies of Israel. Nineveh was the capital city of the Assyrian Empire. This empire would later invade, pillage, and take captive the northern tribes of Israel. Jonah was called, yet was reluctant to go. Nineveh was approximately 550 miles northeast of Samaria on the Tigris River, in what is now modern-day Mosul, Iraq. Jonah instead traveled as far in the opposite direction as he knew to go. Tarshish was a city in the furthest reaches of the Mediterranean, probably on the Iberian Peninsula. The narrative of Jonah is much more than the story of a disobedient missionary. It is an account of the love and mercy of God to a gentile nation, who through the preaching of the Word of God, came to repentance (Kaiser Jr. 65 ff). Many lessons can be learned in the book of Jonah, not the least of which is the sovereignty of God in directing the course of the one He has sent, even through abject disobedience. Many missionaries today suffer from an aliment called the "***Jonah syndrome***," in which they, through unpleasant life events and cultural stress, become bitter, jaded, angry, and even experience hatred towards the very people that God has sent them to witness to. This attitude often occurs in both new and veteran missionaries. Jonah is seen in all his humanity as a testament to what God can do and what a missionary should not do.

Israel: The Light to the Gentile Nations

Old Testament Scripture declares repeatedly that Israel was God's chosen nation to bring light and salvation to the world (Kaiser Jr. 51 ff). The commands and promises of the Lord that attest to this fact are both clear and explicit. There may be no other verse that is clearer than that of Isaiah 49:6 which states, "And he said, It is a light thing that thou shouldest be my servant to raise up the tribes of Jacob, and to restore the preserved of Israel: I will also give thee for a light to the Gentiles, that thou mayest be my salvation unto the end of the earth." Truly, the Lord Jesus Christ did come of the seed and line of Israel, and He was the true light of the world. At the same time, the missionary zeal and command of the Lord for Israel to be His witness throughout the pages of the Old Testament is striking when these passages are studied in the light of a theology of mission. God is a God of mission. God is a God with a mission heart, and mission is at the heart of His plan for the world.

Survey of Mission Work in the Gospels

To understand the mission of God is to understand the meaning of the act of the Father sending His Son (Terry, 65). John 3:16 is the quintessential mission verse. "For God so loved the world, that he gave his only begotten Son, that whosoever believeth in him should not perish, but have everlasting life." Christ Himself declared that the Father had sent Him in John 20:21, "my father hath sent me," and that act of sending the Son was an act of grace. Grace defined is "the free unmerited love and favor of God" (Webster). In the act of sending Christ into the world to die for mankind, the words in John 3:16 stating that the Father "gave his only begotten Son" become much more meaningful. The Father not only <u>sent</u> Jesus Christ, but also <u>gave</u> Jesus Christ as an act of unmerited favor towards a world that had rejected Him. Through that grace, John writes, "But as many as received him, to them gave he power to become the sons of God, even to them that believe on his name" (John 1:12).

As local churches today send out missionaries into the world, they must recognize the connection of mission and sacrifice, exemplified by the mission of God in the sacrifice of Jesus Christ. God is a God that saves by sacrifice, and "the 'Mission of God' implies sacrifice" (Van Rheenen 19). Jesus Christ sacrificed His life on the cross to save the lost, and the Lord is honored and glorified by sacrifice. When a missionary is sent to the field, much must be sacrificed. Just as Christ left heaven, a missionary must leave his home. Just as Christ suffered, so too must His servants suffer. As Christ was despised and rejected, so too will a missionary experience rejection of the words which he preaches. A missionary must however remember the words of the Savior who said, "If the world hate you, ye know that it hated me before it hated you" (John 15:18). A true missionary serving God will most certainly live a life of sacrifice.

An act of mission is an act of sacrifice. However, not all acts of sacrifice are acts of mission. For an act to be a mission, there must be several factors present. First, there must be an authority from which the mission is enacted. Next there must be one who is sent. Finally, there must be an objective or goal to the mission. In the case of *missio Dei* (the mission of God), the authority is God the Father. The one sent is Jesus Christ, God the Son. Christ Himself declares the purpose of the mission in Matthew 18:11, and again in Luke 19:10, "For the Son of man is come to seek and to save that which was lost." The objective of the mission is two-fold: first, the Lord comes to seek out that which was lost; next, He comes to save that which was lost (Ashford 48 ff).

The Seeking of that which was Lost

The Son of Man, Jesus Christ, was sent from heaven by the Father to seek out the lost. After His ascension, Christ imparted the Holy Spirit, whose mission it is to convict the sinner. Through the conviction of the Holy Spirit, Christ still seeks out those who are lost. The sending of the Spirit and His work of conviction is plainly stated by Christ when He said, "Nevertheless I tell you the truth; It is expedient for you that I go away: for if I go not away, the Comforter will not come unto you; but if I depart, I will send him unto you. And when he is come, he will reprove the world of sin, and of righteousness, and of judgment: Of sin, because they believe not on me" (John 16:7-9). The Father sent the Son to seek and to save (through His sacrifice). The Son sent the Spirit to seek and to save (though conviction and sealing). The Lord sent the church to seek out the lost and promised that He would go with them, because as the church seeks, the Lord saves. It is the job of the church to seek the lost and to disciple the saved.

The Saving of that which was Lost

The mission of saving the lost falls squarely on the shoulders of the Lord, for no man can save another from sin. Nor can any man save himself from sin. No work nor making of merit is sufficient to pay for the penalty of sin. Only Christ can redeem the lost soul, and that redemption was paid for by the shedding of the blood of Jesus Christ upon the cross of Calvary.

The message is clear: the wages of sin is death (Rom. 6:23). Death is defined as separation (Webster), and sin brings two types of death. The first type of death is a physical death in which the spirit is separated from the body. Next, the Bible speaks of a second death as the sinner is cast into the Lake of Fire. This is separation also. In the second death, the sinner is eternally separated from God. Only One could pay such a high price for the sin debt of the world. Jesus Christ suffered both physical and spiritual death. The spiritual separation from God the Father and God the Holy Spirit constituted a spiritual death upon the cross. This occurred as Christ took upon Himself the sin of the world and "...was once offered to bear the sins of many" (Heb. 9:28). As He bore sin upon Himself, the very nature of the holiness of God required that the other two persons of the Godhead turn their faces from Jesus. The sky became dark. The Father and the Spirit were separated from the Son, for holiness demands separation from sin. With a loud cry, Christ quotes Psalm 22:1 proclaiming, "My God! My God! Why hast thou forsaken me?" Through this cry of abject loneliness and horror, Christ proclaims to the world that He has suffered separation from God the Father and God the Holy Spirit, hence the double cry. The question that followed was rhetorical. Christ in His infinite wisdom knew the answer. Within that three-hour span of time, our infinite and eternal God was separated from God. Only an eternal being could pay an eternal price. After Jesus suffered a spiritual death (separation), He then dismissed His spirit from His flesh and suffered a physical death.

This same Christ which descended, also ascended into heaven, sprinkling His own blood on the mercy seat of the temple in heaven. "But Christ being come an high priest of good things to come, by a greater and more perfect tabernacle, not made with hands, that is to say, not of this building; Neither by the blood of goats and calves, but by his own blood he entered in once into the holy place, having obtained eternal redemption for us" (Heb. 9:11-12). The redemptive work of Christ, however, could not be complete without the resurrection. Paul tells us in 1 Corinthians 15:17, "if Christ be not raised, your faith is vain; ye are yet in your sins." Christ rose from the dead in victory over sin, death, hell and the grave, and because He has life, the sinner may have life also.

The Gospel Message and the Sin Curse

For a person to hear and accept the good news of the gospel message of salvation through Jesus Christ he must first realize that he is a sinner. There is a universal sin curse upon mankind. Because of that curse, all are destined for eternal damnation in hell, separated from God. John 3:16-18 declares both good news and bad news from the lips of Christ Himself.

> *For God so loved the world, that he gave his only begotten Son, that whosoever believeth in him should not perish, but have everlasting life. For God sent not his Son into the world to condemn the world; but that the world through him might be saved. He that believeth on him is not condemned: but he that believeth not is condemned already, because he hath not believed in the name of the only begotten Son of God.*

Condemnation is a foregone conclusion for humanity. Death is certain, and hell is destined. It is only by the intervention of a loving Father sending a willing sacrifice that man might be saved.

The Missionary Heart of Christ

Christ was moved with compassion when He saw the multitudes. (Matt. 9:36) As Dottie Rambo writes in the song of the same name, "He looked beyond my fault and saw my need," the Lord looked upon the masses of humanity and saw their spiritual need. The word in Greek translated "saw" is εἴδω *eido* (Strong's G1492).

This word not only has the connotation of "seeing" but also perceiving with the senses, turning one's attention toward, and examining (Thayer). Christ was able to peer into the hearts of the multitudes and see their underlying spiritual condition and need. The need of the multitude was three-fold. First, Christ saw that they fainted. This meant that they were weary from exhaustion and without strength (Thayer). The spiritual reality of the lost is that they are without strength or ability to affect their own lost condition. No one can by any intrinsic means nor personal merit be able to save himself from the damnation of the sin curse. Second, Christ saw that the people were scattered abroad. The word translated "scattered abroad" is ῥίπτω *ripto* (Strong's G4496), meaning to be carelessly cast or thrown down (Thayer), This was not in reference to their physical location, but to the fact that the effects of sin had chaotically driven them in all directions but the one path that they should travel. This effect of sin on the heart of mankind is what has caused the emergence of divergent religions and religious thought, all traveling in disparate ways from the truth of God's Word. The third need that was seen by Christ in the hearts of the multitude was inseparably linked to the second. The people were scattered abroad because they had no one to guide them. They were lost sheep with no leader and no direction. Seeing these needs in the lives of the multitude, Christ was "moved with compassion." This yearning, inner pity that Christ felt toward man was not just a mere passing emotion. Christ's compassion motivated Him to action. Lamentations 3:51 states, "Mine eye affecteth mine heart because of all the daughters of my city." Christ's compassion affected His missionary zeal and caused Him to not only seek and save the lost, but to call upon his disciples to labor in the harvest of souls also. It is interesting to note that Christ relates the magnitude of the mission when stating that the "harvest truly is plenteous," and uses that fact as a segue in His call for laborers. Even more interesting is that He tells His disciples to pray that God will send forth laborers, and those who prayed were the very ones who were sent.

The Great Commission of the Church

And Jesus came and spake unto them, saying, All power is given unto me in heaven and in earth. Go ye therefore, and teach all nations, baptizing them in the name of the Father, and of the Son, and of the Holy Ghost: Teaching them to observe all things whatsoever I have commanded you: and, lo, I am with you alway, even unto the end of the world. Amen (Matthew 28:18-20).

The Great Commission as given by Christ to His church in Matthew 28 is the central commandment of mission work and the governing mission statement of local churches in this present age. In it, Christ expressed His authority and then bestowed that authority upon His church to be the executor of the commandment (Brooks 7). There are four verbs that are used in the commission. The first is πορευθεντες *poreuthentes* (Strong's G4198) translated as "go." The second is μαθητευσατε *mathayteusatay*, (Strong's G3100) translated "teach." This word carries the meaning of "making disciples" of all nations. The third verb in the Great Commission is βαπτίζοντες *baptidzontes* (Strong's G907) translated "baptizing." The fourth and final verb is διδάσκοντες *didaskontes*, (Strong's G1321) which is translated as "teaching" and has the meaning of indoctrination. Of the four verbs in the Great Commission, only one is an imperative, meaning a command. The other three are participles (Robinson). In English participles are usually words ending in "-ing." These words are supporting verbs that describe the imperative command of the Commission. That imperative command is μαθητευσατε *mathayteusatay*, translated "teach." Literally, this command means to "disciple" (Thayer). The other three verbs are participles which describe how to disciple. They are *going, baptizing,* and *indoctrinating*. The full meaning of the commandment is to "Disciple all peoples, by the process of *going, baptizing* in the name of the Father, Son, and Holy Ghost, and *indoctrinating* them to observe all things whatsoever Christ has commanded." So, as they were going, they were to teach all nations. What were they to teach? They were to teach all nations of the gospel of Jesus Christ. This point of the Great Commission may be referred to as "evangelization." Secondly, converts were to be baptized in the name of the trinity: the Father, the Son, and the Holy Ghost. This was to be both an outward expression of the inward conversion of the sinner and also an illustrative memorial of the death, burial and resurrection of Christ. The last point of the Great Commission was that of indoctrination. Christ commanded them to teach them to "observe all things, whatsoever I have commanded you." Again, to clarify - the two words for "teach" found in verses 18 and 20 are different in the Greek. The first instance is the word μαθητευσατε *mathayteusatay*, which gives the sense of teaching to make a disciple. The second word "teach" found in verse 20 is διδάσκω *didaskō*, which implies the meaning of "instilling doctrine into." All four verbs are functions of what missionaries must do as they plant churches. Since salvation and baptism are both prerequisites of church membership, and the command to disciple the believer in the teachings of the Word of God is a function of the local church, the planting of churches is implicit in the Great Commission.

> *Since salvation and baptism are both prerequisites of church membership, and the command to disciple the believer in the Word of God is a function of the local church, the planting of churches is implicit in the Great Commission.*

The Great Commission is also found in the books of Mark, Luke, John, and Acts.

> *And he said unto them, Go ye into all the world, and preach the gospel to every creature. (Mark 16:15)*

Then opened he their understanding, that they might understand the Scriptures, And said unto them, Thus it is written, and thus it behoved Christ to suffer, and to rise from the dead the third day: And that repentance and remission of sins should be preached in his name among all nations, beginning at Jerusalem. And ye are witnesses of these things. And, behold, I send the promise of my Father upon you: but tarry ye in the city of Jerusalem, until ye be endued with power from on high. (Luke 24:45-49)

Then said Jesus to them again, Peace be unto you: as my Father hath sent me, even so send I you. (John 20:21)

But ye shall receive power, after that the Holy Ghost is come upon you: and ye shall be witnesses unto me both in Jerusalem, and in all Judaea, and in Samaria, and unto the uttermost part of the earth. (Acts 1:8)

Missionary Methods in the Book of Acts

The book of Acts gives us a wonderful insight into the mission endeavors of the early churches. As we follow the missionary journeys of the Apostle Paul, they provide us with a basic pattern of mission work. Though Paul's methods are not stringent commands for modern missionaries, they give us a fundamental framework of how the Lord intended mission work to be employed. In 1 Corinthians 11:1, Paul said, "Be ye followers of me, even as I also am of Christ." If we follow the pattern laid out in scripture rather than strategies developed by man, our mission endeavors are certain to be more successful. According to the Biblical example, those who were called into the position of a missionary, employed their time in evangelism, church planting, and discipleship. This involved developing church leaders, teaching principles of autonomy to churches that were established, visiting and edifying believers and reporting back to their sending church and other churches of like faith. The job of the missionary is to be the external arm of outreach of the local church, fulfilling the section of the church's commission to go to the "uttermost part of the earth," proclaiming the name of Jesus Christ (Reed 79).

The following thirteen steps are a Biblical pattern of mission work as outlined in the first missionary journey of Paul in the book of Acts. Each one of the steps expounded upon in this chapter are not only methods employed by the first century missionary team, but also a workable pattern of modern mission work. The book of Acts provides a Biblical precedent of what a missionary ought to do. For further reading on the missionary methods of Paul, David Hesselgrave expounds his own "Pauline Cycle" of church planting in the book *Planting Churches Cross-Culturally: North America and Beyond.*

Establish the Calling
(Acts 13:1-2)

The first two verses of Acts 13 outline the missionary call. Barnabas and Paul were among the various ministers who were faithfully serving in the church of Antioch. Etched in the eternal pages of God's Word, there can be no doubt that they were called of the Lord for mission work. A person who wishes to be a missionary and wants to do mission work according to the Biblical pattern must establish whether or not he is called of the Lord. Establishing your calling is very important because the last place you want to be is on a foreign mission field out of the Lord's will. But how can you know if you're called? Can a person know for certain that the Lord has called him into the field of mission work? This is such an important subject that an entire chapter in this book is devoted to it. For more on this topic, refer to Chapter Ten: "Establishing the Call of a Missionary."

Be Sent Through a Local Church
(Acts 13:3)

The next step in Paul's missionary methodology in the book of Acts is being commissioned by a church. In Acts 13:3, the local church at Antioch (of which Paul and Barnabas were members) sent the

BIBLICAL STEPS OF MISSION WORK IN THE BOOK OF ACTS

1. **Establish the Calling**
   (Acts 13:1-2)
2. **Be Sent Through a Local Church**
   (Acts 13:3)
3. **Work as a Team**
   (Acts 13:2; 13:4-5)
4. **Work with Known Contacts**
   (Acts 13:4,5; 13:14; 14:1)
5. **Begin in Large Population Centers**
   (Acts 13:4; 13:13-14; 13:49; 14:6)
6. **Be Bold yet Wise to Opposition**
   (Acts 13:46; 13:51; 14:5-6)
7. **Work with Those Who are Responsive**
   (Acts 13:46-48; 14:21-22)
8. **Plant Churches as People are Converted**
   (Acts 14:23)
9. **Confirm the Souls of the Disciples**
   (Acts 14:22)
10. **Ordain Leaders in Every Church**
    (Acts 14:23)
11. **Teach Principles of Autonomy**
    (Acts 14:23)
12. **Return for Furlough**
    (Acts 14:26-28)
13. **Continue Discipleship with Believers**
    (Acts 15:36)

Figure 11. *Biblical Steps of Mission Work in the Book of Acts*

missionaries out. To do the job of a missionary, you must be sent out as a missionary. Romans 10:15 says, "And how shall they preach except they be sent." The Lord established the institution of the church and vested His authority within it as the sole outlet through which mission work should be done. Though there are many different people on various types of missions today, only those who are sent out in the Biblical way and conducting themselves according to the Biblical pattern can truly call themselves missionaries in the purest sense of the word.

Work as a Team
(Acts 13:2; 13:4-5)

Jesus Christ called many of His disciples in pairs, and in Mark 6:7, He sent the twelve apostles out in pairs. In Luke 10:1, Christ sent out the seventy, two by two. As Christ made His triumphal entry into Jerusalem, He sent two disciples to secure the colt that He would ride upon. Before the final Passover meal, Christ sent Peter and John to prepare the Passover. The Lord called Paul and Barnabas together as a team, and they were not alone. We see that Mark also traveled with them in Acts 13:5. The Biblical precedent of team ministry in mission work is shown throughout the book of Acts. Not only were there the missionary teams of Paul and Barnabas; Barnabas and John Mark; Paul and Silas; etc., there were large groups of believers who accompanied Paul on his journeys. Paul lists several names that he terms συνεργός *sunergos*, translated "companions; helpers; fellow laborers; and fellow workers." Paul mentions the names of those that traveled with, ministered to, or visited him: Priscilla and Aquila, Urbanus, Timothy, Titus, Epaphroditus, Clement, Aristarchus, Mark, Justus, Philemon, Archippus, Demas, Luke, Sosthenes, Stephanas, Fortunatus, Achaicus, and Tertius. This list is certainly not comprehensive as Paul refers to many other fellow workers without mentioning their names.

Why did the Lord send men in teams? There are several reasons. Biblically, there is a principle throughout Scripture that "in the mouth of two or three witnesses shall every word be established" (2 Corinthians 13:1). In the book of Deuteronomy, a single witness was not to be believed, but a man could be put to death for his crimes at the witness of two or three. Missionaries are witnesses for the Lord, and their word must be established in the ears of the mission field. Working as a missionary team has several benefits. First, the missionary doesn't have to work alone. Though no person should ever have to labor alone, we see in Acts 13:4 that a missionary is never truly alone. He is sent forth, led, and guided by the Holy Spirit. Christ promised in the Great commission that He would be with us "alway, even unto the end of the world." Rest assured through His promise in Hebrews 13:5 that the Lord will never leave us, nor forsake us. Even with the promise of His presence, the Lord realizes that there is comfort and encouragement in numbers. Marriage was instituted because the Lord knew that "It is not good that the man should be alone" (Genesis 2:18). In the same way, it is not good that a man serves alone. The pressures of ministry and stress of the mission field can be overwhelming for a man to bear alone. The field can be a very lonely place without fellow helpers to aid in bearing the burden. There are many other benefits: accountability, edification, and companionship with others who share a common culture. In addition, a team working together to further the gospel mission throughout the world will accomplish much more than a single person could ever hope to do. The Bible teaches us the important principle of fellowship and co-labor with other Christians through the institution of local churches. Just as we should not forsake the assembling of ourselves together with other Christians in church (Hebrew 10:25), the missionary would be wise to follow the precedent of co-labor on the mission field.

Work with Known Contacts
(Acts 13:4,5; 13:14; 14:1)

A crucial step in mission work is to make a first point of contact with the target audience. As we follow the precedent laid out in the first missionary journey of Paul, we find that Paul and Barnabas first visited contacts who were known and familiar to them. In Acts 13:4, they first traveled to Cyprus, Barnabas' home. There are other connections also. Some of the people from their next stop, Pamphylia, were most likely contacts who had been in Jerusalem at Pentecost (2:10). Furthermore, Pamphylia was inhabited by Cilicians, Paul's countrymen, who was from Tarsus in Cilicia. They then traveled to Pisidia (Acts 13:14) who were of the same people as Pamphylia. In each city they visited, Paul and Barnabas first visited fellow Jews in the synagogues which, by Jewish custom, was open for anyone to stand and expound upon the scripture in a public setting. Paul and Barnabas began their missionary journeys by visiting known contacts.

Making first contact on a new field is a daunting task, however the missionary method of Paul was to start with the known and then reach out to the unknown. Even Christ Himself set this example by going to the Jew (God's chosen people) first. In Acts 13:46, Paul proclaims to his Jewish brethren, "It was necessary that the word of God should first have been spoken to you." Yet, when they rejected the gospel, Paul continues, "lo, we turned to the Gentiles." Paul started with known points of contact, and worked out from there.

Begin in Large Population Centers
(Acts 13:4; 13:13-14; 13:49; 14:6)

Paul and Barnabas went from city to city. Their first stop was Salamis, the largest and most important city in Cyprus. From there, they traveled to Paphos, the capital of the province. Next, they sailed northwest to Perga, the capital of Pamphylia. Their next stop, Iconium (14:1) was the capital city of Lycaonia, an important city of trade. From there they spread throughout the surrounding area into smaller cities (14:6). Mission efforts should begin in areas of high population and then spread (through the people of that central area) to other areas throughout the region (13:49) Paul chose Antioch as a strategic center for mission work because it was "the military and administrative center for that part of Galatia which comprised the Isaurian, Pisidian and Pamphylian mountains, and the southern part of Lycaonia. It was hence that Roman soldiers, officials, and couriers were dispatched over the whole area, and it was hence, according to Acts 13:49, that Paul's mission radiated over the whole region" (ISBE). The point is to go where the people are. If a missionary can establish a work in a central location, he holds an advantage in getting the gospel into the surrounding rural areas. Seldom is the opposite true. Regardless, a missionary must go where ever he is called, whether it be a large city or a rural village. Yet if the doors of opportunity are open, the area in which the most people can be reached may be the best option.

Be Bold yet Wise to Opposition
(Acts 13:46; 13:51; 14:5-6)

Paul and Barnabas waxed bold in their preaching against opposers of the faith, however they were also wise in fleeing danger. Some missionaries have a hard time differentiating between the two. When Paul preached in Antioch of Pisidia, there were Jews who "spake against those things spoken by Paul, contradicting and blaspheming" (Acts 13:45). In the face of doctrinal error and dissenters who would lead others astray, missionaries must be bold in the faith, declaring the truth of God's Word. The missionary must not back down from the absolute truth of scripture. His preaching must be with authority and power. His words must be guided by the wisdom of God rather than the opinions of man. It is only then that he may, as Paul and Barnabas, "wax bold" in the declaration of truth.

A person must not kid himself into thinking that the mission field will be an easy path to take. There will be opposition from every angle – without and within. The missionary must prepare his heart, strengthen his resolve, and rely fully upon the grace of God to have any possibility at survival and success on the mission field. In Chapter 14, Paul and Barnabas hear of a plot to kill them, so they wisely flee the danger, and preach the gospel in a different region. "And when there was an assault made both of the Gentiles, and also of the Jews with their rulers, to use them despitefully, and to stone them, They were ware of it, and fled unto Lystra and Derbe, cities of Lycaonia, and unto the region that lieth round about: And there they preached the gospel" (Acts 14:5-7). There is wisdom in determining when opposition is spiritual danger (when we should wax bold and fight), or when opposition means physical danger (when the wise action would be to flee). Consider the words of the Lord as he sent out the twelve apostles:

> *Behold, I send you forth as sheep in the midst of wolves: be ye therefore wise as serpents, and harmless as doves. But beware of men: for they will deliver you up to the councils, and they will scourge you in their synagogues; And ye shall be brought before governors and kings for my sake, for a testimony against them and the Gentiles. But when they deliver you up, take no thought how or what ye shall speak: for it shall be given you in that same hour what ye shall speak. For it is not ye that speak, but the Spirit of your Father which speaketh in you. And the brother shall deliver up the brother to death, and the father the child: and the children shall rise up against their parents, and cause them to be put to death. And ye shall be hated of all men for my name's sake: but he that endureth to the end shall be saved. But when they persecute you in this city, flee ye into another. (Matthew 10:16-23a).*

Work with Those Who are Responsive
(Acts 13:46-48; 14:21-22)

When Paul and Barnabas preached to the Jews at Antioch in Pisidia, many of them were at first positively inclined to the message of the gospel (Acts 13:43). By the next sabbath their opinions changed when they saw the large number of Gentiles that came to hear the preaching. When Paul and Barnabas saw that the Jewish people of Perga rejected the gospel, they turned to work with those who were responsive to the gospel.

> *Now when the congregation was broken up, many of the Jews and religious proselytes followed Paul and Barnabas: who, speaking to them, persuaded them to continue in the grace of God. And the next sabbath day came almost the whole city together to hear the word of God. But when the Jews saw the multitudes, they were filled with envy, and spake against those things which were spoken by Paul, contradicting and blaspheming. Then Paul and Barnabas waxed bold, and said, It was necessary that the word of God should first have been spoken to you: but seeing ye put it from you, and judge yourselves unworthy of everlasting life, lo, we turn to the Gentiles. For so hath the Lord commanded us, saying, I have set thee to be a light of the Gentiles, that thou shouldest be for salvation unto the ends of the earth. And when the Gentiles heard this, they were glad, and glorified the word of the Lord: and as many as were ordained to eternal life believed (Acts 13:43-48).*

Then in verse fifty-one we see that "they shook off the dust of their feet against them [the Jews]." They did this according to the commandment of Christ to the apostles in Matthew 10:14-15, "And whosoever shall not receive you, nor hear your words, when ye depart out of that house or city, shake off the dust of your feet. Verily I say unto you, it shall be more tolerable for the land of Sodom and Gomorrha in the day of judgment, than for that city." According to the established custom of the Jews of that day, when a traveler returned home, he would shake the dust of foreign lands off his shoes so as to not contaminate his homeland with the impurities of the Gentiles. This act implied that a missionary was not to waste his time with those who rejected the message of the gospel, but to give them over to God for judgment.

The first Baptist foreign missionary from America, Adoniram Judson spent the first seven years of his ministry in Burma reaching out and trying to gather an audience for whom to preach. It was only after this period of seven years that he saw the first convert to the faith (Anderson 215 ff). Before a missionary can effectively present the gospel message to others, he must win their respect and trust. He must have enough rapport with the people he is trying to reach that they will stop and listen to the message of the gospel that he wishes to convey (Hesselgrave 113). Without a point of contact, the task will be much more difficult. Judson's only point of contact was with the son of William Carey, an Englishman. He spent many fruitless years working with the Burmese. It was only when Judson turned to work with the Karen people, a tribal group in northern Burma, that he saw any substantial fruit. He learned through many hard years of labor to work with those who were responsive.

Plant Churches as People are Converted
(Acts 14:23)

The method is simple in its format: the gospel is preached, sinners are converted, and churches are formed. The job of a missionary is not the conversion of souls to Christ, but rather the effective communication of the gospel and faithful obedience to His commands (Hesselgrave 167). It is God who converts the believer to the salvation of his soul. With that fact in mind, God would not call a missionary to go to a place in which He is not already working in the hearts of the people. The mission belongs to God. A missionary, though an integral part, is only a part of the equation (Ashford 18). The Holy Spirit visits the souls of the heathen, convicts of sin, and sends a messenger to proclaim the gospel of Jesus Christ to those who respond to His leading. If churches, Christians, or missionaries are unfaithful in the command to witness, God Himself is always faithful, and His Holy Spirit will visit every person on earth who have the mental and spiritual capacity to choose righteousness or rejection. John 16:8-11 describes the work of the Holy Spirit in these terms, "And when he is come, he will reprove the world of sin, and of righteousness, and of judgment: Of sin, because they believe not on me; Of righteousness, because I go to my Father, and ye see me no more; Of judgment, because the prince of this world is judged." In the words of Charles Ryrie, "It has been suggested that the world being reproved of righteousness (John 16:8) means that the message of the need for accepting God's grace will be made known by the convicting power of the Holy Spirit" (Ryrie).

In Acts 14:23, we see that the missionary team returned to ordain pastors in the churches that were planted. However, there is no specific reference to the organization of these churches in the previous chapters. It is simply understood that churches were planted in each city that the gospel was received. Church planting is understood because they returned to visit these churches. What we must recognize here is that each time a group of people were converted, they were most certainly, and of necessity, organized into a local body of believers – a church.

In an area void of a church body, conversion should result in the congregation of believers, or the establishment of scriptural, local New Testament churches (Hesselgrave 192). The words local and New Testament should be unnecessary, but with the pervasiveness of the heretical teaching of a universal body of believers, the distinction must be made. There is no other type of church than a local congregation of believers (Reed 37 ff). There is and never has been a universal church, either visible or invisible (Graves 30). The definition of the word church is: a called-out assembly of soundly saved, scripturally baptized believers who have covenanted themselves together to carry out the commands and commission of our Lord Jesus Christ (Cross, Landmarkism: An Update 10 f). The work of a missionary is planting churches. As the gospel is preached and converts are made, those who are saved and baptized should be organized into an autonomous local body of believers; in other words, a church (Reed 18). The authority to organize into a scriptural church lies within the prerequisites of church membership. Before becoming a church member, a person must be saved and scripturally baptized. A person can only receive scriptural baptism though the authority of an established scriptural church. Thus, authority is passed from one scriptural church to the next, and has been so in unbroken succession for the past two millennia.

Confirm the Souls of the Disciples
(Acts 14:22)

In Acts 14:22, Paul and Barnabas returned to their former fields of labor, confirming the faith of the believers (Hesselgrave 219). This portion of the job of the missionary is exhorting, strengthening and encouraging believers as they face the trials and endure the tribulation which will most assuredly come to those who follow the Lord. In Acts 14:21-22, after Paul and Barnabas "had preached the gospel to that city, and had taught many, they returned again to Lystra, and to Iconium, and Antioch, Confirming the souls of the disciples, and exhorting them to continue in the faith, and that we must through much tribulation enter into the kingdom of God." The word translated "confirming" is ἐπιστηρίζω "epistērizō," which means to reestablish, to strengthen, and to render more firm (Strong's G1991). It is easy for the faith of a new believer to waiver in the face of the trials that they will face their lives. The missionary is the one who brought the faith and knowledge of Christ into the lives of the believers, and ought to be the one who regenerates and strengthens that faith. After churches are established, the missionary should return to those churches on occasion (as the ministry will permit) to encourage the brethren.

Ordain Leaders in Every Church
(Acts 14:23)

As Paul and Barnabas revisited the churches that had been established, the ordained new leaders to continue the work in the absence of a missionary. Acts 14:23 states that the missionaries had ordained "elders in every church." No work can continue without a succession of leadership. This principle was passed on from the apostle Paul to his son in the ministry, Timothy. He writes in Second Timothy 2:2 "And the things that thou hast heard of me among many witnesses, the same commit thou to faithful men, who shall be able to teach others also." The job of the missionary is to work himself out of the job (Hodges 41). He must train up others to take his place and disciple those men to disciple others. This is the grand scheme of the perpetuity of the gospel message throughout all generations. This is also why the education of a missionary, the training of a missionary, and the ability of a missionary is of utmost importance. He must not only disciple other Christians, he must disciple leaders (Schnabel 248). Pastors of churches will rely on the missionary for answers to their theological questions. Leaders in the Christian community will turn to the missionary for the explanation of the Scriptures (Schnabel 237). The influence of the missionary will shape entire communities, entire church bodies, and possibly entire nations. He must be apt to teach. He must be Biblically sound. He must be able to perform the duties of discipling spiritual leaders in every aspect of what that entails.

Teach Principles of Autonomy
(Acts 14:23)

After the ordination of new pastors in the churches, Paul then commended those churches to the Lord's care (Hesselgrave 279). There comes a day when every parent must cut the cord that ties them to their children. They must allow their children to become adults, make their own decisions, and even make their own mistakes. The same is true of a missionary and the churches that he plants. For those churches to truly be independent, a missionary must not lord over them, but allow them to be self-functioning bodies of Christ. Modern missiology refers to the practice of "indigenous" church principles. The word "indigenous" means "naturally occurring" (Terry, 303). A better expression for this principle might be "autonomous" church principles. Whatever the name, the principles are as follows:

1. **Churches Ought to be Self-governing**
2. **Churches Ought to be Self-supporting**
3. **Churches Ought to be Self-propagating**

Churches out to be self-governing. If an outside authority governs a church, it has ceased to be a local church, and is practicing a catholic (universal) church doctrine. As soon as a local congregation is able to covenant together to form a local body, they are a church. As a church, they should be self-governing. The idea of "mother churches" lording over "daughter churches" is never found in scripture. However, in Revelation 2:6,15 Christ states that He "hates" the deeds and doctrine of the Nicolaitans (people-conquerors). Though a missionary should have a guiding role in church planting, he is not and should not be the pastor of the church, else the goal of autonomy will be much more difficult. The role of the missionary is that of an organizer in congregating the believers into a functional, self-governing, self-supporting and self-propagating church. The Biblical missionary has an itinerant style ministry of evangelization and organization (Schnabel 258), and after that is complete, he begins the process again in another area.

Churches ought to be self-supporting. He who controls the purse-strings has control. Churches can never be fully autonomous unless they are free from outside finances. Many missionaries face the struggles of churches who have learned to be dependent upon a foreign cash flow. A missionary himself is usually the cause of this problem. He creates a bad precedent by supplying financial aid to a new congregation rather than teaching them that they need to tithe and give offerings. A missionary begins by paying the utility bills for the church rather than teaching them to pay. He may rent or build a building for them. He may pay a salary to the pastor rather than teaching them to support their own leaders. He often feels obligated as a missionary to take care of the needs of the fledgling work. As the people see the money flowing from the missionary or other churches, they become dependent, lazy, and negligent in their obligations. So, what is a missionary to do? Is it wrong to financially help a church? Absolutely not! Yet, the way that it is done will determine the course of the autonomous structure of the church. If a missionary wishes to help a church financially, he must teach them to give. He must teach them to sacrifice. He must teach them that they are obligated to take care of their own pastor. And when it is time to help that local body financially, he ought to give anonymously through the local offering of the church. The pastor's salary should come from church. The bills should be paid by the church. Initially, every missionary will help in the process of planting the church. Yet, when a congregation is taught to give, they will become financially self-sufficient.

Churches ought to be self-propagating. The ultimate goal in discipleship is to make converts who will reproduce themselves. The ultimate goal of church planting is to see that church reproduce itself. It is a mistake by every pastor or missionary that wants to see church growth to be inward-focused. Only churches who are focused outwardly upon the worldwide mission of God will see true growth. A truly autonomous church is a self-propagating church. Dr. Clyde Lanier stated, "It doesn't matter how many you bring in. It matters how many you send out." A church focused on mission work is a church that is growing, both spiritually and numerically. From the very inception of a new church plant, a missionary should get the people involved and excited about mission work.

Return for Furlough
(Acts 14:26-28)

After Barnabas and Paul's first missionary journey, they returned home to report back to both their sending church (14:26-28) and other churches (Acts 15:3-4). In between the missionary journeys of Paul, he returned to his home church to report of the blessings of the Lord on the mission field. Today, missionaries enjoy a period of furlough where they come back to their own country, spend time with their families and sending church, and report to those who have partnered with them in the ministry both financially and prayerfully (Lederleitner 22). Many missionaries in the past went to foreign fields and never returned to their home country. William Carey spent forty-one years serving the Lord in India and died there, having never taken a furlough (Wellman 124). Nevertheless, the principle is a Biblical one, and had Carey come home on occasion, his wife Dorothy might not have suffered the mental anguish and breakdown (Wellman 83) that eventually led to her death. Even Christ is recorded in the gospels as saying to his disciples, "Come ye yourselves apart into a desert place, and rest a while" (Mark 6:31). There are many reasons that furlough is more than just a good idea. It is a time of rest and refreshment for a missionary who gives of himself for years at a time in a mentally, physically, spiritually, and culturally stressful environment. It is a time of spiritual renewal for a missionary and his family. It is a time to visit with family, friends and the church family of home. It is a time to relate back to the sending church and other churches what the Lord has done, not only as a matter of responsibility but as an encouragement to the churches of his home country. And finally, furlough is a time to rest and detoxify from the constant stress of battling on the front lines of spiritual combat on the mission field. No one can endure prolonged and unrelenting stress for an indefinite period of time (Koteskey). Without furlough, missionary attrition rates become higher, physical health begins to wane, spiritual fitness becomes stagnant, and the overall attitude of a missionary become like that of Jonah, who despised the very people to whom God called him to preach. Furlough is not a vacation. Furlough is a part of the job requirements of a missionary and has its foundations in Scripture.

Continue Discipleship with Believers
(Acts 15:36)

The next principle of Paul's missionary method is found in Acts 15:36, "And some days after, Paul said unto Barnabas, 'Let us go again and visit our brethren in every city where we have preached the word of the Lord, and see how they do.'" Hesselgrave states that "relationships continue" (Hesselgrave 293). Though the churches were loosed from the oversight of the missionary to continue autonomously on their own, there was no break in fellowship between the planters and the planted. Paul desired to go back and check on the progress and wellbeing of the churches. Verse 41 of the same chapter states that Paul "went through Syria and Cilicia, confirming the churches" once again. Fellowship amongst Christians and especially among churches is a Biblical principle that was practiced in the time of the apostles and should not be ignored today, with one caveat: there can be no delegation of authority, no combining of authority and no hierarchy of churches and clergy lording over the Lord's heritage. The relationship between a missionary and the church in which he has planted and labored may feel like a paternalistic one, yet must be a familial fellowship between brethren on equal footing and not that of master and slave (Hodges 148).

PART II

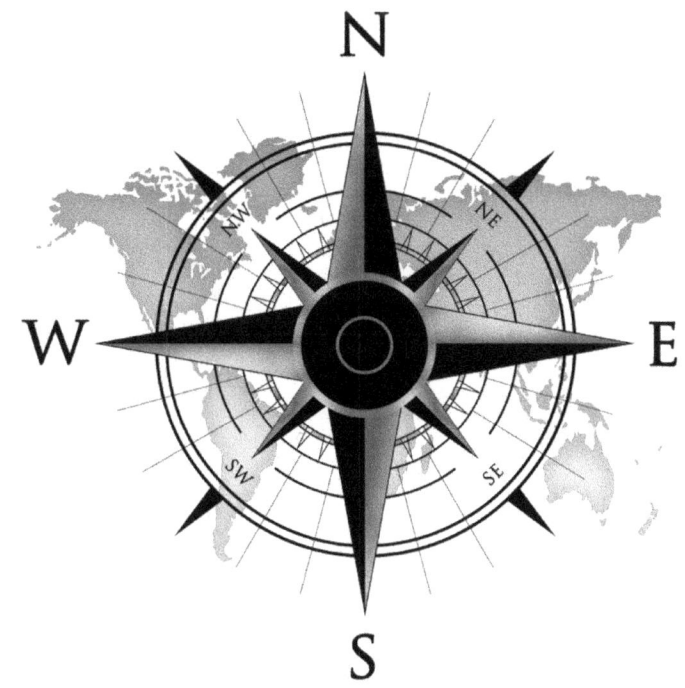

A HISTORICAL SURVEY OF MISSION WORK

Chapter Six

MISSION WORK IN THE FIRST CENTURY A.D.

Apostolic Mission Work

The book of Romans, believed to have been written only twenty-six years after Christ's resurrection, records a striking statement. Romans 10:18 states, "But I say, Have they not heard? Yes verily, their sound went into all the earth, and their words unto the ends of the world." The early Christian churches of the first century were highly motivated evangelists, carrying out the Great Commission of Christ with a fervor and zeal that has not been duplicated since. Many of the early Christians were martyred, giving their lives for the propagation of the gospel of Jesus Christ. The third century historian, Eusebius, records the missionary work of the apostles,

> *Meanwhile the holy apostles and disciples of our Savior were dispersed throughout the world. Parthia, according to tradition, was allotted to Thomas as his field of labor, Scythia to Andrew, and Asia to John, who, after he had lived some time there, died at Ephesus. Peter appears to have preached in Pontus,*

Galatia, Bithynia, Cappadocia, and Asia to the Jews of the dispersion (Maier 93).

The book of Acts records the persecutions of the early churches, beginning with the martyrdom of James, the son of Zebedee, who was arrested and imprisoned by King Herod Agrippa I. To appease the hatred of the Christians by the Jewish leaders, Agrippa beheaded James (Acts 12:2). Herod would have done the same with Peter, but an angel of the Lord led Peter out of prison and to freedom (Acts 12:6-19). The stories of the rest of the apostles may be gleaned from history. However, much of the history of the apostles has been embellished over the years or simply consigned to legend. Sorting through many ancient texts and histories, and confirming the facts by the churches they left behind, the lives and ministries of these apostles can be followed.

Andrew

The apostle Andrew, according to history, became a missionary, taking the gospel message of Christ to Scythia (modern Russia) and then preaching and planting churches in Pictland, which is modern day Scotland, beyond the border walls of the Roman Empire (Maier 93). Legend states that Andrew was crucified in Greece on an X shaped cross. To make his death a lingering and torturous one, Andrew was tied rather than nailed to the cross by the Roman soldiers (Dvornik).

Philip

Philip became a missionary to the Gauls in what is modern day France. In a book written by the Frankish historian Freculphus Lexoviensis, Philip is believed to have traveled to Britain to preach the word and plant churches (Natumewicz 5-54). Philip died as a martyr, being stoned to death in the city of Hierapolis in Asia Minor, eight years after the death of James, son of Zebedee (Schaff 92).

THE FIRST CHRISTIAN MARTYRS

STEPHEN
stoned to death

JAMES, SON OF ZEBEDEE
beheaded

JAMES THE LESS
thrown from temple, then beaten to death

MATTHEW
burned at the stake in Ethiopia

MARK
dragged through the streets until dead

LUKE
hanged

PETER
crucified upside down

ANDREW
crucified by being tied to an X-shaped cross

PHILIP
stoned to death

BARTHOLOMEW
flayed alive, then crucified

THOMAS
pierced through with a lance in India

JUDE
shot to death with arrows

MATTHIAS
stoned to death

THADDEUS
clubbed to death

PAUL
beheaded

Figure 12. *The First Christian Martyrs*

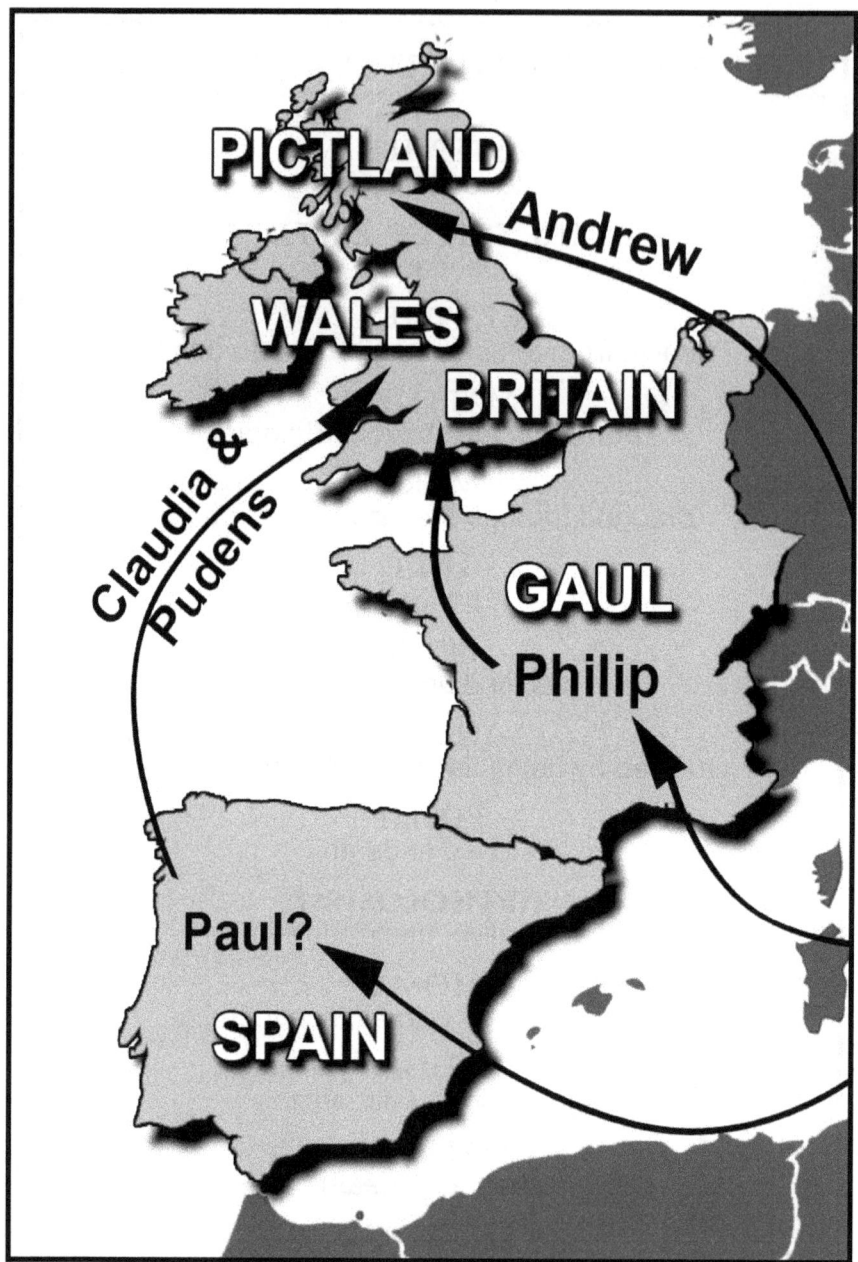

Figure 13. *Map of the evangelization of Western Europe in the first century AD.*

Spain, Gaul (modern France), and the British Isles were evangelized during the lifetime of the apostles. Converts under Paul, Claudia and Pudens took the gospel back to Wales. Andrew went to Scythia (modern Russia) and to the Picts in modern day Scotland. Philip went to Gaul (modern France) and Britain.

The Brethren of the Lord

Several of Jesus' disciples were related to the earthly family of Christ. It is written by the second century writers Papias and Hegesippus that Cleophas was the brother of Joseph, which would make him the uncle of Christ on Joseph's side. Eusebius of Caesarea also states in his *Church History,* Book III, Ch. 11, that Joseph and Cleophas are brothers, and that his son Simeon became pastor of the church of Jerusalem after the destruction of the temple in AD 70. The Bible speaks of Mary, the wife of Cleophas (John 19:25) being the mother of James the Less and Joses (Matthew 27:56). Cleophas is a Hebrew name - Alphaeus being the cognate form of the word in Greek (Hovey). James the less is also noted as being the son of Alphaeus (Luke 6:15), therefore, there is Biblical evidence that Cleophas and Alphaeus are one in the same. Though we know nothing of his brother Joses, it is probable that James the Less was the cousin of our Lord on (as it was supposed) His father Joseph's side of the family. Since Christ's half-brother was named James, and there was also the apostle James (son of Zebedee) this would explain the appellation "the Less" to differentiate this James from others. The Bible also lists Levi (Matthew) as the son of Alphaeus (Mark 2:14). If Matthew's father is the same Alphaeus, then Matthew and James the Less are brothers, and we find that a second apostle was related to the earthly family of Christ. There are three accounts of the names of the twelve apostles in the synoptic gospels. In each of these lists, Matthew, Thomas and James are found together. Thomas in Hebrew is the word for "twin." He is also called Didymus in the New Testament, which is the Greek word for "twin." Could Thomas possibly be the twin brother Matthew as many speculate because they are listed together often in scripture? These are interesting suppositions to ponder, yet a person must be careful not to be too dogmatic in this arena of study since much is mere conjecture, and there were many people in Bible times who bore the same name.

There are, however, other family connections which can be deduced by Bible study. John lists a fourth woman at the cross along with Mary (wife of Cleophas), Mary Magdalene, and Mary, mother of Jesus. John does not list her name, but states that this fourth woman is the sister of Mary, Christ's mother (John 19:25). However, her name can be found in the gospel of Mark, which calls her Salome (Mark 15:40), The gospel of Matthew calls this same woman "the mother of Zebedee's children" (Matthew 27:56). Piecing together the synoptic gospel accounts, this fourth woman at the cross is Salome, the sister of Jesus' mother Mary, wife of Zebedee, and mother of James and John. This would make Salome and Zebedee the aunt and uncle of Jesus Christ and James and John, His cousins.

Jesus is listed as having four brothers and at least two sisters (Mark 6:3). The sisters are not named in Scripture, but His brothers are: James, Joses, Simon, and Judas (Matthew 13:55). James, the half-brother of the Lord, and son of Mary and Joseph became the pastor of the church in Jerusalem after the ascension of Christ (Acts 12:17; 15:13). Nothing more is spoken of Joses. Simon is sometimes equated with the apostle Simon Zelotes (Bechtel), also called Simon of Canaan in Scripture, though this connection is mere conjecture and has no Biblical nor historical evidence to back up the claim. The fourth brother of Christ is, however, mentioned in both Scripture and extrabiblical historical texts. His name is Judas, or Jude, and is the author of the epistle of the same name found in the New Testament. Many theologians equate Jude with the apostle Thaddaeus Lebbaeus since Luke lists a "Judas the brother of James" and Matthew and Mark omit the name Judas and replace it with Thaddaeus in the listing of the twelve apostles.

This familial relationship between Christ and His disciples is an important point. There was a time in Christ's earthly ministry when even his brothers did not believe in Him. Family relationship does not necessarily guarantee that one will know Christ. John states in John 7:5 "For neither did his brethren believe in him." However,

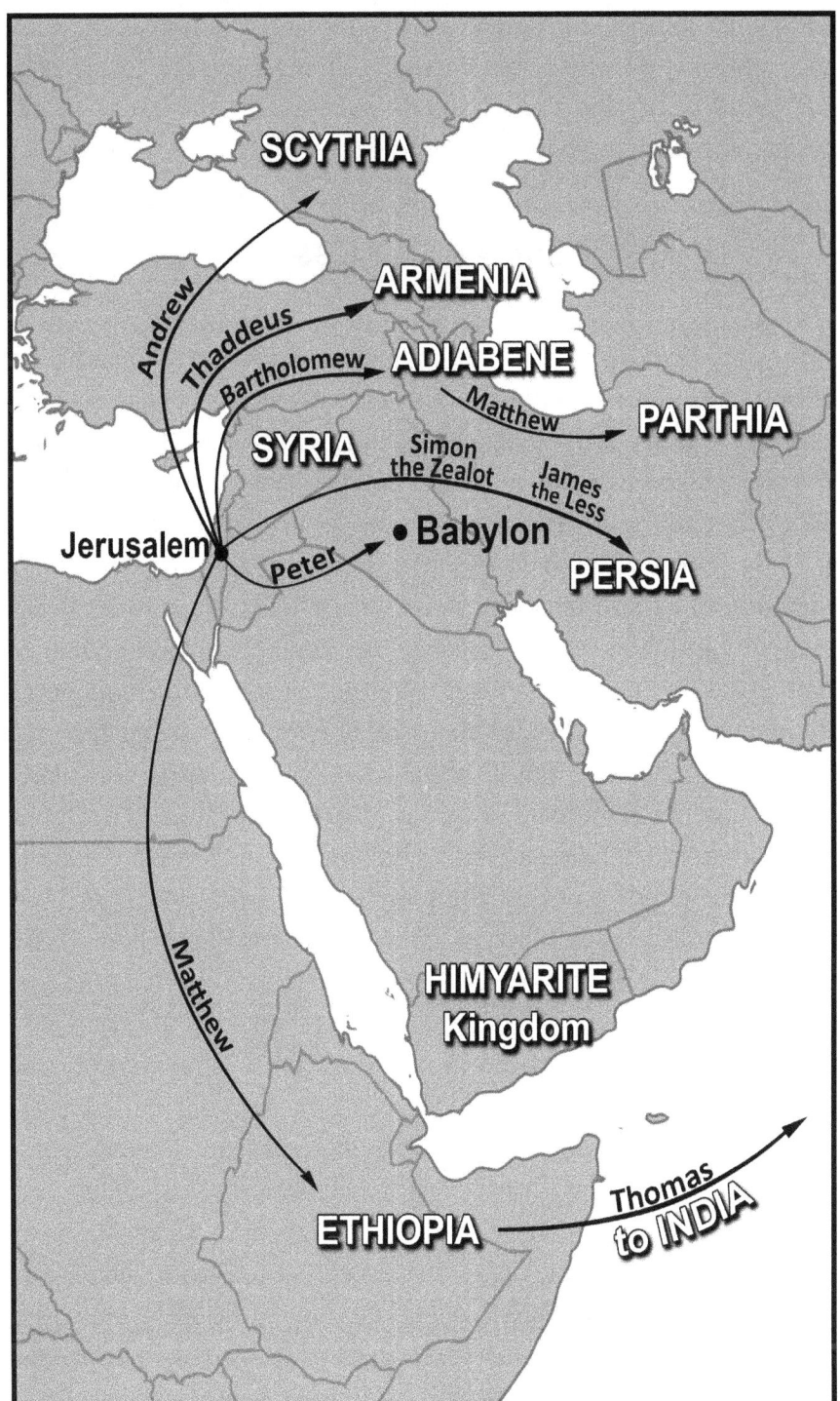

Figure 14. *Missionary journeys of the apostles in the Middle East.*

after Christ arose from the dead and ascended into heaven, these men not only believed, but carried Christ's message to the ends of the earth, giving their lives as martyrs for the cause of the propagation of the gospel message.

James the Less

James the Less, as he is called in Scripture, ministered among the Israelites in Jewish settlements in both Syria and Persia. During the first century AD, there was a vassal nation of the Armenian Empire which lie on the northern borders of Persia name Adiabene. According to the Jewish historian, Josephus, Adiabene had a very large Jewish population which had settled in the area during the mass deportation of the Babylonians in 586 BC (Josephus 20.2.1). The Babylonians had a policy of removing people from their homeland and resettling them to control revolts and uprisings from conquered nations. The rulers of Adiabene were converted to Judaism by the influence of the large Jewish population of the country in the early part of the first century. The queen of Adiabene, Helena had gone so far as to move to Jerusalem to be able to worship there, having built palaces just south of the temple mount for herself and her sons (Ibid). Adiabene played a large role in the First Great Jewish War between Israel and Rome in AD 66-73. This Jewish kingdom aided Israel as they fought for independence from Rome (Ibid). The Jewish War culminated in the destruction of the temple and the sacking of Jerusalem in AD 70. All told, over one million Jews lost their lives during the destruction of Jerusalem. James the less ministered to his Jewish brethren in the nation of Adiabene, and established churches throughout that kingdom. Adiabene, even in the first century after Christ, was converted from Judaism to become a primarily Christian nation. James the Less died as a martyr sometime before AD 70, being thrown from the temple and beaten to death by the Jews in Jerusalem as he preached. He was then buried beside the temple (Carroll, 11).

Matthew

Matthew, the author of the first gospel in the New Testament, also known as Levi left his occupation as a tax collector for the Roman Empire to become a missionary to the scattered Jewish people throughout the world. His missionary journeys, according to extrabiblical accounts, took him to Persia and Parthia in the east, Syria and Macedonia to the north, and Ethiopia to the south. Matthew suffered a martyr's death, being burned at the stake for his stand for Jesus Christ while serving as a missionary in Ethiopia (Herbermann).

Thomas

Much has been written about the missionary exploits of the apostle Thomas, who sailed along the trade routes of the "silk road" between the far east and Roman Empire (Fahlbusch 285). At a very early point, Thomas was imprisoned and later sold as a slave. He was purchased by a merchant named Abbanes, a man from India, who took Thomas back with him to India. Later, it is written that Thomas became a servant of the Indo-Parthian King, Gondophares (Ibid). This brought Thomas to the western coast of India in approximately the year AD 52. It is written that he landed at the port city of Muziris which is in the area of the modern-day cities of North Paravur and Kodungalloor in the Indian state of Kerala. Thomas traveled there to minister to a Jewish settlement in the area, and from there planted at least eight churches in the areas of Kodungallur, Palayoor, Kottakkavu, Kokkamangalam, Niranam, Nilackal, Thiruvithacode and Kollam (Medlycott 157 ff). These churches were all located along the Malabar coast, which is the western coast of the Indian peninsula. They were all found along the tributaries of the Periyar River, where Thomas visited the settlements of scattered Jewish people (Slapak 27). The Syriac author Bardaisan, who lived in the latter half of the second century, writes of Christians in India during his day who trace their heritage and conversion to Christianity to the apostle Thomas (Brock). Of special note is the sect of Christians in southwest India today known as the Saint Thomas Christian churches. These churches claim to be of decent of the first churches planted by Thomas in the first century (Fahlbusch 285). The people of this sect have a marked Jewish culture, which gives evidence to the conversion of early Jewish settlements in India to Christianity (Slapak 27). According to the tradition of these churches, Thomas evangelized western India and then traveled to the opposite side of the Indian peninsula to the Coromandel Coast of south-east India, where he continued his missionary activities. (Medlycott) Thomas was martyred c. AD 72 in the city of Chennai, India, being run through with a lance (Farmer 418).

Bartholomew

Bartholomew traveled as a missionary to the east, his ministry being attested by both the writings of Jerome and Eusebius of Caesarea as having ministered first in the areas of Armenia, Persia and India (Nasranis). Bartholomew and Thaddeus worked as a missionary team, and are credited with having brought Christianity to the kingdom of Armenia early in the first century. Armenia later became the first country in the world to adopt Christianity as their state religion, even before the Roman Empire (Fenlon). Polymius, the king of Armenia converted to Christianity under the ministry of Bartholomew, which angered the king's brother, Astyages. Astyages subsequently had Bartholomew executed by first being flayed alive and then crucified upside down. Bartholomew is also known as Nathaniel, the brother of the apostle Philip (Fenlon).

Thaddaeus

Thaddaeus Lebbaeus, one of the twelve apostles, is said to have worked alongside of Bartholomew to bring Christianity to Armenia. Adiabene would have been the central kingdom in Armenia that the missionary efforts of Thaddaeus, Bartholomew (Nathaniel) and

James the Less were carried out. Thaddaeus is said to have preached the gospel as a missionary to many various places: Judea, Samaria, Idumaea, Syria, Armenia, Mesopotamia, and Libya. He healed the king of the city of Edessa, preached as far away as Persia, and is said to have been clubbed to death for his faith in the modern-day city of Beirut, in Lebanon in the year AD 65, along with his fellow martyr Simon the Zealot (Chapman).

Simon the Zealot

Some historians have tried to equate Simon the Zealot with Simon, brother of Christ (Chapman). However, there is no external evidence to support this claim. The book of Matthew refers to him as "Simon the Canaanite," from the Hebrew יאנק *kanai*, meaning *zealot*. The Zealots were a Jewish sect who fought for the independence of the nation of Israel from the Roman Empire. Many Zealots saw the Messiah as a patriotic figure who would lead the Jews to freedom from Roman rule. The Zealots incited violence, led in the Jewish War, and even killed many other Jews for siding with Rome. Simon left this sect to follow Christ, however, the name "Zealot" is stuck with him, having been recorded in Scripture for all eternity. According to tradition, Simon first took the gospel across the sea to the isles of Britain, along with others such as Joseph of Arimathea, to convert the native population from their traditional belief in Druid paganism. Simon later became a missionary to the country of Egypt, and after leaving those parts, joined up with the apostle Jude to do missionary evangelism and church planting in Persia, Armenia (possibly Adiabene), and in Syria, where they both were martyred in modern day Beirut, Lebanon in AD 65.

John the Beloved

John the Beloved, the son of Zebedee and brother of James was given charge of Mary, the mother of Jesus (John 19:27). It is known that

John became the pastor of the church at Ephesus later in his ministry (Zahn). Toward the end of the first century, John was arrested for disseminating the religion of Christianity during the reign of emperor Domitian, the brother of Titus who destroyed Jerusalem and tore down the temple block by block in AD 70. During the reign of Domitian, the Flavian Amphitheater, also known as the Colosseum of Rome was finally completed. John was taken to the amphitheater to be executed. Placed into a giant vat of boiling oil, it is recorded that John was miraculously unharmed, and all the witnesses of this miracle were converted to Christianity (Roberts Vol. III 260). If this story is true, it would have been a huge boost for the ever-growing number of Christians in Rome. The Colosseum was estimated to hold between 50,000 to as many as 80,000 spectators (Byrnes IV 1043 ff). Upon realizing that John would not be killed, he was banished to live on the Isle of Patmos, a prison colony of Rome (Roberts Vol. III 260). There, John lived in a cave and would pen the book of the Revelation of Jesus Christ. Sometime after this, John was freed and returned to live out the rest of his days in Ephesus, dying sometime after the year AD 98 (Zahn). John is the only one of the twelve apostles that did not die a martyr's death. Two of the disciples of the apostle John wrote works that are still in existence today. Polycarp, the pastor of the church at Smyrna, wrote much of what we know about the extrabiblical history of the life and ministry of John. Ignatius, who later became the pastor of the church of Antioch in Syria also relates that his teacher in the ministry was none other than John the Beloved apostle of Jesus Christ.

Paul

The book of Acts focuses on the life of Paul the apostle. Through the pages recorded in God's Word, Paul's missionary work spanned Syria, Asia minor, Macedonia, Greece, the island of Cyprus, Italy and Judea. Paul spent his early ministry in Damascus, a city of the Nabateans, and dwelt three years in Arabia. He then returned to his home in Cilicia, no doubt preaching the gospel there, until he was fetched to Antioch by Barnabas. Paul planted no less than twenty churches during his ministry. Three missionary journeys are recorded in the Acts of the Apostles, and Paul possibly went on a fourth missionary journey, as it is speculated from the New Testament Scriptures and extrabiblical historical writings. On this fourth journey, Paul may have journeyed west to Spain and then north through Gaul (modern day France and Belgium), and possibly even passing over the English Channel to the Isle of the Britons. The historian, Tertullian, who lived AD 155-222 wrote in his book *Adversus Judaeos* of the conversion of Hispaniola, Gaul and the Britons which had already occurred before his lifetime, "all the limits of the Spains, and the diverse nations of the Gauls, and the haunts of the Britons—inaccessible to the Romans, but subjugated to Christ" (Roberts Vol III 158). The fact that the apostles of the first century had already established churches in Britain is also attested by Hilary of Poitiers (AD 300–376) and Eusebius of Caesarea, (AD 260–340) who wrote in the book *Demonstratio Evangelica* that "some have crossed the Ocean and reached the Isles of Britain." (Ferrar 130) Joseph Belcher writes:

> *It is believed that the Gospel of Jesus Christ was introduced into Britain about the year 63, by Claudia, a Welsh princess, converted under the ministry of the apostle Paul, at Rome. Her exertions to extend the reign of Christ were constant and successful. Bishop Burgess tells us, that the early British churches bore a striking resemblance to the model Institution at Jerusalem; and Mosheim tells us that 'No persons were admitted to baptism, but such as had been previously instructed in the principle points of Christianity, and had also given satisfactory proofs of pious dispositions and upright intentions.' (Belcher 157)*

Claudia, also known as Rufina, was the daughter of a Welsh King and was the wife of the Roman Senator Pudens. Pudens and Claudia are mentioned by Paul in Rome in Second Timothy 4:21. Pudens (or Pudence) was a member of the household of Caesar, and the couple exerted their authority to bring the gospel to Wales (Camden 54). It is possible that Paul traveled to Briton to meet with them and the new churches on his fourth missionary journey, after going to Spain.

> *"Under the first epoch, Stillingfleet and Burgess have collected the ancient documents extant, to prove that "St. Paul advanced into Spain," and "into the utmost bounds of the West," and "conferred advantages upon the islands which lie in the sea." And Henry Spelman quotes a passage out of Fortunatus, bishop of Poictiers, stating that "St. Paul passed over the ocean, even to the British Isles." (Brownlee 59)*

Peter

The history of the missionary ministry of Peter is recorded partially in the first few chapters of the book of Acts, and the rest can be inferred by his writings in the epistles that bear his name. In Acts 2:9-11, the Bible lists the countries that were represented on the day of Pentecost. These people would certainly have been either Jews by blood or proselytes to the Jewish faith who had traveled to Jerusalem to worship and to celebrate the feast days. Parthia, Media, Elam, Mesopotamia, Judea, Cappadocia, Pontus, Asia, Phrygia, Pamphylia, Egypt, in the parts of Libya around Cyrene, Rome, Crete and Arabia were all present on the day of Pentecost. Peter, being called to the ministry of the Circumcision (an epithet for the Jewish people) was the speaker on that day when 3000 of those present were converted to Christianity. It was to these people that Peter ministered. Most, if not all who were present and saved that day were pilgrims who did not live in Jerusalem, but eventually returned to their homes, being scattered throughout distant lands. It is recorded in First Peter 1:1 that Peter wrote to some of these very people, "Peter, an apostle of Jesus Christ, to the strangers scattered throughout Pontus, Galatia, Cappadocia,

Asia, and Bithynia." Peter's second epistle records that he is writing from Babylon. According to Roman Catholic belief, "Babylon" is a code word for the city of Rome, which is compared to one another because of the wickedness of that city, the pagan worship there, and the persecution of Christians by the Roman Empire (Stravinskas 18). However, there is no Biblical nor historical foundation for this belief. The Catholics conveniently place Peter in Rome because of their belief that he was the pastor of the church of Rome, and therefore the first pope of the Roman Catholic church (Ibid). This belief stems from a misinterpretation of the passage of Scripture where Christ is speaking to Peter and states, "And I say also unto thee, That thou art Peter, and upon this rock I will build my church; and the gates of hell shall not prevail against it" (Matthew 16:18). The problem is the confusion of the words that Christ used in this verse. The name Peter comes from the Greek word Πέτρος *Petros*, (Strong's G4074) meaning pebble or little stone. However, Peter was NOT the rock upon which Christ build his church. The word used for "rock" here is πέτρα *Petra* (Strong's G4073) meaning a large rock, boulder or cliff. The solid rock and foundation upon which Christ build His church upon the earth was not in the frailty of a sinful human being. The church was not established upon Peter, as the Roman Catholic church teaches, but rather upon the rock of Christ himself. Jesus here is contrasting the fact that Peter is but a small stone, but Christ would build His church upon the unfaltering, unwavering solid rock of Jesus Christ Himself. There is no account of Peter ever traveling to or ministering in the city of Rome. If the Word of God is to be taken literally, and there is no reason either doctrinally, contextually or historically that it should not be taken literally, then Peter was most certainly writing from the actual city of Babylon, which was situated on the Euphrates River in ancient Persia. Though there are many who would argue that Babylon was nothing more than a city of ruins by the first century AD, historical writings show evidence that there was a large population of people still living there, including a colony of Jewish people who had been displaced by the Babylonian captivity some six centuries earlier. Taking these facts into consideration, it is determined that the apostle Peter traveled and ministered to the converts in the areas of Asia Minor and also Persia, in the city of Babylon. Christ signified in John 21:18-19 that Peter would die a martyr's death by crucifixion.

> *Verily, verily, I say unto thee, When thou wast young, thou girdedst thyself, and walkedst whither thou wouldest: but when thou shalt be old, thou shalt stretch forth thy hands, and another shall gird thee, and carry thee whither thou wouldest not. This spake he, signifying by what death he should glorify God. And when he had spoken this, he saith unto him, Follow me.*

According to both Albert Barnes and John Wesley, Peter would suffer crucifixion some thirty-four to thirty-six years after this prophecy sometime between AD 64-66 (Wesley 273). According to Catholic tradition, he was executed in AD 67 along with Paul in Rome (Stravinskas 18). This however is disputed, and even though Peter was certainly executed, his presence with Paul and his presence in Rome is not only doubtful, but highly improbable.

Chapter Seven

POST APOSTOLIC MISSION WORK

Early Mission Work to the Rise of Catholicism

Christianity quickly spread to the ends of the earth in every country and area where people existed. This fact is attested to by the book of Romans, which states in Romans 10:18 "But I say, Have they not heard? Yes verily, their sound went into all the earth, and their words unto the ends of the world." By the year 64, just thirty-four years after the ascension of Christ and the giving of the Great Commission to the church, the first Christian missionaries arrive in China. According to the World Christian Encyclopedia, the first Christians in Tunisia and Gaul are reported in AD 80 (Barrett 23). By the year 100, Christianity has spread through northern Africa, and Christian congregations are found in the areas of Morocco and Algeria (Ibid). In the year 112, Pliny the Younger writes that the Christian community is spreading quickly in the area of Bithynia (Neill 28). The book The Shepherd of Hermas, though non-canonical, states that by the time of its writing in AD 140, that "The Son of God... has been preached to the ends of the earth" (Barrett 23). By 150, the gospel message has been preached to the western ends of the known world on both the western coast of the Iberian Peninsula in present day Portugal and also on the western coast of the continent of Africa in what is now Morocco (Ibid). By the year 166, it is written by Soter, the pastor of the church at Rome that the population of Christian converts has exceeded that of the entire Jewish population scattered throughout the world (Neill 30). The following year, in AD 167, Lucius, one of the kings of the Britons who ruled from a small area not yet conquered by the Romans, pleaded to have Christian missionaries sent to Brittany to convert the Britons (the ancient Celtic tribes of Britain) to Christianity (Ingram 10). Influenced by the small, but growing Christian community that had been established there over one hundred years earlier, Lucius himself was a new believer in the Lord Jesus Christ. At his request, the church at Rome sent two missionaries named Fuganus, also known as Phagan, and Duvianus, who is also called Deruvian, who were natives of the country of Wales, but had been converted to Christianity on their travels to Rome (Ibid). In the following decade, Christian missionaries would penetrate the northern forests of Germania, and by 174, the first Christian churches were planted in what is present day Austria (Barrett 23). Early Christian historical works tell us of the presence of the Gaulish churches in what is modern day France, as churches in the cities of Lyon and Vienne began to suffer persecution in AD 177 (Neill 24). In 190, the Christian churches that had been planted under the ministry of Thomas and had thrived for over a century and a half called for Christian teachers to come work with them in southern India. In response to this call, Pataenus of Alexandria becomes a missionary to the country of India (R. H. Glover 20). By AD 196, the Syriac author Bardaisian writes that Christianity has spread wildly throughout Assuristan, which is Parthian ruled Assyria, as well as Parthia, Bactria and all areas of Assyria (Dickens). Quintus Septimius Florens Tertullianus, a prolific author who lived from circa AD 155 – 240 wrote that by the year 197 Christianity had spread throughout all of Northern Africa, in both the common people and the upper ranks of society (C. G. Herbermann

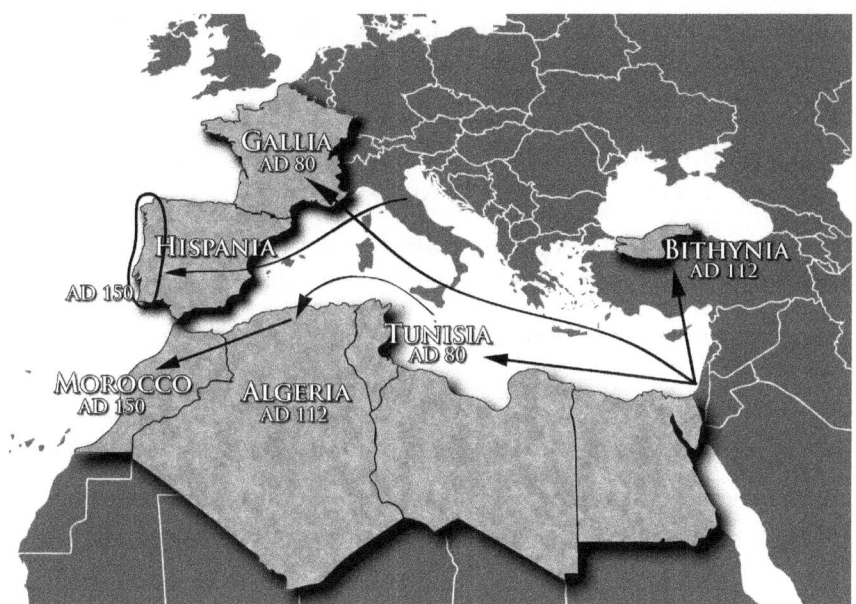

Figure 15. *Dates from historical records showing the spread of Christianity in Northern Africa, Gaul, Hispania, and Bithynia.*

385). At the end of the second century, in approximately 198 or 199, churches in China send missionaries, known as the Kungyueh who arrive by boat to bring the gospel to the Japanese (World Heritage Encyclopedia).

By the year AD 200, the first Christian communities appeared in Switzerland (Barrett 23). Herbermann writes that in 206, Abgar, the Syriac King of Edessa has been converted to Christianity (C. G. Herbermann 282). Tertullian notes that believers in Christ are found beyond the boundaries of Hadrian's Wall in Pictland (Modern Scotland, or Britain north of the Firth of Forth) and also in Hibernia, which is present day Ireland by the year AD 208 (Neill 31). In AD 250, before the papal system of Roman apostasy had corrupted the church at Rome, the Christians there were very mission minded and sent seven missionaries led by Dionysius to plant a church in the city of Paris which at the time was a Roman garrison built on the settlement of the Celtic tribe known as the Parisii, a sub-tribe of the Celtic Senones (C. G. Herbermann 481). Dionysius, also known as Denys was beheaded in Paris for refusing to renounce his faith in

Christ (Ibid). During this same time, a missionary by the name of Gregory Thaumaturgus began ministering in the area of northern Asia minor known as Pontus, and experienced a great revival there. Tradition states that when Gregory first went to Pontus, there were only seventeen Christians, yet by his death in AD 270, there were but seventeen people in all of Pontus that were not Christian (Latourette Vol. I 89). By the year AD 280, there are rural churches that are being planted throughout northern Italy and elsewhere in the world (World Heritage Encyclopedia). By this date, most of the large urban centers have established churches and missionary efforts begin to increase into regions of smaller populations. By the end of the second century AD, it is estimated that over ten percent of the world's population has converted to Christianity, and efforts are being made to translate the Word of God into many different languages, of which ten are available by the year 300 (Barrett 24).

The Rise of the Roman Catholic Church

In AD 304, Armenia becomes the first nation in the world to declare Christianity as its state religion, even before that of the Roman Empire, which did not officially declare the Roman Catholic church as the religion of the empire until February 27, AD 380 (Coleman 466). On that date, the emperor Theodosius issued the "Cunctos Populos" decree, known in English as the Edict of Thessalonica (Ehler 6-7). In that decree, Theodosius declared that the only legitimate brand of religion was that of Nicene Trinitarian Christianity, establishing it as the state religion of Rome (Ibid). Roman apostasy slowly evolved over the centuries, with its beginnings in the heresy of what John wrote in the book of Revelation as the "deeds of the Nicolaitans," which Christ expressly declared that He hated. This heresy can be explained in the translation of the word "Nicolaitans" which means "people conquerors" (Vincent Vol. II 439). It was the practice of ecclesiastical hierarchy, in which pastors would lord over the laity or membership of their churches. This later evolved into pastors of large metropolitan

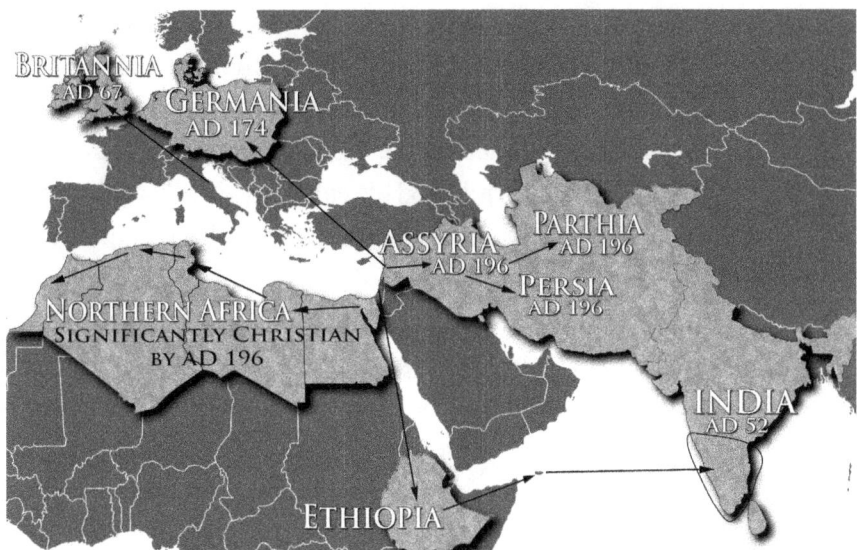

Figure 16. *Map listing the dates of a significant Christian population in the selected areas.*

According to one source, Christianity had spread to "the ends of the earth" by AD 140.

churches holding sway over smaller, rural church bodies. The Roman Empire, in accepting Christianity as a state-run religion would find that this practice suited its need of control, and therefore created a hierarchy among the clergy to exert power from the top down throughout its newly formed bureaucracy of churches. This began with the call of Constantine to enact the Edict of Milan in February 313, which ceased all hostility and persecution of Christians throughout the empire (Frend 137). Constantine was no doubt influenced by his Christian mother, the empress Helena. Helena was the wife of Emperor Constantius Clorus and mother of Constantine the Great. British legend (not historically accurate) says that she was a princess and daughter of King Cole, the King of the Britons of the nursery rhyme "Old King Cole" (Harbus 73). As a Christian, she made a pilgrimage to the Holy Lands and lived some time in Jerusalem, known at the time as the city of Aelia Capitolina (Ibid). The Catholics revere her as a saint and have a legend that she found the true cross. The historical record, however, teaches only that she met Constantius during her time in Jerusalem and married (Ibid). It was her faith that brought her son to respect Christianity and embrace the religion. In AD 325, Emperor Constantine called a council of bishops in the Bithynian city of Nicaea to obtain a universal consensus of what would be adopted by the Roman Empire as its religion (Eusebius 928 ff). Constantine sent invitations to over 1800 pastors of all the known churches within the boundaries of the Roman Empire, however, the vast majority of true churches rejected his call, knowing that submitting to the Roman Empire was not only a politically dangerous move, but was also doctrinally incorrect (Ibid). Of the 1800 pastors who were called to the council, Eusebius records that approximately 250 attended the meeting (Ibid). This was the beginnings of what evolved into the Catholic church. The point should be made, however, that by definition the word Catholic means "universal," (Merriam Webster) and the Roman church was by no means a "universal" church. At the time of its founding, the true churches of Jesus Christ were much more numerous than those who had sold out to Rome (Eusebius 928). Many churches agreed to Roman authority for various purposes. The pastors of the churches at Rome, Antioch and Jerusalem were given special power over wide areas, and held authority over all other churches in those areas (Ibid). They submitted to Roman rule to achieve power. Others came because they were promised a salary from the government, and still others were enticed to Roman control for the promise of beautiful edifices and cathedrals. Despite this, the true churches that did not submit were greater in number, and many factions such as the Donatist churches of Northern Africa would not yield to the power of Rome (Cantor 51).

Eastern Churches Reject Roman Rule

During the following centuries, there was a great push from the churches of the east, especially that of the churches in Syria, to evangelize and send missionaries eastward towards Persia, India, China, and Mongolia. These churches rejected Roman apostasy and later followed a man by the name of Nestorius, and therefore became known as the Nestorians (Bosch 204). These churches in later centuries united with the Eastern Orthodox Catholics and still exist today as the

"Holy Apostolic Catholic Assyrian Church of the East" (Binns 28). However, in the early centuries, there is evidence that these churches and their missionary efforts held to scriptural doctrine. Nestorius was branded a heretic by the Roman papal system, and accused of teaching that Christ's human nature and Divine nature were actually two separate persons. Nestorius himself denied these claims. He in fact taught the doctrine of the hypostatic union – the belief that Christ is both fully man and fully God. He preached against the use of the word *Theotokos*, or "Bringer-forth of God," describing Mary. This phrase gave rise to Mariolatry and the Catholic title for Mary as "the Mother of God" (Britannica, Nestorius).

Persecution as a Stimulus for Mission Work

From the beheading of John the Baptist to the present age, followers of the Lord have been persecuted and martyred. In the words of J.M. Carrol,

> *Following their Savior in rapid succession fell many other martyred heroes: Stephen was stoned, Matthew was slain in Ethiopia, Mark dragged through the streets until dead, Luke hanged, Peter and Simeon were crucified, Andrew tied to a cross, James beheaded, Philip crucified and stoned, Bartholomew flayed alive, Thomas pierced with lances, James, the less, thrown from the temple and beaten to death, Jude shot to death with arrows, Matthias stoned to death and Paul beheaded (Carroll 11).*

Persecution of Nero

One of the first great persecutions of the early Christians happened in Rome in AD 64, after the great fire of Rome. Sometime on the night of the eighteenth of July, AD 64, a fire broke out in the urban streets of one of the largest cities on earth (Kline 269 ff). The fire burned

ROMAN PERSECUTION OF CHRISTIANITY
• Nero - AD 64 • Domitian - AD 89 - 96 • Trajan - AD 109 • Hadrian - AD 117 • Marcus Aurelius - AD 161 • Maximinus - AD 235 • Decius - AD 250 • Valerian - AD 257 • Diocletian - AD 303 • Galerius - AD 311

Figure 17. *A list of Roman persecution of Christianity by date and the emperor under which the persecution occurred.*

for six days, and Nero was accused of having set Rome ablaze to make room for new construction plans that he had made. Angered at being publicly accused of the fire, Nero blamed the destruction on the growing Christian community and instituted an intense persecution of Christians in Rome. (Kline 269 ff)

Flavian Persecution

Both the Christian churches and the Jewish community were persecuted towards the end of the reign of the Flavian emperor Domitian (Smallwood 51). It was Domitian's father Vespasian and later his brother, Titus who had warred against the Jews and destroyed both Jerusalem and Herod's temple. Towards the end of his reign, in AD 96, Domitian began persecuting the churches, attempting to execute the apostle John, by then an elderly man. According to the church historian, Eusebius, the Roman consul and cousin of Domitian, Flavius Clemens was executed for being a Christian. The Consulship was the highest elected position in the empire, right under that of the emperor himself. After his execution, Flavia Domitilla, the wife of the consul was exiled to the island of Pandateria for also being a Christian (T. D. Barnes 36).

Trajanic Persecution

In 109, the emperor Trajan began yet another persecution of Christians, ordering the governor of Bithynia, Pliny the Younger, to execute all who would not curse the name of Jesus Christ and embrace the ancient Roman religion (Canfield 86-99). The record of the letters between Pliny and Trajan have survived, documenting the persecution and martyrdom of those who refused to renounce Jesus Christ in Bithynia. In the face of this persecution, Pliny writes that by AD 112, the Christian community has spread rapidly throughout the area.

Hadrianic Persecution

The emperor Hadrian was much more lenient in his attitude toward Christians during his reign. Justin Martyr records in his work, First Apology, in AD 155, that Hadrian required that any legal action against a Christian would only be taken if they had committed an act against Roman law, and that naming the name of Christ was insufficient for prosecution. Hadrian also went a step further, decreeing that anyone who brought charges against a Christian, but failed in the suit was to be prosecuted for "slanderous acts" (W. H. Frend 7).

Persecution of Marcus Aurelius

Marcus Aurelius, the Roman emperor from 161-180 reinstated the persecution of Christians (D. Farmer). According to Eusebius, Christians in Lugdunum, which is modern-day Lyons in France, were arrested and tried for professing Christ. There, they were taken to the amphitheater, tortured and fed to lions. Though many equate this punishment as having taken place in the Colosseum of Rome, Christians were probably never fed to wild beasts there. It did, however, occur in many similar arenas throughout the Roman Empire (Ibid).

Persecution of Maximinus

The next major persecution of the churches occurred during the reign of Maximinus, from AD 235-238 (Bowman 28). Recorded by Eusebius, Maximinus the Thracian emperor of Rome began an intense campaign to root out pastors of local Christian churches. Eusebius writes that in 235, Hyppolytus and Pontian, pastors of two different churches in Rome, were both sent into exile on the isle of Sardinia (Ibid).

Persecution of Decius

In the year 250, the Roman emperor Decius decreed an empire-wide persecution of all who would not sacrifice to the Roman gods and the "genius" (the divine nature) of the emperor (W. Frend, The Rise of Christianity 319). Christians were especially targeted, and for eighteen months many Christians were executed. Others renounced their belief to escape death. Those who apostatized were forced to make a public sacrifice to the Roman gods, accept the divinity of the emperor of Rome, and publicly curse Jesus Christ. After this persecution, a division arose among the churches over whether or not to accept those pastors back into the pulpit who had renounced and cursed the name of Christ so they could escape execution. The Donatists of Africa took a hard-line stance on the issue and would never accept those men, stating that they had disqualified themselves from the ministry (Cantor 51).

Persecution of Valerian

The emperor Valerian, in AD 257 ordered another great persecution of Christians, seeking them out and forcing them to sacrifice to the Roman gods (W. H. Frend 325). The pastors and preachers of churches were to be put to death. Christians in the Roman government were removed from their positions, stripped of their titles, and forfeited their property. They were then made to sacrifice to the Roman gods. Upon refusal to do so, they were executed or sold into slavery (Ibid).

Diocletianic Persecution

During the period of the Roman Tetrarchy, the four co-emperors of Rome, Diocletian, Maximian, Galerius and Constantius Chlorus issued several decrees that hoped to wipe out the Christian religion once and for all (T. D. Barnes, Constantine and Eusebius 22). The edicts ordered a policy known as universal sacrifice, in which all subjects of the Roman empire were to worship and sacrifice to the Roman gods only. This culminated in the feast of the Terminalia, celebrated on February 23, AD 303, in which Diocletian declared that the Christian religion would forever be terminated (T. D. Barnes, Constantine and Eusebius 21). He then issued an "Edict against the Christians," which ordered the death of all Christian leaders, forbade the assembly of churches, seized the property of known Christians, ordered the destruction of any Christian houses of worship and the burning of all Bibles. Christian church members, even if not executed, were stripped of all legal rights as citizens. This Diocletianic persecution was the most intense persecution of Christianity in Roman times. Many believers throughout the empire were martyred because of their faith, and many of the early writings and Biblical manuscripts were lost.

Figure 18. *An antoninianus (double denarius) coin of emperor Diocletian who tried to exterminate the Christian community in the Roman Empire.*

Persecution of Galerius

Galerius, who only two years before had recommended that Christians be burned at the stake, saw the futility of the persecution. Even the non-Christian Roman populace began an outcry against the severity of the state-sponsored murder of their neighbors. Christianity was widespread, and very few populations in the Roman empire were unaffected by the persecution. Rather than wiping out the Christian religion, Christianity flourished during the time of persecution. Many saw the undying faith of those who were martyred and converted to faith in Jesus Christ. The intense persecution of the saints by the Roman Empire may have very well been the stimulus of the explosive growth of churches and missionary endeavors throughout the world, as Christians fled for their lives, taking their faith with them to distant lands. Galerius issued the Edict of Toleration in AD 311, effectively ending the persecution of Christians (Bowman 589 ff). The following year, Constantine the Great would embrace this religion and carry the cross as his banner at the Battle of Milvian Bridge where he commanded his troops to emblazon Christian symbol of the Chi-Rho (the first two letters of Christ in the Greek language) on their Roman shields, declaring "Εν Τούτῳ Νίκα" (with this sign, you shall conquer) (Eusebius 55).

Chapter Eight

CHURCH PERPETUITY THROUGH MISSION WORK

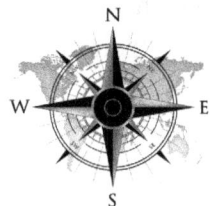

The Spread of Christianity Throughout the East

The missionary activity of the early churches spread throughout every country in the world. Though not regularly taught in the course of ecclesiastical history, Christianity was a world religion at a very early date, having established a foothold in places such as China and India, Mongolia and even Japan. The missionary activity of the Syrian churches must not be disregarded in this respect. In AD 498, missionaries from the Eastern Syrian churches begin ministering to the Hephthalite Huns of the central Asian steppes of Turkestan, teaching them to read and write with the Greek alphabet (Olson 102). Syrian missionary labor also resulted in the conversion of the Najranian Arabs of southern Arabia to Christianity (Trimingham 287). At that time, the country of Yemen was known as the Himyarite kingdom, which was Jewish ruled. The Jewish Himyarites were intolerant of the Christian community and persecuted them, resulting in a war in which the Najran Christians begged for assistance from the Christian kingdom of Ethiopia. The Jewish Himyarites defeated the Ethiopian army and completely wiped out the Christian population in southern Arabia (Ibid).

According to an inscription found on an archaeological artifact termed the Xi'an Stele (or Nestorian Stele) found in Chang'an, China, Syrian and Persian missionaries led by Alopen came from the Roman Empire to bring the gospel to China in 635. Alopen and his team of missionaries were sent to preach the gospel along the silk road by the early Nestorian churches. They were welcomed by the emperor Taizong, who had the Scriptures translated into Chinese and distributed throughout the land. The Xi'an Stele was erected in AD 779 as a monument in central China to the missionaries and their church planting efforts (Moffett 14 f). Several ancient manuscripts known as the Jesus Sutras were discovered in the Mongao caves of central Asia dating from the time of Alopen. The efforts of these eastern missionaries multiplied over many generations. Many of the people of China, Mongolia and Eastern Central Asia were converted to Christianity. The Uighurs of western China, which today are almost completely Muslim, were, during the twelfth and thirteenth centuries considered completely Christian (joshuaproject.net). The Mongol tribes of the Kara Khitai, the Naimans, the Keraits, and the Merkits had significant Christian populations for several centuries. In Mongolia, Hulagu, the grandson of Genghis Khan and brother of Kublai Khan along with his wife, Dokuz Khatun, were the Christian emperor and empress of the Mongol Empire (Hildinger 148). When Marco Polo traveled throughout China and visited the court of the Mongol emperor along with his father and uncle, he found many in those lands to be Christian. It was not until the fall of the Mongol rulers, which were defeated by the Ming dynasty of China in 1368 that Christianity lost its foothold in this part of the world (Moule 216-40). After the takeover by the Ming dynasty, they persecuted and killed most of the Christians in the country, destroying church buildings and building Buddhist temples on top of their ruins. Recent archaeological discoveries have proven that several Buddhist

CHURCH PERPETUITY THROUGH MISSION WORK 153

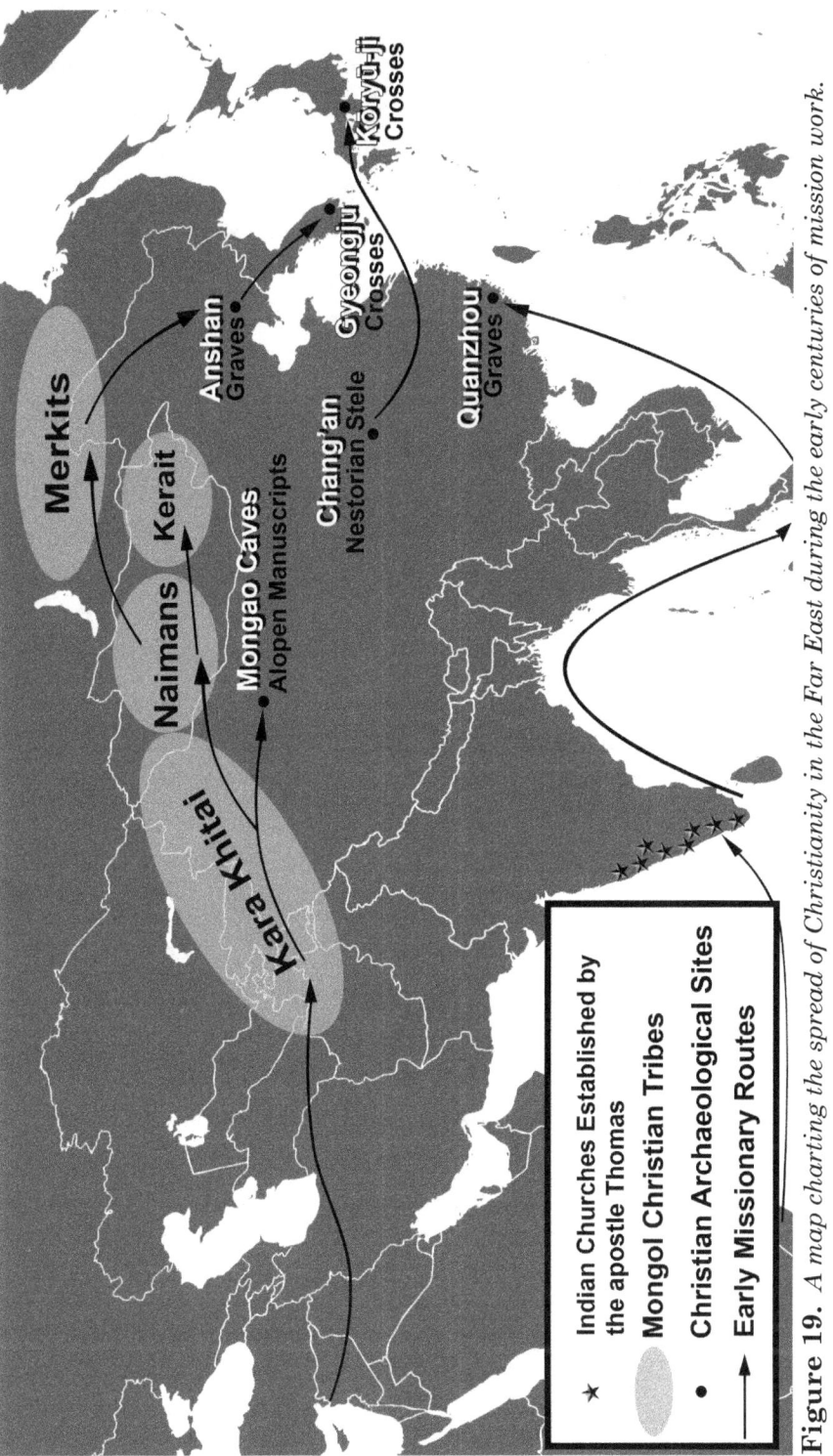

Figure 19. *A map charting the spread of Christianity in the Far East during the early centuries of mission work.*

monasteries and temples in China, Korea, and Japan were built atop of the ruins of Christian churches such as the Kōryū-ji temple in Kyoto, Japan built in AD 603 and Gyeongju in Korea (Joseph Jr.). Christian grave markers have been found in Anshan and Quanzhou, China. China, Mongolia and the Far East had a large population of Christians for a period of almost seven hundred years.

The Novatians

The names given to groups of early Christians who refused to identify with the church of Rome are numerous. These names were given, not by the churches themselves, but by their enemies - usually the Roman Catholic church. One such group was named the Novatians. The Novatians were named after Novatianus, who, like the later Donatists of Africa, stated that pastors who denied Christ during the persecution of Decius in AD 250 should be disqualified from the pastorate. Novatianus was a champion of local church discipline against those who sacrificed to idols and cursed the name of Christ to escape death. The Novatian churches refused to readmit any of the *lapsi*, those who lapsed into idolatry and renounced their faith under Roman persecution (Hisel, 78). They were strict in the doctrine of holiness and moral purity. Like most of the early churches, they practiced baptism by immersion, rejected infant baptism, rejected the Roman church, and each church governed themselves independently. The churches of the Novatians were similar in doctrine and practice to the Baptist churches of today. Doctrines and practices are the measure that must be used to differentiate true churches throughout the ages from false religion.

The Donatists

The Donatists were early Christian churches in Northern Africa who refused to join the Roman church, stating that they had no authority over them (Cantor 51 f). The Donatists were named for Donatus Magnus, a Berber theologian who championed the fight against

Rome. After the intense persecution that occurred during the reign of the emperor Diocletian, the churches in Africa that followed the teachings of Donatus refused to reinstate those pastors who had publicly cursed the name of Christ to escape execution, or those who had handed over copies of Scripture to be burned to avoid execution. The Donatists called these men "traditores" meaning "those who had handed over the holy things" (Lindberg 45). Other doctrinal positions of the Donatist churches set them apart from those churches who embraced Roman apostasy. Donatists practiced baptism by immersion, rejected infant baptism, rejected the Roman church, and each church governed themselves independently. They would, by all accounts, be doctrinally identical with the Baptist churches of today (Hisel).

The Paulicians

The Paulicians were the name given to the true churches of Jesus Christ in Armenia, tracing their history to apostolic times (Hisel 124). Armenia was the first true Christian nation. The churches there predate the Catholic church and rejected Catholicism. The Roman church called them Paulicians because they held to the pure doctrine of the church written in the Epistles of Paul. John T. Christian states,

> *Turning to the doctrines and practices of the Paulicians we find that they made constant use of the Old and New Testaments. They had no orders in the clergy as distinguished from laymen by their modes of living, their dress, or other things; they had no councils or similar institutions. Their teachers were of equal rank. They strove diligently for the simplicity of the apostolic life. They opposed all image worship which was practiced in the Roman Catholic Church. The miraculous relics were a heap of bones and ashes, destitute of life and of virtue. They held to the orthodox view of the Trinity; and to the human nature and substantial sufferings of the Son of God. Baptist*

> *views prevailed among the Paulicians. They held that men must repent and believe, and then at a mature age ask for baptism, which alone admitted them into the church. "It is evident," observes Mosheim, "they rejected the baptism of infants." They baptized and rebaptized by immersion. They would have been taken for downright Anabaptists (Allix, The Ecclesiastical History of the Ancient Churches of Piedmont. Oxford, 1821). (Christian 55)*

The Paulicians were driven from their native Armenia by severe persecution and spread throughout Europe. Many of them settled in what is present day Bulgaria. There, they were called the Bogamils. Though their Catholic enemies accused them of many heresies, such as embracing Gnosticism and the dualistic theology of Zoroastrianism or the mysticism of Manichean beliefs, nowhere in their original Armenian writings do the Paulician churches ever state that they hold to those heresies (Hisel). On the contrary, the Paulicians held to sound, Biblical doctrine such as salvation by grace through faith, baptism by immersion, and a rejection of the Catholic heresies of infant baptism, worship of Mary, and ecclesiastical hierarchy (Ibid). W.F. Adeney called the Paulicians, "Ancient Oriental Baptists... these people were in many respects Protestants before Protestantism" (Adeney 219).

The Petrobrussians, Arnoldists, and Henricians

Another name given to the pure and true churches of Christ during the middle ages is that of the Petrobrussians. The Petrobrussians were churches in southern France who were named after Peter of Bruys. Petrobrussians were opposed to pedobaptism and the veneration of idols by the Catholic church. They also preached openly against the doctrine of transubstantiation, in which the Catholics believe that the bread and wine, when blessed by a priest, becomes the actual body and blood of Jesus Christ (Vedder 15). Petrobrussians were opposed to the Catholic doctrine of praying for the dead (Livingstone 1264). Another popular preacher in France under the influence of Peter de Bruys was Henry of Lausanne. The Catholics gave rise to calling these churches Henricians also, after the name of Henry. These French Baptists were severely persecuted by the Catholic church during the period of the Inquisition, and many were martyred for their faith (Hisel).

Arnold of Brescia was another disciple of Peter de Bruys which preached boldly against the Roman church. S.H. Ford writes of Arnold, "He was a Baptist. For holding just what Baptists now hold, and for no other charge, he was arrested, condemned, crucified, and then burned, and his ashes thrown into the Tiber. The Arnoldists, the Henricians, and Petrobrussians we have found, and by their enemies, showed them to be Baptists" (Ford 57 f). The Arnoldists, as they were called preached against the Catholic doctrines of pedobaptism and salvation by the efficacy of partaking in the Eucharist. The disciples of Arnold were termed Publicans and Poplecans, both names probably derivations of the original name Paulicians (Lambert 72). In the book History of the Baptists by John T. Christian, it is written, "By the year 1184 the Arnoldists were termed Albigenses, a little later they were classed as Waldenses. Derckhoff, one of the German writers on the Waldenses affirms: There was a connection between the Waldenses and the followers of Peter de Bruys, Henry of Lausanne and Arnold of Brescia, and they finally united in one body about 1130 as they held common views" (Christian 67).

The Waldenses

The churches known as the Waldenses or Waldensians inhabited the Piedmont area of Northwestern Italy. Their confessions of faith identify them scripturally with the beliefs of modern day Baptist churches. The Waldenses claim to have an ancient pedigree dating to the time of the apostles (R. Robinson 302). Even the Catholics agree that the Waldenses predated the Protestant movement by many centuries, and had adherents to their doctrine in every country. Modern Protestant scholarship attributed the name Waldenses to Peter Waldo. However, the sect was not named after Peter Waldo as is commonly assumed, but took their name for the Italian word *valdesi*, meaning "valley" (R. Robinson 302). The name predates Peter Waldo and refers to the fact that they lived in the valleys of Piemont (or Piedmont), Italy. The Waldenses were heavily persecuted in the Middle Ages by the Roman church. Samuel Moreland recorded a history of this persecution, especially of a bloody massacre of entire villages of the Waldenses in 1658 by the Catholics. For many centuries, the Waldenses worshiped and preached the true gospel of Jesus Christ apart from the apostasy of the Papal system. They believed in salvation by grace through faith and practiced believer's baptism. In their written creeds from the twelfth century, the Waldenses rejected pedobaptism, transubstantiation, praying to saints, worship of Mary, and the Catholic doctrine of purgatory. As their faith spread they were given other names throughout Europe, yet the common thread of doctrine and fellowship identified these believers as the true Baptist churches of their day.

Other Names given to True Churches

Many other names were given to these true churches throughout the ages who continued to practice and preach the pure, unadulterated Word of God. According to Samuel Morland, they were often known by the region they inhabited, by a well-known preacher of their number or some other epithet given to them by the surrounding population or by the Catholic church (Morland 12 f). Waldensian churches of like faith in the region of Albie were known as the Albigenses. Those in England went by the name of the Lollards. In the southeastern French province of Dauphine these brethren were mockingly called Chaignards. In the Swiss Alps, they were known by the name of

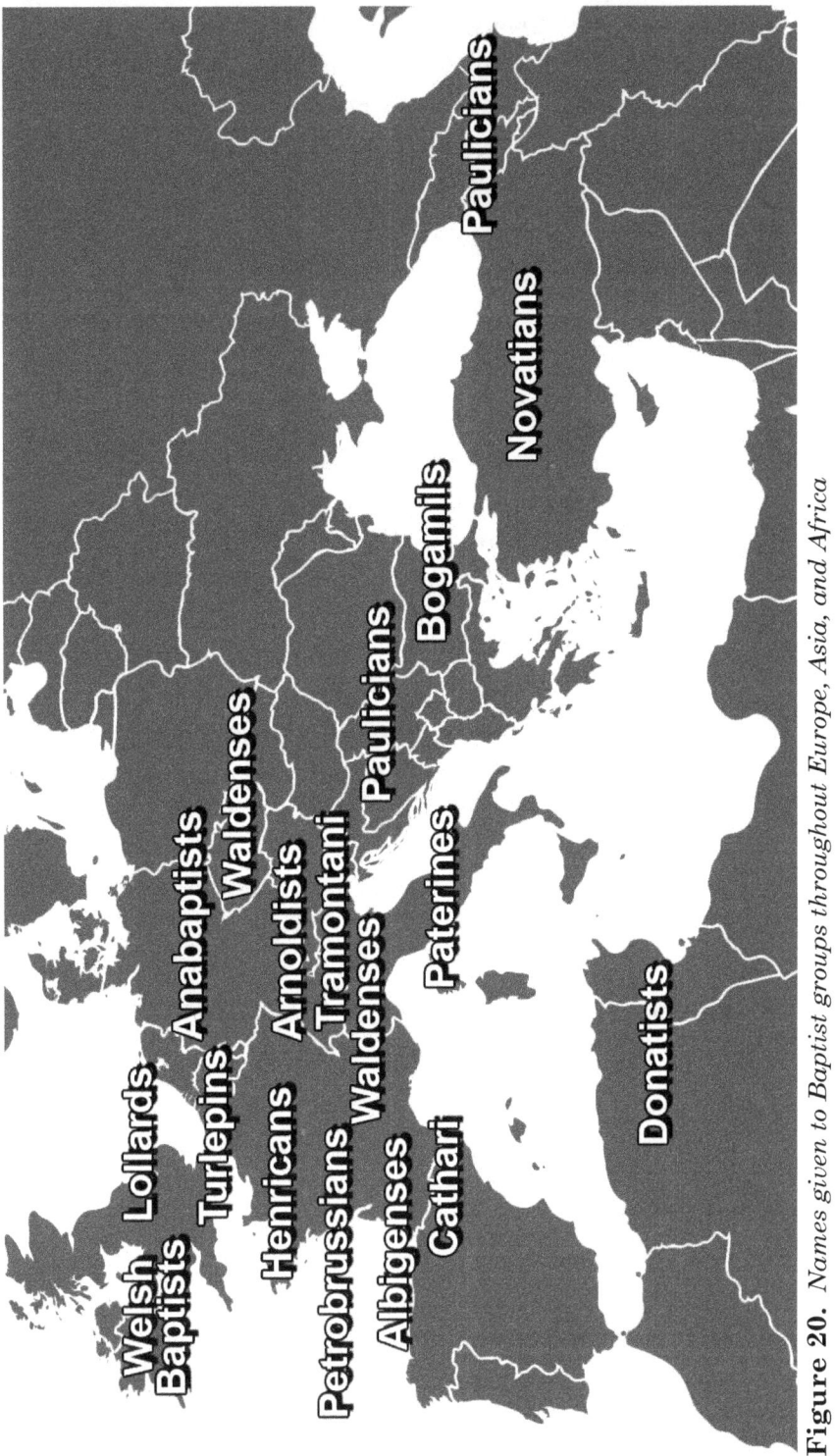

Figure 20. *Names given to Baptist groups throughout Europe, Asia, and Africa*

Tramontani. They were called the Siccars in the French region of Provence. The Germans called these faithful Christians Gazares, which means "wicked ones." They were known as the Turlepins in the region of Flanders, Belgium. The term *Turlepin* denotes those who live in the wild among the wolves, for certainly these faithful followers of Christ were often forced to flee for their lives on threat of execution from their enemies and would hide out in the uninhabited regions of the forests and wilderness to be able to practice their faith in peace (Ibid). In the book Alien Baptism and the Baptists, William Nevins speaks of the relation of all these various groups,

> *On the French side of the Pyrenees was the little village of Abby in the province of Albigeois. Here came the Novatians and Donatists, and later the Paulicians, and later still, the Waldenses. But as they all held identical views, in opposition to the Roman Church, they mingled and blended into one harmonious whole, and became known as the Albigenses, from the town near which they lived, and then the name was given to others with like views that inhabited the surrounding provinces (Nevins 55).*

Of all these groups, one single name was also used to describe them throughout the ages by the Catholic church: Anabaptists. Of these Anabaptists, John Lawrence Mosheim, a Lutheran historian writes,

> *Before the rise of Luther and Calvin, there lay concealed, in almost all the countries of Europe, particularly in Bohemia, Moravia, Switzerland, and Germany, many persons who adhered tenaciously to the following doctrine, which the Waldenses, Wickliffites, and Hussites, had maintained, some in a more disguised and others in a more open and public manner; viz. 'That the kingdom of Christ, or the visible church which He established upon earth, was an assembly of true and real saints, and ought therefore to be inaccessible to the wicked and unrighteous, and*

> *also exempt from all those institutions which human prudence suggests, to oppose the progress of iniquity, or to correct and reform transgressors"* (Mosheim 491).

Several modern groups including the Mennonites and the Amish are direct descendants of Anabaptist groups that moved to America during the reformation period. This fact has been used by modern historians to disprove the connection between the ancient sects of Anabaptists and that of modern day Baptists. The point, however, still stands that the relationship is not direct genetic and physical lineage, but similarity in doctrine and practice between that of modern day Baptist churches and those of ancient times. Christ certainly promised the perpetuity of His churches when He proclaimed that "the gates of hell shall not prevail against it" (Matt. 16:18). This does not mean that individual churches would not cease to exist, but that the truth of the gospel would be proclaimed by an unbroken heritage of scripturally pure churches throughout all the centuries, from the first church in Jerusalem to the rapture of the saints. Charles Haddon Spurgeon spoke on the issue of Baptist Perpetuity,

> *We believe that the Baptists are the original Christians. We did not commence our existence at the reformation, we were reformers before Luther or Calvin were born; we never came from the Church of Rome, for we were never in it, but we have an unbroken line up to the apostles themselves. We have always existed from the very days of Christ, and our principles, sometimes veiled and forgotten, like a river which may travel underground for a little season, have always had honest and holy adherents* (C. H. Spurgeon 225).

Again, Spurgeon commented on the Anabaptists,

> *History has hitherto been written by our enemies, who never would have kept a single fact about us upon the record if they could have helped it, and yet it leaks out*

every now and then that certain poor people called Anabaptists were brought up for condemnation. From the days of Henry II to those of Elizabeth we hear of certain unhappy heretics who were hated of all men for the truth's sake which was in them. We read of poor men and women, with their garments cut short, turned out into the fields to perish in the cold, and anon of others who were burnt at Newington for the crime of Anabaptism. Long before your Protestants were known of, these horrible Anabaptists, as they were unjustly called, were protesting for the "one Lord, one faith, and one baptism" (C. H. Spurgeon 249).

Chapter Nine

MODERN BAPTIST MISSION WORK

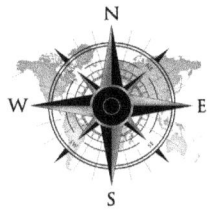

According to most modern historians, it was Roger Williams, the founder of the colony of Rhode Island who founded the first Baptist church in America - in Providence, Rhode Island in 1638 (Brackney 23). This has been called into question by many Baptist scholars. The First Baptist Church of Newport, Rhode Island, planted by John Clarke, also claims the title of the first and oldest Baptist church in the United States, having its beginnings in 1638 (Adlam 15). There is, however, evidence that Baptist congregations from England and Europe had fled persecution and emigrated to America even before the founding of those two churches. "Before Roger Williams was baptized, or his Church organized, there were Baptist churches and Baptist ministers throughout New England" (Ford, 9). With the founding of the Rhode Island colony, many Anabaptist people who were experiencing persecution by the Puritans in Massachusetts fled to the new colony to practice freedom of worship. "But in Virginia were Baptists ere Rhode Island had its charter. In Massachusetts were Baptist congregations before Williams was baptized" (Ford, 11).

Entire congregations of Welsh Baptists along with their ministers were recorded to sail across the Atlantic Ocean to the New World, establishing an old line of pure, Baptistic churches with a history that stretched back to apostolic times (Ray 64).

The Father of Modern Mission Work

Among modern Baptist missionaries, William Carey is of special note. Carey has been called by many historians the "Father of Modern Missions" (Gonzalez 419). Born in 1761, William Carey grew up as a member of the Anglican Church in Northhamptonshire, England (Wellman 12). When he was fourteen, Carey became an apprentice cordwainer in Piddington, England. There, he met a man named John Warr who would become a close friend and influence the rest of his life (Wellman 20). Warr was a dissenter of the Church of England, and convinced Carey that the teachings and practices of that church were unbiblical. Not long after, Carey, Warr, and other dissenters began a Congregational church in the village of Hackleton, England. Though not formally educated, Carey was an extremely intelligent man. He worked as a shoemaker in his early adult years. While employed as a shoemaker, Carey learned to read and write in Greek, Hebrew, Italian, Dutch, and French (Wellman 26). At the age of twenty-two, Carey left the Congregationalists to join a local Baptist church. On October 5, 1783, Carey was baptized and dedicated his life to the gospel ministry (Wellman 21 f). The church he joined was a Particular Baptist church, meaning that they believed in Calvinistic doctrine. This exposure to Calvinism may have been the catalyst that pushed Carey to first think about mission work for the first time. The Particular Baptists believed that since God had elected some to salvation and all others were doomed to damnation, spreading the gospel message was a futile activity. They held to the belief that God would do all the mission work, and that men should not concern themselves about the souls of the heathen around the world. While at a Bible study one day,

Carey posed the question of whether or not the Great Commission of the Lord Jesus Christ was still in effect and if churches should still carry the gospel to the ends of the earth. John Ryland, the pastor and minister that baptized Carey, responded "Young man, sit down; when God pleases to convert the heathen, he will do it without your aid and mine" (Wellman 27). This, however, was just another push for William Carey in the opposite direction. He was a voracious reader and obsessed himself with stories of faraway lands and missionary efforts to those areas. He read the journal of Captain James Cook and *Account of the Life of the Late Rev. David Brainerd* by Johnathan Edwards. Captain Cook was an explorer, and Brainerd was a missionary to the native Americans (Carpenter 529). These stories along with his study of the Word of God inspired a missionary zeal that led him to write his own work, *An Enquiry into the Obligations of Christians to Use Means for the Conversion of the Heathens*. Determined to become a missionary himself, he set his eyes on the expansive British Empire which at the time stretched around the world. He decided that British controlled India would be the best place to begin a work. Carey founded the Baptist Missionary Society, which would support the mission effort (Smith 52). In 1793, Carey sailed for the shores of India. It was not until seven years later, in 1800, that Carey saw his first convert (Pal 11). During those seven years, he worked to support himself at an indigo factory in India and translated the Bible into the Bengali language (Wellman 84). Carey suffered terrible loss on the mission field, sacrificing for the cause of Christ. His son, Peter, contracted dysentery and died on the field, and a short time later, Dorothy, Carey's wife, had a nervous breakdown from which she never recovered. Dorothy had at first been unwilling to move to India. She was illiterate and had never traveled more than a few miles from her home in England. In 1807, Dorothy Carey died, having been completely insane for many years (Wellman 109). Carey's diligent labor and sacrifice was not without its reward. By the time of his death, William Carey spent 41 years on the mission field, having never returned to his home, nor having ever taken a furlough. During those 41 years, over 700 converts were recorded. Carey's Bible translation work was prolific. Carey personally translated the Scriptures into the languages of Bengali, Oriya, Assamese, Arabic, Marathi, Hindi and Sanskrit (Galli 244).

The First Baptist Missionary from America

William Carey's influence on modern mission work was widespread, and his exploits were known throughout the world. In 1810, a student movement in the Congregationalist churches of America formed what would become known as the American Board of Commissioners for Foreign Missions (Goodsell 6). Samuel Mills was the leader of the movement which, inspired by Carey in India, decided to send out missionaries of their own. The first missionaries to be sent included a group of men by the names of Samuel Newell, Samuel Nott, Gordon Hall, Luther Rice and Adoniram Judson (Ibid). Having no experience in sending or supporting missionaries, Adoniram Judson was sent by the commission to ask for advice and possible support for the missionaries from the London Missionary Society. Unfortunately, this was a volatile time. The newly formed United States had won its independence from Britain not many years before, and hostilities broke out again with the War of 1812. Sailing across the ocean during this time would prove both dangerous and futile. Judson's ship was attacked by French privateers (Anderson 89). Judson was taken prisoner and sailed on the French vessel to the mainland. He was able to escape after not too long a time and flee to England, where he finally was able to contact the London Missionary Society (Ibid). The English, wanting nothing to do with Americans at this time, sent Judson on his way and told him that the Americans should support their own missionaries. This first overseas trip was just the beginning for Adoniram Judson. After he returned home to the States, the Congregationalist mission board decided that the best course of action was to send their men to work with an established missionary, so they wrote letters asking William Carey to accept them as associates in the work in India. Carey agreed to receive them, and the new missionaries set sail for India. While sailing over the ocean, which would take them many months, two of the missionaries, Luther Rice and Judson, decided that they would have to debate the Baptist missionaries that they were going to work with in India over several points of doctrine. Congregationalists practiced pedobaptism, the baptism of infants for salvation. Knowing that Carey and the other Baptist missionaries in India were opposed to pedobaptism, the two decided to undertake an in-depth Bible study on that particular topic, looking into the original Greek and comparing all the Bible passages on the subject to the modern practices of baptism. After the painstaking study, both Adoniram Judson and Luther Rice came to the conclusion that the Baptists were Biblically correct. By the time they arrived in India, they had decided to cut all ties with the Congregationalists and associate themselves with churches that lined up with scriptural doctrine and practices. Both Luther Rice and Adoniram Judson consented to be baptized on landing in India by the Baptist missionary William Ward. This created a dilemma for the two because they had cut ties with their sole means of support. After discussing their options, the pair decided that Judson and his wife should remain on the mission field while Luther Rice would return to the United States to secure financial support for the mission work. Felix Carey, son of William Carey had determined to begin a new work in the British colonial area of Burma. Judson agreed to travel to Burma with Felix and try to establish a foothold in that new area (Ibid).

It was in 1813, at the age of 25 that Judson and his wife moved to the country of Burma (Anderson 170). Judson was also very adept in the study of languages. He knew Greek, Hebrew and Latin, which he used in Bible study. (Ibid). The Burmese language was very different, however, from everything that he had previously learned. It took Judson three years, studying twelve hours a day with a language tutor to master the Burmese language. At the time, conversion to Christianity was punishable by death in Burma. It was four years before Judson ventured to hold a public service. At first, he decided to wear the yellow robes of the Buddhist monks to show that he was a teacher of religion. This however, proved to be fruitless. The Burmese thought that he had converted to Buddhism. Afterward, he tried wearing a white robe, but white robes are reserved in that country for the nuns of Buddhism. Finally, Judson decided that no matter what he wore, the Burmese would only see him as an outsider, and that wearing garments to show he was a teacher of religion was just an artificial show. Judson's first true public meeting was not until April of 1819 (Anderson 215). There were fifteen people in attendance. That same year, Judson baptized the first Burmese convert, six years after moving to Burma, and seven years after moving to the mission field. After twelve years on the field, he had only 18 converts to Christianity. Judson continued working tirelessly for the Lord, and had completed a translation of the New Testament in the Burmese language in 1823. During the British-Burmese War which broke out the following year, Judson was arrested and dragged off to the Ava death prison where he suffered seventeen months of torture and starvation. Judson was later marched along with other westerners to a village outside of Mandalay where he was kept for an additional six months (Anderson 302). Of all other prisoners in the camp, all but Judson and one other man died. Judson had left his wife Ann alone in a hostile environment to care for their two children. Ann was expecting their third child at the time of Judson's arrest. Not long after his release, Ann Judson died, on October 24, 1826 (Ibid). Six months later, their third child also died. Judson spent the rest of his life working with the Karen people of Northern Burma. Unlike the Burmese nationals, the Karens, which were a nomadic hill tribe, eagerly received the Word of God. Some of the ancient oral traditions of the Karen tribe seemed to be variations of Old Testament stories (Ibid). This may be evidence that they had been exposed to Christianity in previous generations by ancient missionaries who traveled to the East. When Judson died, he left a legacy of over 100 Baptist churches and 8,000 believers in the country of Burma. Many other missionaries followed Judson to continue the work, and today Burma has one of the largest Baptist populations in the world (Ibid).

The Organization of Baptists in America

Mission work within the United States was growing quickly along with the growth of the new nation. In 1790, the year of the first American census, there were 872 Baptist churches in the United States with 64,975 members, 722 ordained preachers and an additional 449 licensed ministers. In the next four decades, these numbers would grow significantly. By 1836, there were 372 Baptist associations in the U.S., 7,299 Baptist churches, 4,075 ordained ministers, 966 licensed ministers, and church membership numbers totaled 517,524 (Hiscox 253).

Luther Rice had returned to America and began traveling among Baptist churches to raise support for Judson, who was hailed as the first Baptist foreign missionary to be sent out from America. While on deputation, Luther Rice met a minister in Georgia by the name of Richard Furman. Furman convinced Rice to organize the missionary efforts among Baptist churches nationwide. The zeal of the preaching of Luther Rice, along with the stories of the foreign field with the Judsons and Careys excited the churches. Through the efforts of this one man, the General Missionary Convention of the Baptist Denomination in the USA was formed in May 1814 (Wardin). Richard Furman became the first president of the new Baptist convention, Luther Rice became the first mission promoter of the convention, and Adoniram Judson became the first missionary (Rogers).

Within the next few years, most of the other protestant denominations in the United States would follow the missionary efforts of the Baptists to create missionary societies of their own: the Methodists in 1819, the Episcopalians in 1821, the Presbyterians in 1831, and the Lutherans in 1837.

Two different types of Baptist churches existed at this time, divided by the doctrine of Calvinism (Ray 24). The missionary efforts of Rice and Judson brought the issue of Calvinism to the forefront,

Early Baptist Churches in America

- 1st Newport, RI 1638
- Providence, RI 1639
- 2nd Newport, RI 1656
- 1st Swansea, MA 1663
- 1st Boston, MA 1665
- North Kingston, RI 1665
- 7th Day Newport, RI 1671
- South Kingston, RI 1680
- Tiverton, RI 1685
- Smithfield, RI 1706
- Hopkinton, RI 1708
- Great Valley, PA 1711
- Cape May, NJ 1712
- Hopewell, NJ 1715
- Brandywine, PA 1715
- Montgomery, PA 1719
- New York City, NY 1724
- Scituate, RI 1725
- Warwick, RI 1725
- Richmond, RI 1725
- French Creek, PA 1726
- New London, CT 1726
- Indian Town, MA 1730
- Cumberland, RI 1732
- Rehoboth, MA 1732
- Shiloh, NJ 1734
- South Brimfield, MA 1736
- Welsh Neck, SC 1738
- Leicester, MA 1738
- Middletown, NJ 1688
- Lower Dublin, PA 1689
- Piscataway, NJ 1689
- Charleston, SC 1690
- Cohansey, NJ 1691
- 2nd Swansea, MA 1693
- 1st Philadelphia, PA 1698
- Welsh Tract, DE 1701
- Groton, CT 1705
- Piscataway, NJ 1707
- Southinton, CT 1738
- West Springfield, CT 1740
- King Wood, NJ 1742
- 2nd Boston, MA 1743
- North Stonington, CT 1743
- Colchester, CT 1743
- East Greenwich, RI 1743
- Euhaw, SC 1745
- Heights Town, NJ 1745
- South Hampton, PA 1746
- Scotch Plains, NJ 1747

Figure 21. *A list of early Baptist churches in America*

with many Calvinists preachers condemning the preaching of the gospel to the heathen. This led many churches to adopt the name "Missionary Baptist" to distinguish themselves from the Calvinists who held on to the doctrines of unconditional election, irresistible grace and limited atonement (Ray 33). The Calvinists adopted names such as "Sovereign Grace Baptists," "Old Line Baptists," "Primitive Baptists," and "Hardshell Baptists."

The Southern Baptist Convention

The General Missionary Convention of Baptists eventually split prior to the civil war, over the issue of whether a missionary could also be a slave owner. In 1845, delegates from the South met in Augusta, Georgia to form the Southern Baptist Convention. Today, the Southern Baptist Convention is the largest Baptist group in the world and the second largest denomination in America. In 2016, the SBC reported that there were 47,272 churches and a total membership of 15.22 million. Their mission outreach is centralized in two main mission boards, the North American Mission Board and the International Mission Board. NAMB reports 5,684 missionaries in North America (NAMB) and the IMB reported 3,596 international missionaries (IMB).

Landmarkism: A Return to Biblical Mission Work

In the 1850s, conservative Baptist preachers spoke out against the tide of progressive, liberal theology and the practice of some Baptist churches in accepting pedobaptism and pulpit affiliation with other denominations. Missionary T.P. Crawford wrote the booklet *Churches to the Front*, it was a call for Baptists to return to scriptural church practices of mission work (Crawford). J.R. Graves, a prominent Southern Baptist theologian, began writing articles on "returning to the ancient landmarks" in his Tennessee newspaper (Graves). It was a call for Southern Baptists to return to Biblical ecclesiology. Graves preached that the ancient view of Baptists was that there was not an invisible, universal church of all the saved. Only local churches had authority to baptize, to administer communion, to send missionaries, and to ordain ministers. The Landmark Baptists called for the Convention to give back the authority to local churches in mission work by rejecting the board system and adopting local church sponsored mission work (Cross, Landmarkism: An Update 21).

At the beginning of the twentieth century, a large portion of Southern Baptists still held to Landmark doctrine such as local church autonomy, rejection of alien baptism, and the practice of restricting the ordinance of communion to the members of the local church. These doctrines were debated and argued between fundamental and progressive Baptists. However, one main point of contention was that of what was termed "Gospel Missions." Gospel Missions referred to the practice of mission work being done directly through the authority of a local church rather than through the authority of a mission board system. In 1859, there was a push in the Southern Baptist Convention to do away with the Foreign Mission Board. Then, in 1892, T.P. Crawford, a Baptist missionary to China penned the book, *Churches to the Front*, in which he criticized the board system as an encroachment upon the authority of the local church's commission to carry out mission work (Weaver 157). The Gospel Mission movement, which held the board system accountable to Biblical principles, was a significant catalyst in the split between Landmark churches and Convention churches.

The term Landmarkism has its roots in Proverbs 22:28, "Remove not the ancient landmark, which thy fathers have set." Many Baptist churches of that day were succumbing to the ecumenical movement of protestant denominations. During the period of the Second Great Awakening, a revival of unprecedented proportions swept through America, and many unchurched people were saved (Clark 16). This revival swelled the ranks of all denominations, and Baptist preachers saw that the gospel of salvation by grace was being preached in churches who had previously taught that works and sacraments were required to enter heaven. Some Baptist pastors opened their doors to these people, accepting baptism from protestant churches. Some even accepted those who had been baptized as infants. This open-door policy of ecumenicity continued to permeate the Baptist ranks. Methodists, Church of Christ, and preachers from many other denominations were preaching in Baptist pulpits (Graves 144).

Landmark Baptist preachers began earnestly speaking out against the practices of ecumenism and the board system of missionary work, stating that these practices violated the sovereignty of church authority and Biblical doctrine. Three "Landmarks" were emphasized:

1. Church succession of an unbroken lineage of authority and doctrine from the time of the founding of the first church by Jesus Christ when He called the disciples in Galilee to the present age.

2. The local, visible assembly of saved, baptized believer, covenanted together to carry out the work of the Lord is the only type of church. There is no universal body of believers, and scriptural authority is only given to local bodies, each congregation being recognized as the body of Christ.

3. Baptism, administered by scriptural authority (a local church) to a scriptural candidate (a person professing faith in Christ) by a scriptural mode (immersion in water). This ruled out pedobaptism, sprinkling, and any baptism administered by a denomination or congregation that is not of like faith and practice.

Later in the Landmark Baptist movement, which was a revival of scriptural practices among Baptist churches rather than an organization of new doctrines and practices, the Landmarks of the faith were further enumerated:

1. Salvation by grace through faith

2. Eternal Security of the believer

3. Baptism by immersion of a believer by a scriptural church

4. Administration of the Lord's Supper by a scriptural church, given only to members of that local church

5. The church defined as a called out local assembly of saved, scripturally baptized believers covenanted together to carry out the commands and commission of Christ

6. The perpetuity of scriptural churches in an unbroken line of succession from the founding by Christ in Galilee until the present day, and that true Baptists were never part of the Roman church.

7. Since authority was vested in the church body, church government was to be congregational and democratic

8. Bridal identity of believers is earned by faithfulness to the commands of the Lord, including baptism, church membership and faithfulness in Christian living (Graves)

These Baptist distinctives became a test of fellowship not only between Baptists and other denominations, but also among the Baptist ranks. Landmark Missionary Baptists began to see that the ever-growing bureaucracy of the mission board system was extra-biblical in its practice and, like the ancient Roman hierarchy of centuries past, began to exert authority over local churches. At the end of the nineteenth century, many of these churches left the convention Baptists and continued to do mission work on a local level, through individual churches and local associations of churches.

Associations of Landmark Baptist Churches

Pioneers in the Landmark Baptists included the preachers Benjamin Marcus Bogard (March 9, 1868 – May 29, 1951) and Doss Nathan Jackson (July 14, 1895 – November 29, 1968). These two men were instrumental in their state associations of Arkansas and Texas, respectively. The Baptist Missionary Association of Texas was begun in 1900 as a way for sound, Landmark Baptist churches to conduct mission work on a state level away from what was seen as the corruption of the convention board system (C. N. Glover 99). This was followed by a departure of the Baptist churches in Arkansas from the convention and founding of the Arkansas Baptist State Association in 1902. In the year 1905, a nationwide association of Landmark Missionary Baptists was formed. It was called the General Association of Baptist Churches (C. N. Glover 100). In 1924, the Baptist Missionary Association of Texas joined this association, and the named was changed to the American Baptist Association (C. N. Glover 124).

The first interstate missionaries of the General Association (later the ABA) were sent out in 1905. They were J.A. Scarboro, ministering in Summit, GA, and C.R. Powell who was a missionary in Jacksonville, TX. The first foreign missionaries were I.N. Yohannon, a Jewish missionary to the Jews in Urmia, Persia (present-day Iran); S.M. Jureidini serving in Beirut, Syria; Jennie Edwards serving in Cuba; M.M. Munger, missionary to Mexico, and the following missionaries to the country of China: M.F. Crawford, W.D. King, T.J. League, Charles Tedder, Blanch Rose Walker, D.W. Herring, Alice Herring, L.M. Dawes, J.V. Dawes, G.P. Bostick, T.L. Blalock and Wade Bostick. Po-Chow, An Hwei, Taian Fu and Chining Chow were also supported as national missionaries in China (C. N. Glover 117 ff).

According to reported statistics, the American Baptist Association of landmark missionary Baptist churches grew substantially, despite a split with the Baptist Missionary Association of Texas in 1950. In 1935 there were a reported 1,734 preachers, 2,662 churches with a total of 263,484 members. Thirty years later, in 1965 these numbers had grown to 3,150 preachers, 3,227 churches and 726,112 members. The American Baptist Association reached its height of growth in 1980, when they reported an estimated total of 5,700 preachers, 5,000 churches and 1,500,000 total church members (Melton). In the 1980s and 1990s these numbers began to drop dramatically, with many churches leaving the association to fellowship with convention churches or independent Baptists. Many other rural churches closed their doors as both population and interest in church declined in the scattered areas where these rural churches existed. By 2009, the American Baptist Association reported that there were 1,700 preachers among 1,600 churches with a total attendance of 100,000 members (Melton). The current numbers represent a remnant of only seven percent of the peak of the association. In 2017, the ABA had 44 interstate missionaries, 36 foreign missionaries, 71 national missionaries, and 10 missionary helpers. In addition, there are many other missionaries sent out by local ABA churches who do not report statistics through the associational mission office.

In 1950, The American Baptist Association annual meeting convened in Lakeland, FL. That year, a growing rift among the churches concerning church representation by proxy messenger, among other issues, resulted in hundreds of messengers walking out (C. N. Glover). Those messengers met together in Little Rock, Arkansas and formed the North American Baptist Association, now known as the Baptist Missionary Association of America. By 1968, The BMAA reported 3,000 preachers, 1,550 churches with a combined membership of approximately 200,000. According to their website (BMA Missions), the association now has 1,300 churches with a membership of 230,000. They support 36 American international missionaries, 29 North American church planters, 680 national missionaries, and 200 support workers. Their main offices are in Conway, Arkansas.

Several of the churches that split from the American Baptist Association in 1950 joined together to create the Interstate and

Foreign Missionary Baptist Associational Assembly of America. This association is commonly referred to as Faithway Baptists, after the name of their Sunday school literature ministry. The Faithway Baptists claim 168 churches with a total membership of over 30,000.

Independent Baptist Churches

In the late 1800s, there was a large break from the convention system because of issues such as progressive liberalism and the sovereignty of mission boards apart from the authority of local churches. Thousands of churches across America slowly withdrew from larger denominational conventions such as the Southern Baptists and the Northern Baptist Convention. The Landmark movement and the Gospel Mission movement spurred this break. Though many separate groups were formed, the majority of these churches identified themselves as independent Baptists. Because of the nature and autonomy of independent churches, statistics are difficult to report, however, a 2014 study by the Pew Research Center found that independent Baptists comprise approximately 2.5% of the population in America (Pew Research Center).

Many Independent Baptist churches chose not to fellowship with Landmark Baptist associations because they felt their mission structure betrayed the principle of Gospel Missions, or direct local church mission work. Despite this fact, several mission organizations began in the first half of the twentieth century among independent Baptists with similar mission structures to that of other Baptist groups. Among these groups are The World Baptist Fellowship, Baptist Bible Fellowship International, as well as mission organizations such as Baptist International Missions, Inc.

The World Baptist Fellowship originally organized in 1933 as the Premillennial Missionary Baptist Fellowship. Many leaders in the American Baptist Association encouraged Norris to merge his group with the ABA, but that never became a reality. In 1950, a conflict between Norris and George Vick created a split in the WBF. That year, Vick and approximately one hundred other pastors met at Central Baptist Church in Denton, Texas to form the Baptist Bible Fellowship International. Today the World Baptist Fellowship has 945 churches and 83 missionaries. The Baptist Bible Fellowship is a fellowship of pastors rather than churches, yet there are approximately 4,500 churches with 1.2 million members that are associated with the BBFI. Many of these churches consider themselves "Bible Baptists." Today, there are 838 active missionaries in 97 fields serving under the BBFI.

Among other independent Baptist groups, many fellowship in circles or "camps" divided by schools such as Bob Jones University, Liberty University, Pensacola Christian College, (the former) Tennessee Temple University, West Coast Baptist College, Hyles-Anderson College, etc. In 2011, David Cloud wrote an article about Independent Baptist Church mission work. There were sixteen Independent mission agencies listed: Baptist Bible Fellowship International, Association of Baptists for World Evangelism, Baptist Mid-Missions, Baptist International Missions Incorporated, Central Missionary Clearinghouse, Baptist World Mission, World Baptist Fellowship, Evangelical Baptist Missions, Macedonia World Baptist Missions, Maranatha Baptist Missions, Independent Baptist Fellowship International, Baptist Faith Missions, International Baptist Missions, Baptist Missions to Forgotten Peoples, Baptist Evangelistic Missions Association, and Fairfax Baptist Temple Missions. Their total combined missionary force was 3,640 foreign missionaries (Way of Life).

There are certainly more missionaries among the independent Baptist ranks than are reported in the statistics here. Missionaries from churches who hold to the principle of local-church only mission work are usually not reported in official statistics, yet they form a large portion of Baptist mission work around the world.

PART III

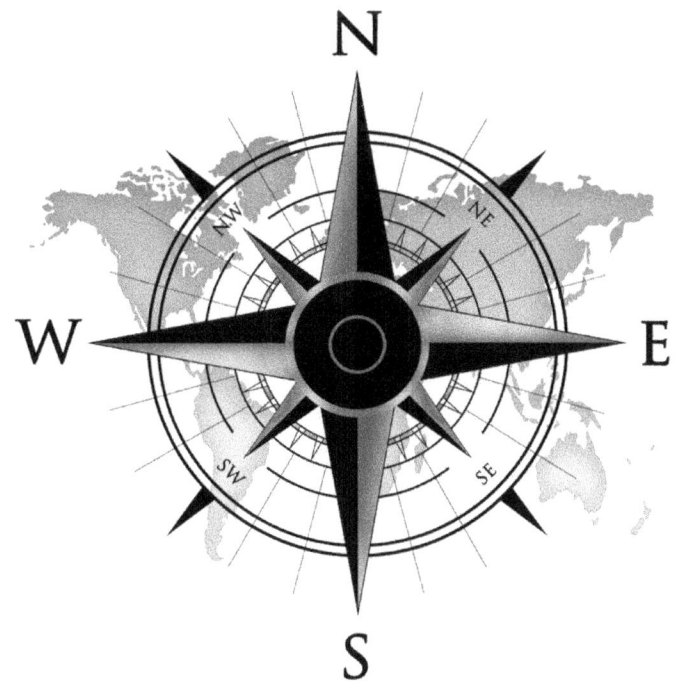

A PRACTICAL GUIDE TO MODERN MISSION WORK

Chapter Ten

Establishing the Call of a Missionary

The Commission Verses the Call

It must first be established that the Great Commission was given as a commandment to the local church and is the purpose for which the church exists (Reed 78). The command to evangelize, baptize and disciple was not given to the individual, but to the church body; to be executed corporately by the church body. Some may say that there is no need of an individual calling to mission work by the Lord because it is already commanded. However, that command is not given to individual persons, but rather the body of the local church as a whole (Ibid).

The individual, specific calling upon a person's life to mission work is different that the commission of the church to mission work (Sills 83). Though all Christians are called to be a witness, the saying that "all Christians are missionaries" is simply not true (Hoke 22). The role of a missionary is a specific task given to a specific person who is called of God to that task, sent out by the express authority of a church, and lead by the power of the Holy Spirit in the execution and accomplishment of that task. Consider the following quote:

> *We are convinced that missionary is not simply a generic term for all Christians doing everything the church does in service to the kingdom of God. We do a disservice to the term by universalizing its use, oversimplifying a rich vocabulary and theology of gifting and vocation. While all believers are witnesses and kingdom servants, not all are missionaries. While all believers must be committed to and involved in mission, not all are missionaries. (Hoke 22)*

Many will ask themselves the question, "How do I know that I am called?" Over the years, I have counseled many prospective missionaries and addressed this question. The normal answer from most pastors or other missionaries is that "you just know." This, of course, is not helpful at all. The following advice may be found more practical: If a person struggling with the call to ministry can do anything else in life, and be truly happy in doing it – then they ought to that instead (C. Spurgeon 26). The man who is out of God's will on the mission field will be the most miserable man in the world. Yet, if the one struggling with a question of God's call cannot find peace in their heart with any other employment, yet peace comes as he surrenders his will to the tugging of God's Spirit upon his life, then he has been called. There are several Biblical principles that can shed light on the subject. These principles developed from Scripture are as follows.

Principles of the Calling of God

The Principle of the Faithful Servant

The first principle of knowing the calling of God is found in Acts 13:2. I call this The Principle of the Faithful Servant. The Principle of Faithful Servant states that God will call those whom He finds faithfully serving Him to take the next step in their Christian service.

ESTABLISHING THE CALL OF A MISSIONARY

Acts 13:2 states, "As they ministered to the Lord, and fasted, the Holy Ghost said, Separate me Barnabas and Saul for the work whereunto I have called them." The verse states that "as they ministered," God's Holy Spirit called. These men were found faithfully doing what they knew to do. This principle teaches that God will entrust further responsibility to those who are already serving. This principle is often found in the workplace. Bosses, almost without exception, will pick those who are the best workers for promotion. God does the same. If a person wants to be called of the Lord to further service, he ought to busy himself in the tasks that he knows to do now. Many of these tasks are clearly outlined in the Word of God. First, a person must be saved. "Marvel not that I said unto thee, Ye must be born again" (John 3:7). Next, they must be baptized, "Repent, and be baptized" (Acts 2:38). Thirdly, they must join a church and be faithful in attendance, "Not forsaking the assembling of ourselves together" (Heb. 10:25). They should also maintain a life of faithful service to the Lord, "This is a faithful saying, and these things I will that thou affirm constantly, that they which have believed in God might be careful to maintain good works. These things are good and profitable unto men" (Titus 3:8). If a person does what he already knows to do, and executes those tasks faithfully, God will choose that servant for even greater things.

> *God will call those whom He finds faithfully serving Him to take the next step in their Christian service.*

The Principle of the Seeking Servant

The second principle of knowing the will of God and His calling is The Principle of the Seeking Servant. The principle of the seeking servant states that to find the will of God, a person should be actively and seriously searching for the will of God. This principle is also found in Acts 13:2 where it states that they not only ministered but fasted. Fasting is a practice taught in Scripture but seldom observed in today's world. Fasting, or focusing on spiritual things by denying

> *To find the will of God, one should be actively and seriously searching for the will of God.*

oneself of food and worldly pleasures is never commanded in Scripture, but is implied to be a part of the life of the believer. Fasting is a means by which a person seeks the fellowship of God, turning away from worldly needs to seek the fulfillment of spiritual needs. The implication here is that these men were actively seeking the will of God in their lives. A person may occasionally stumble upon a spiritual truth, but, "he that seeketh findeth" (Matthew 7:8). To find the will of God, a person must be actively seeking the will of God. Fasting, though not a popular practice, is a Biblical one, and this practice shows the seriousness of the person who is actively seeking the will of the Lord. In Acts Chapter six, at the ordination of the seven deacons, there was no fast that was recorded, however at the ordination of the missionaries in Acts 13, there is a record of two fasts, one before the call of the Holy Spirit and one after the call. Those who were fasting in verse two were the ministering servants in the church seeking the will of the Lord on their lives. After the call, verse three records that the church performed the fast. "And when they had fasted" refers here to the church body (Clarke, Adam). This shows not only the seriousness of the call of the missionary, but also of the desire to know the specific will of God by both the individual men who were called and the church who was to send them.

The Principle of the Sacrificial Servant

Next is The Principle of the Sacrificial Servant, which states that before the perfect will of God can be known, a person must deny the world and yield completely to God. The apostle Paul states that sacrificial living is inextricably linked to the will of God. The Bible explains that a living sacrifice is made by denying the world and taking on the mind of Christ. The transformational power of Christ can take a worldly, sinful mind that cannot know God's will and change it into a spiritual and holy mind that is in perfect harmony with God's will. Romans 12:1-2 states,

> *I beseech you therefore, brethren, by the mercies of God, that ye present your bodies a living sacrifice, holy, acceptable unto God, which is your reasonable service. And be not conformed to this world: but be ye transformed by the renewing of your mind, that ye may prove what is that good, and acceptable, and perfect, will of God.*

God's will for the believer is to live and walk by faith in the Lord. God wishes for His servants to rely upon Him. To be able to live by faith and rely upon the Lord, a missionary must surrender self and embrace the Divine as all-sufficient. It is one of the hardest lessons to learn in the life of a believer. God teaches this lesson in our lives over and over again, sometimes by taking everything that we rely upon so that there is nothing else to turn to but God. This passage gives the means by which anyone can discern God's will. First, the Christian must yield himself through surrender. Paul writes that the life of the Christian should be presented to God as a living sacrifice. Just as Christ sacrificed Himself in death for mankind, the believer should sacrifice himself in life to the Lord, not by dying, but by living for Christ. This is not only acceptable to God, it is a reasonable thing to do. The next step is to deny the world by refusing to pattern yourself after the fleshly and sinful attitudes of the society and culture that surrounds us. Christians are in the world, but are not of the world. There should be a marked difference in the life of a child of God and that of a lost person. The third step is a transformative changing of the thought patterns, ideas, and opinions within the soul of the child of God. In the flesh the

> *To know the perfect will of God, one must yield oneself completely to the Lord, denying the world and conforming oneself to the image of the Lord by taking on the mind of Christ.*

thoughts of the mind are controlled and steered by sin. In Christ, the mind is driven by the righteousness of God. To know the will of God, the believer must know the mind of God. To understand the mind of God, a Christian must think as God thinks rather than as the world thinks. When a person reaches the point of surrender, denial, and transformation, he will know the "good, and acceptable, and perfect, will of God."

The Principle of the Willing Servant

The Principle of the Willing Servant states that knowing the will of God rests, in a large part, in the willingness of the believer to do the will of God. God is under no obligation to reveal the knowledge of His will to a person who is not willing to do His will. This is the lesson that Christ taught in John 7:17, "If any man will [is willing to] do his will, he shall know of the doctrine, whether it be of God, or whether I speak of myself." The verse states that those who are willing to do God's will shall be given that knowledge. This theme runs all throughout Scripture. The Lord placed man in the garden and told him to obey. However, God gave Adam the choice to disobey, because God wants obedience with a willing heart. He wants mankind to serve Him out of love, not obligation; out of desire, not compulsion; out of a willing heart, not force. God desires both obedience and a willing heart. Exodus 25:2 states, "Speak unto the children of Israel, that they bring me an offering: of every man that giveth it willingly with his heart ye shall take my offering." In the wilderness, God told the children of Israel to bring an offering, but to Moses, He commanded that he only accept offerings given willingly. In the book of Isaiah, Chapter one, God said that the offerings of Israel were an abomination to Him because they were offered out of a sense of duty and requirement (Isa. 1:12) rather than a willing heart (Isa. 1:19). In the New Testament, Paul writes to "give

> *Knowing the will of God rests, in a large part, in the willingness of the believer to do the will of God.*

> ## OBEDIENCE AND WILLINGNESS
>
> Willingness is having a desire to do something. Obedience is actually doing it. If you desire to serve God but you don't serve Him, it's like saying "be warmed and filled" to a person who is cold and hungry, but you don't cloth him or give him food. Desire without obedience is like faith without works. It's useless. But how about obedience without willingness? It's like all the other religions out there - works without faith. It will get you nowhere. God demands both. There will certainly be days that you don't feel like serving, but you do it anyway because it's the right thing to do. That's sacrifice, and God is pleased with it. However, when everyday ministry becomes a drudgery that you have no desire for, there is probably a more serious heart problem at stake. You might need to check your spiritual condition and relationship with the Lord. God wants you to obey; and God wants you to *want to* obey. This theme runs all throughout Scripture... sometimes with different names, but all the same truth. Love and Submission. Faith and Works. Spirit and Truth. Willingness and Obedience. They go hand and hand.

Figure 22. *Missionary Insights: Obedience and Willingness*

cheerfully, not of necessity, for God loveth a cheerful giver"; and again, he writes in Second Corinthians 8:12, "For if there be first a willing mind, it is accepted according to that a man hath, and not according to that he hath not." In the book of First Chronicles, David gives Solomon sound advice to follow the Lord. He told him to serve God with a perfect (i.e. whole, undivided) heart and a willing mind. He wanted his son to "want to" serve God, not just to do it because he said so. David hoped that the desire of Solomon's heart was to serve the Lord. He explained that God knows every thought and even the motivation behind the thoughts and actions. David knew that God would always be there for Solomon unless he rejected the salvation of the Lord to be cast off from God for eternity. "And thou, Solomon my son, know thou the God of thy father, and serve him with a perfect heart and with a willing mind: for the LORD searcheth all hearts, and understandeth all the imaginations of the thoughts: if thou seek him, he will be found of thee; but if thou forsake him, he will cast thee off forever" (1 Chron. 28:9). Psalms 40:8 says, "I delight to do thy will, O my God: yea, thy law is within my HEART." As a servant grows closer to the Lord, his wants, desires, and wishes become conformed to the will of God. The desires of his heart begin to change. The desire to do worldly things diminishes. His personal will begins to line up with God's will. This process occurs in the life of those who allow the Spirit to control their lives. The Bible speaks of it as a relational position, known as being "In Christ," which is the goal in Christian maturity. Salvation is "Christ in you." Yet when the Christian is "in Christ," he is walking in God's will. Paul calls it being "filled with the Spirit." The theological term for the process of conforming man's will to the will of God is known as sanctification: becoming more and more like Jesus Christ.

The Desire to Do Mission Work

First Timothy 3:1 states, "This is a true saying, If a man desire the office of a bishop, he desireth a good work." Desire is one marker of the calling of God on the life of an individual to enter the ministry (C. Spurgeon 28). There should be a desire in the heart of a man called to mission work to serve the Lord on the mission field. If there is no desire for the spiritual aspects of missionary service, i.e. sharing the gospel, a genuine love for people, a desire to teach and disciple others to be more like Christ, a love for the Word of God, etc., then the candidate must ask himself what his actual driving desire to do mission work might be. Many people go to the mission field hoping to fulfill some carnal desire. Some may go because of a love of travel, a love of adventure, or a romantic notion of the missionary life. Still others may go with more insidious intentions. There are missionaries who have gone to the field

> *If there is no desire for the spiritual aspects of mission work, one must ask himself what his true desire to do mission work might be.*

to flee from legal trouble. There are missionaries who have gone because of affairs. Others might see the missionary life as a way to live abroad and get paid to do so. Regardless, the true spiritual desire residing in the heart of a Christian to surrender their life to foreign mission work for the honor and glory of the Lord cannot come from the flesh. Therefore, a prospective missionary ought to examine the true desire and motivation for going to the field. If that desire is of the flesh, it cannot be of God. If that desire is of God, it cannot be of the flesh.

Confirmation of a Specific Calling

The calling of the missionary can and ought to be confirmed by several factors, all with Biblical foundations. The first of which is the overwhelming sense of urgency as to the Lord's calling which comes with an unmistakable compulsion from the Lord (C. Spurgeon 27). The prophet Jeremiah described this passionate zeal, "Then I said, I will not make mention of him, nor speak any more in his name. But his word was in mine heart as a burning fire shut up in my bones, and I was weary with forbearing, and I could not stay" (Jer. 20:9). Next, there should be evidence of the calling of the Lord by the display of the gifts that God has given to that person to perform the work in which He has called him to. God has set forth qualifications to each of His ministerial positions. If there are specific qualifications of a pastor or a deacon, it should be doubly so for the missionary who is called to train the pastor and the deacon. Many of the necessary skills can be learned, practiced and sharpened, but some abilities will reveal themselves from birth, in the life of the man who is called. "Before I formed thee in the belly I knew thee; and before thou camest forth out of the womb I sanctified thee, and I ordained thee a prophet unto the nations" (Jer.

1:5). There should also be a confirmation from others with the spiritual insight to recognize the calling, the desire, and the gifts upon the life of a missionary (C. Spurgeon 34). The book of Proverbs states that wise counsel can validate the intentions of the heart. "Without counsel purposes are disappointed: but in the multitude of counsellors they are established (Prov. 15:22). The counsel of man should never be considered over the Word of God. A man who is truly called will show evidence of that calling. It can be clearly seen by others with a spiritual perception to which the man who is called is sometimes blind.

Ability Versus Availability

It is a popular saying among many preachers today that "God does not care about your ability. He cares only about your availability." We certainly cannot limit the work of the Lord nor the power of God to confound the wise by showing His power through those who are limited in personal ability. There are endless examples of how God has used the weak to prove His own power. Nor should we rely on our own skill and talent to the exclusion of our reliance upon the Lord. Considering this fact, we must also remember that God placed very specific qualifications in the New Testament for those who would be spiritual leaders. The qualifications for a missionary should be no less than that of a pastor or deacon seeing that the missionary will be the one who trains pastors and deacons (C. Spurgeon 32,34). Availability, without any ability would not be a qualifier for any other profession: a surgeon, mechanic, nuclear engineer. Nor should we confuse availability of a worker with one who is uniquely qualified by the Lord to carry out the work to which God has called him. Another popular saying in modern pulpits is, "God doesn't call the qualified, He qualifies the called." If a man knows that he is called to be a missionary, he should learn all he can to increase his skill and knowledge in that field of labor. Many men may be unqualified and unprepared when they answer the call of the Lord. Only the person who chooses to stay that way is truly unfit for labor. Ministers should seek education and training to be qualified for the calling with which they are called.

Availability, if taken to mean surrender to the Lord's will, is essential to the call of the missionary. However, once the call is confirmed, the hard work begins. Much of the success of a missionary will be determined by the preparation that he has put into his missionary training. This training is the honing of the God given abilities that the Lord has bestowed upon that individual. Once a person has determined what his specific gifts are, he should compare those talents with a list of the skills that are needed to carry out the work. Where he is lacking, an effort must be made to form and increase those skills.

Assessing the Character of the Missionary

Mission work is a demanding position both spiritually, physically and emotionally (Moreau 172 ff). It requires expert knowledge of Scripture and theological questions. It requires spiritual maturity and sensitivity to the leading of the Holy Spirit. It requires physical stamina and strength. It requires emotional stability and wellness, as well as a penchant for enduring long-term, high stress situations. In assessing a missionary's specific call to the mission field, it must be pointed out that there are three main points of missionary training. These points are: 1) What a missionary ought to be 2) What a missionary ought to know 3) What a missionary ought to do. In other words, the focus of training a missionary for the work of the Lord on the mission field consists of three primary areas: character, knowledge, and skill.

A missionary must have moral character if he is to be entrusted with the enormous task of mission work (Moreau 174-181). It is the job of a missionary to not only evangelize the lost, but disciple the saved, train Christian workers, indoctrinate believers, and instruct an entirely new generation of pastors and churches in the ways of Christ. He is to be looked to not only as a leader, but an example of what a Christian

> *A missionary is an example of what a Christian should be - in doctrine, in practice, and in character.*

should be, in doctrine, in practice, and in character. A missionary with poor moral character could do irreparable damage to the ministry and the cause of Christ. He could, by his lack of character, turn an entire population of souls away from the truth. He could also corrupt the principles and practices of new churches, new believers and possibly generations of converts to come. It is said that character can be defined as who a person is when no one else is watching. A man's character lies in the true attributes of the heart with neither pretense nor show.

A Personal Walk with God

The most important attribute of a missionary's moral character is his personal walk with God. Dr. Clyde Lanier, theologian and the pastor of Westwood Missionary Baptist Church of Winter Haven, Florida for over forty years stated, "You can no more teach that which you do not know, than you can come from a place which you've never been" (W. C. Lanier). For a missionary to be able to tell others about Jesus Christ, he must first know Jesus Christ himself. A missionary must be saved (Terry, 589). He cannot introduce a person to someone that he does not know himself. Not only must a missionary know Christ, but he must also have a personal walk with Christ. As an example to every convert on the mission field, he must exemplify what a Christian ought to be. Paul told the church at Corinth in First Corinthians 11:1 to "Be ye followers of me, even as I also am of Christ." To be this example, he must spend quality time with the Lord on a daily basis.

The presence of God in the life of the believer is evident in both the person's character and attitude. Just as a congregation can quickly tell when a pastor has not sufficiently prepared for a sermon, others can sense when a missionary is not walking with the Lord. Through the countless trials which a missionary faces, neglecting a personal relationship with the Lord can spell certain doom. It is only through the power of God upon his life and ministry that a missionary is able to succeed in the work to which the Lord has called him. A.W. Tozer put it this way,

> *There is today no lack of Bible teachers to set forth correctly the principles of the doctrines of Christ, but too many of these seem satisfied to teach the fundamentals of the faith year after year, strangely unaware that there is in their ministry no manifest Presence, no anything unusual in their personal lives. They minister constantly to believers who feel within their breasts a longing which their teaching does not satisfy. (Tozer 5)*

Spiritual Discipline

A missionary must possess spiritual discipline (Moreau 178). He must constantly be working on his spiritual life. The two main disciplines of spirituality in the life of every Christian are a constant prayer life and the study of God's Word. There must be a constant, open line of communication between a missionary and the Lord. Sin causes this communication to cease. The missionary needs God's provision, God's protection and God's power upon his life. This can only be accomplished through the life of a spiritually disciplined disciple of the Lord. Many ministers find themselves in constant study of the Scriptures as they prepare lessons and sermons for others, yet neglect their own personal devotions. It is often very easy for a missionary to get so caught up into the work of the ministry that they neglect their own personal relationship with the Lord. The consequences often exhibit themselves in an inability to handle the stress of the ministry, resulting in feeling overwhelmed, anxious and bitter. To succeed on the mission field, a missionary must win the battle on a spiritual front. Keeping a disciplined life on a spiritual level is vital for the work to prosper, the missionary to thrive, and the gospel to flourish.

> ## EXAMINING MY SPIRITUAL CONDITION
>
> ***2 Corinthians 13:5 "Examine yourselves, whether ye be in the faith; prove your own selves. Know ye not your own selves, how that Jesus Christ is in you, except ye be reprobates?"***
>
> "So, you've traveled halfway around the globe to come and help other people," I said to myself, "Yet how is your own spiritual life? Are you where you should be in your personal walk with the Lord?" Many people think that mission work is the height of spiritual living, yet what I found in my own heart when I came on the mission field was the exact opposite. Thailand is an idolatrous nation, and the devil has never cared for anyone invading his territory. The struggles we faced sometimes seemed overwhelming. Yet, when I lost focus of Christ in my life, it was then that I was truly overwhelmed. Satan could win the battle in my heart because my eyes were focused upon my problems rather than the Lord. Our sin nature can easily shift our focus away from Christ. Each day we must examine ourselves to guard against losing focus.

Figure 23. *Missionary Insights: Examining my Spiritual Condition*

Self-Discipline

A missionary must have self-discipline (Gardner 111). Discipline must be exercised not only on the spiritual front, but also in all practical aspects of life. On the mission field, a missionary will most likely be his own boss, set his own schedule, and work at his own pace. There is usually no one lording over him, supervising his every move. Because of this fact, it could be very easy for a missionary to become slack in his work. No one will know when he rises late. No one will know when does not put in the proper amount of language study. No one will know when he decides to not go out to visit, to witness, or even to attend a church meeting. There are many who go to the foreign field and become lazy, indifferent, and reclusive. The culture can sometimes become so overwhelming that a missionary decides to close himself off from it, lock his doors, and stay secluded in his home. Only a man with the self-discipline to press on in the face of uncertainty can make it on the mission field. He must move when he does not have the energy to move. He must go when he does not have the power to go. He must witness when he does not have the courage to witness. He must keep fighting when all that is in him has been exhausted. He must do all this and much more. The only way that a missionary can persevere is through the power of the Lord in His life. He must rise when it is time to rise. He must preach when it is time to preach. He must study when it is time to study, and he must have courage when he walks into the unknown.

Personal and Spiritual Maturity

A missionary should possess both personal and spiritual maturity (Moreau 173 ff). First Timothy 3:6 states, "Not a novice, lest being lifted up with pride he fall into the condemnation of the devil." Though this is a qualification of a pastor, it should be even more so for a missionary. The satanic war that is waged against the life of the man of God who endeavors to propagate the gospel is intense and unyielding. A missionary battles on the front line of spiritual combat. Every inch of ground that is won for the gospel is bought with a heavy price of sacrifice and labor. Every soul that is saved from the jaws of hell through the blood of Jesus is won in the context of unceasing spiritual warfare in the lives of those

> *The missionary battles on the front line of spiritual combat. Every inch of ground that is won for the gospel is bought with a heavy price of sacrifice and labor.*

who would brave the battle against the principalities and powers of Satan himself. No army would ever send an untrained soldier into battle. Nor should any church send a novice to fight where seasoned men of God have fallen. Just as John Mark left the mission field, so too have many young missionaries who had no clue of the cost of service until it was too late. Physical maturity (or age) has less of a correlation with missionary attrition rates as does spiritual maturity. Age does not always bring wisdom. Sometimes, age comes alone. The Word of God brings spiritual wisdom and experience brings practical wisdom. Missionaries must highly abound in both. The novice is unqualified for the titanic task of training pastors, planting churches, and discipling new populations in the ways of Christianity. Only those who possess a marked maturity in both worldly cares and spirituality should ever be considered for the position of missionary.

Moral Purity

A missionary must be a morally pure man of God. Two qualifications in First Timothy Chapter three touch on this point. First, a man must be blameless. This does not imply that he is to be without sin, but that he must not have a mark against his name. Though no man is perfect, his character must be considered unspotted. If any point of moral impurity or ethical uncertainty can be laid to his charge, he is unfit to be the representative of Christ. A missionary must lead by the example of his character. The second qualification which directly relates to the moral purity of a missionary is First Timothy 3:7, "Moreover he must have a good report of them which are without; lest he fall into reproach and the snare of the devil." Not only must his name be spotless, but his testimony among the lost must be decent, upright and respectable. On the mission field, I have worked with many other missionaries over the years. Some had a spotless character. Others caused the people on the field to question the lives and faithfulness of all Christians by the testimony of their character and behavior. Can a penitent minister who had fallen into sin be restored to his former position? If the sin which was committed brings a reproach upon the ministry and becomes a snare which drives the hearts of others away from the Lord, that man should be disqualified from the position. Certainly, God is a God of second chances, yet that man may be better suited for a position elsewhere.

Personal and Family Wholeness

> *The family of the missionary make up an indivisible team that will live and experience the joys and pressures of the mission field together.*

There must be personal and family wholeness in the life of a missionary. In First Timothy 3:4, Paul writes, "One that ruleth well his own house, having his children in subjection with all gravity." Many men commit their lives to serve on a foreign field, not taking into consideration the impact that this decision will have on their families. William Carey is a prime example. His wife Dorothy at first refused to accompany him onto the field, only agreeing to go after her sister promised to move with her. Her refusal, along with the death of a child on the field, led to a nervous breakdown, insanity, and finally, death. The importance of the marriage relationship of a missionary cannot be overemphasized. Whatever problems exist in the marriage at home will exponentially increase on the mission field. Neither family nor marital issues will be solved by moving to another country. The family unit of a missionary (husband, wife, children) make up an indivisible team that will live and experience the joys and pressures of the mission field together. The missionary would be wise to consider this fact and discuss the future impact that his calling will have on the lives of his family. The sacrifice that he makes is not his alone to bear. His wife will also sacrifice. His children will also sacrifice. Issues in the marriage or family of a missionary ought to be resolved before leaving for the field.

A Servant's Attitude

A missionary is a servant of God, and he must possess a servant's attitude (Terry, 591). Humility is a trait that can only be acknowledged externally. When someone recognizes that they have it, they have immediately lost it. It is a temptation for every missionary on deputation to begin to "think more highly of himself than he ought to think." Churches and church members often see the passing foreign missionary as a "spiritual giant" or a "super Christian." They heap gifts and praise and honor upon the one who would dare to leave his family, his homeland, and his former life behind, to serve the Lord on distant shores. It takes very little praise to make a person begin to think that he is something special. However, reality strikes him incredibly hard when he reaches the field and finds that no one there cares about his credentials or sacrifice. He must keep a servant's attitude through it all. The word *minister* is defined as "a servant." The verb form, *to minister*, means "to serve." A missionary is not the boss of everyone around him. He should not lord over God's heritage like an authoritarian despotic dictator. A missionary is there to serve the spiritual needs of the people around him. The lack of humility and a proper attitude of service often exhibits itself in another form on the mission field. One of the greatest difficulties of a missionary is not necessarily the native population on the field, but rather the interpersonal relationships with other missionaries and Christian workers. Missionaries often feel a sense of ownership over the ministries that they have begun. This feeling often develops from a genuine desire to protect the new work and new converts from harmful influences. This desire, however often results in many missionaries being extremely territorial and often hostile towards others working in the same area. Among the servants of the Lord who are of like faith and practice, this ought not to be so. To serve the Lord, a missionary must exemplify the humble, obedient, servant's attitude that the Lord Himself displayed as an example for us to follow.

Teachability

A missionary must be a man who is teachable (Moreau 176). Learning is a lifelong process. It does not stop after a person graduates from Bible college, nor does a degree or title confer all the knowledge that will be needed in the ministry. A missionary must be teachable. Even a seasoned minister who has preached or pastored for many years in his home country, when moving to a foreign field, becomes as helpless as a child. His years of experience is of no help when he cannot relate that experience to the new environment. A missionary must be willing to learn. For example, in language learning in a foreign culture, sometimes the best teachers are young people, who are willing to spend time teaching the basics when others feel that it is beneath them. Pride is the enemy of education. If a missionary thinks he knows it all, he can never be taught. He should be capable of gleaning knowledge from anybody - from the smallest child to the greatest teacher.

Adaptability

A missionary must be adaptable (Terry and Payne 240 f). Robert Burns wrote these words in his often-quoted poem "To a Mouse," "The best laid schemes o' mice an' men / Gang aft a-gley." In other words, the best laid plans of mice and men often go awry. It is important to plan and set goals as long they do not become more important than the mission. A missionary must be flexible and learn to adapt to the constantly changing situations that he faces on the mission field (Moreau 177). Having the wrong attitude toward the obstacles that change a missionary's plans will only bring anger and bitterness. However, when a missionary looks to the Lord and His providential wisdom as the catalyst of those changes and obstacles, he can see that the hand of the Lord is in all that he does, directing as He sees fit and changing the course for the better. James eloquently teaches the Biblical attitude that a missionary ought to have.

> *Go to now, ye that say, Today or tomorrow we will go into such a city, and continue there a year, and buy and sell, and get gain: Whereas ye know not what shall be on the morrow. For what is your life? It is even a vapour, that appeareth for a little time, and then vanisheth away. For that ye ought to say, If the Lord will, we shall live, and do this, or that. But now ye rejoice in your boastings: all such rejoicing is evil. (James 4:13-16)*

Compassion for Others

A missionary must show that he has compassion for others (M. Barnett 78). This is the quintessential motivation for mission work. Christ Himself showed compassion for the lost. A missionary does not preach the gospel to the world because of a feeling of pity or affection that originates from his own feelings. A missionary is sent out to preach the gospel to the world because of God's love and compassion on them. When a missionary expresses compassion on others, he is exhibiting the love and compassion of Christ rather than his own fickle emotions. Matthew 9:36-37 speaks of Christ's compassion on the lost,

> *But when he saw the multitudes, he was moved with compassion on them, because they fainted, and were scattered abroad, as sheep having no shepherd. Then sayeth he unto his disciples, "The harvest truly is plenteous, but the laborers are few; pray ye therefore the Lord of the harvest, that he will send forth laborers into his harvest.*

It is very easy for any minister who is not carefully guarding his heart and relationship with the Lord to become bitter against those very people to whom he has been called to minister. When a missionary first enters the field, he feels an obligation, and rightly so, to give of himself to others. He may give away personal items to those whom he sees as less fortunate than himself. He gives of his time, often to the expense of his own family, and others are more than willing to take all that he has to give. If, however, the spiritual, mental and physical resources that have been expended are not resupplied in his life, he becomes bankrupt, exhausted, and overdrawn. His attitude becomes jaded and bitter towards the very people to whom he is ministering. When the day comes that a missionary doesn't feel like ministering, giving, and loving people, he must remember that it is because of God's love and compassion and not his own that he is there.

Identifying and Implementing Spiritual Gifts

A missionary must identify and implement his personal spiritual gifts (Terry, 335). Spiritual gifts refer to the God-given abilities and talents that a person possesses which can be used in the service of the Lord. These gifts are also known as "grace gifts" because of the use of the Greek word *charis*, (Strong's G5486) in Scripture translated "gift" in English (Rom 12:3-8). *Charis* means a gift given by divine grace. A grace gift would, by definition, imply that the talent or ability possessed is not something that has to be developed or practiced, nor is it naturally occurring in the flesh, but is given to a person by the Lord through the element of grace. In other words, the gift is unmerited, unearned and did not originate from the person that possesses it, but rather from God. A proper attitude of spiritual gifts will not allow the Christian to become puffed up or prideful of the gift that he exhibits, because of the recognition that it is a gift from God, and not a natural talent from himself. Elmer Towns has developed a spiritual gift inventory which helps to identify a person's specific spiritual gifts. An inventory of a person's gifts and abilities is vital in determining the area in which he will excel. It will also determine what areas of ministry he needs to work on. There are many demanding areas of ministry for the foreign missionary. Not only must a missionary excel in the regular areas of ministry: preaching, evangelism, teaching, discipleship, etc., he may be demanded to perform in other areas such as construction, music, counseling, medicine, administration, logistics, language learning, cultural adaptation, and much more. A spiritual gifts assessment is a vital part of missionary preparation.

I Shall Not Slide

Psalms 26:1 "Judge me, O Lord; for I have walked in mine integrity: I have trusted also in the Lord; therefore I shall not slide."

David held integrity as his principle, and walked in it as his practice. He was able to boldly tell the Lord that he had walked in integrity in the past, and in verse 11, he said he would continue to walk in integrity. In a world where the fields are white and laborers are few, we see more and more men of God falling by the wayside, and even fewer men of integrity taking their place. We as servants of the Lord are like the helium balloon, when filled, climb ever upward, but when the helium is released, quickly falls. The balloon is nothing more than a vessel for the expression of the helium to reveal its characteristics, just as we as God's servants are vessels for the expression of our Lord Jesus Christ to reveal Himself to the world through us. When we are filled, we climb ever upward. When we empty our lives of God's working and fill it with sin and cares of this world, we quickly fall. David stated plainly, "I shall not slide!" That means he would not stumble, he would not waver, he would not stagger, he would not falter, he would not fall. I took my kids to a playground and watched as they labored to climb the steps up the ladder, and then a moment was all it took to slide back down again. Isn't that so true? All of your labor, all your toil, all of your ministry and your testimony can vanish in one quick moment by one false step. Sliding is always quick and it's always down. Yet David boldly made the decree, "I shall not slide!" Then he called upon the Lord to help him make that commitment a reality. David reveals to us two principles that he relied upon and upon whose foundation his commitment to never slide rested upon:

1. **He had, and would continue to walk in integrity**
2. **He placed his trust in the Lord**

Figure 24. *Missionary Insights: I Shall Not Slide*

Knowledge and Skill Assessment

Biblical and Theological Knowledge

It is important for a missionary to be well versed in Biblical and theological knowledge. He must be expertly equipped to handle the Word of God (C. Spurgeon 28 f). He must, as listed in First Timothy 3:2, be "apt to teach." One of the main responsibilities of a missionary is to disciple others in the doctrines and commandments of the Bible. Since a person cannot teach that which he does not know, it is of the utmost importance for a missionary to be educated in Scripture. For him, it is a Biblical commandment, "Study to shew thyself approved unto God, a workman that needeth not to be ashamed, rightly dividing the word of truth" (2 Tim. 2:15). The book of Hebrews states that those who are unskilled in God's Word are spiritually immature. "For everyone that useth milk is unskillful in the word of righteousness: for he is a babe" (Heb. 5:13). Those who are unskilled in the Word of God are unprepared for the ministry. "Not a novice, lest being lifted up with pride he fall into the condemnation of the devil" (1 Tim. 3:6). A missionary must know the Word of God.

Culture, Geography and Demographics

In addition to Biblical knowledge, a missionary must be educated in the culture, geography and demographics of the people groups and land in which he will minister. No missionary will ever be able to effectively minister to a people unless he is able to break through the cultural barriers that separate him from the people. Different races and ethnicities are inherently dissimilar in their worldview, their religious views, their norms, and even their thought processes. An in-depth study of the cultural habits, customs, and taboos will help the cross-cultural missionary in crossing that divide.

> *The Word of God transcends all cultures, and is relevant to all people.*

Geographic and demographic knowledge can help pinpoint various needs of the people on the mission field. Keep in mind that the Word of God transcends all cultures, and is relevant to all people. God understands every person in every culture. "For the ways of man are before the eyes of the LORD, and he pondereth all his goings" (Proverbs 5:21). Yet, it is also the job of a missionary to understand the culture of the people to whom he is ministering (Elmer, Cross-Cultural Servanthood 93).

Communication

The importance of fluency and effective communication cannot be overemphasized. A missionary must be able to communicate with and relate to the people on the field. This includes two aspects: language and interpersonal communication. Much of language learning is simply rote memory. Vocabulary, spelling, and grammatical rules must be memorized. However, communication is much more than the pronouncement of memorized words. A missionary must be versed in the colloquialisms, slang, and innuendos of the culture. He must understand the meaning behind the words that are said. This knowledge can only come with experience in the culture. However, much can be learned in study prior to going to the field. Interpersonal communication is vital to the ministry of a missionary. Missionaries cannot teach others unless they can effectively communicate with others. In a humorous look at the problems of ineffective communication, Osmo Wiio lists four laws of communicative confusion: (Wiio)

- A) **If communication can fail, it will.**

- B) **If a message can be understood in different ways, it will be understood in just that way which does the most harm.**

- C) **There is always somebody who knows better than you what you meant by your message.**

- D) **The more communication there is, the more difficult it is for communication to succeed.**

The gospel message of Jesus Christ must be effectively communicated (Hesselgrave 142). There is a difference between proclamation and communication. There are those who stand on the street corner yelling out the message of salvation to passing vehicles. Most, if not all, have their windows up and are driving much too fast to hear a single word that is being spoken. There is proclamation taking place, but not effective communication. If the gospel message is to be effectively communicated, it must be presented to the listener in a fashion that is understandable, and that message must be received and processed (Gregory 18 f). This does not mean that the receiver must believe the gospel for communication to take place, but that he or she must comprehend the message which is given in the way that it was intended to be understood. Here, another important principle can be learned by a missionary intending to serve on the foreign mission field. That principle is this: a missionary cannot minister to a person that he cannot communicate with. Learning both the language and the culture of the target audience is essential in effective mission work. If the gospel message is to be communicated to a certain people group, the language of the people group must be learned by the missionary. Not only should the vocabulary and grammar of that field be learned, but also the cultural mindset and worldview of the people there (Terry, 278). There are many missionaries who have learned the basics of a language, only to find that they are still not effective in their communication, because they do not understand why the people think the way they think, act the way they act, nor do they comprehend the idiosyncrasies and colloquial jargon of the culture (Burnett 11 ff).

A missionary must strive for effective communication, because he will never be able to effectively minister to a person who he cannot effectively communicate with.

Ministry Experience

A missionary should be well equipped for practical ministry (C. Spurgeon 34 ff). First Timothy 3:6 declares that he must not be a novice. It would be foolish for a church to send out a missionary with no ministerial experience, as he will be the one organizing churches and teaching others how to minister. He must know how to preach and how to develop a proper message. For a missionary, this is doubly true since he must prepare a message that will transcend the cultural and language barrier. There can be no colloquial phrases or culture-specific illustrations to which the people will not be able to relate. He must know how to properly conduct a worship service, and teach others to do the same. He must be versed in the pageantry of weddings and the solemnity of funerals. It would be wise for a sending church to allow the prospective missionary to serve on the staff of the church first, not only to allow for ministerial training and experience, but also to prove his qualifications in the ministry.

Leadership, Servanthood, and Discipleship

A missionary must be a leader, a servant, and a discipler (Elmer, Cross-Cultural Servanthood 155 ff). Some of the best leaders are those who are hesitant to lead. Many leaders are easily corrupted by the power of the office, but a missionary must be a humble man. Some are tempted to drive their congregations by force, as a cowboy would drive his cattle with a whip or an ox goad, but a missionary must lead by example as a shepherd leads his sheep. To be a good leader, a missionary must learn to be a good servant. The term "minister" simply means servant, and he that wishes to be leader of all must become a servant of all. In addition, he must possess the knowledge of how to disciple others in the ways of Christianity. The principal responsibility of the missionary is discipleship, that is, to teach others to follow Christ. Discipleship encompasses salvation, indoctrination, and edification. To make a disciple of Christ, a missionary must lead him to the Lord by presenting the gospel. Next, he must teach him the Word of God. For a missionary, discipleship is a continuous process. He must continue to encourage and build up the believers in the faith which is a lifelong endeavor.

The Faith Aspect of Mission Work

The most important principle that a missionary must learn is that he must live by faith (Gardner 13). Every aspect of a missionary's life revolves around the concept of a life which is governed, guided, and controlled by faith in the Lord. From the very beginning, a missionary's call is a testament to surrendering self-control to the control of God. Without believing that God can and will take care of him and his family, there can never be true surrender to the call of the Lord. A missionary must believe that the Lord who called him to the mission field is the same Lord that will take care of him on the mission field. To have true faith in the Lord, the missionary must realize what that type of faith entails. Hebrews 11:1 is the perfect Biblical definition of faith. "Now faith is the substance of things hoped for, the evidence of things not seen." In this verse, there are two main attributes to a Christian's faith: substance and evidence. A missionary who serves and worships the one true God has a faith that is different than the faith of heathen religions. The faith of the Christian has substance. Substance is something that is tangible, something that is real, and something that is truly there. Believers in a false god or false religion can never have this type of faith, for their hope is not a tangible hope, and their faith is placed in something that is not real. True Christianity is not wishful thinking nor is it a pipe dream. It is the knowledge of the reality of what God will bring to pass, even though it has not yet happened. The true missionary does not walk by blind faith with uncertainty in the hope of the watch-care and deliverance of God. The faith of a missionary not only has substance, it also has evidence. In a court of law, evidence is that which is admissible as testimony to the truth. A man should never be sent out as a missionary if he is a novice, lacking the experience of God's power in his life. This experience is the very evidence that a missionary is to draw upon as he lives and walks by faith. He

> *The most important lesson that a missionary must learn is that he must live by faith.*

should be able to look back upon a back log of answered prayers and a lifetime of God's providential intervention. This is the lesson that is taught in First Samuel 7:12, "Then Samuel took a stone, and set it between Mizpeh and Shen, and called the name of it Ebenezer, saying, Hitherto hath the LORD helped us." Ebenezer was a monument of the help of the Lord in the lives of the Israelites. Samuel, in erecting the stone, declared that the Lord had helped them "Hitherto," or up until that point in time, with the point being inferred that since God had brought them this far, He would carry them the rest of the journey. It was evidence of the providence of the Lord. The faith of a missionary is never blind faith, but is secured by the blessed hope that faith in Christ has true substance and a lifetime of evidence to prove that the Lord will never fail.

> 1. The Principle of God's Presence
> 2. The Principle of God's Provision
> 3. The Principle of God's Protection
> 4. The Principle of God's Power

Figure 25. *The Four Principles of Faith*

Four Principles of Faith

There are four Biblical principles of faith that a missionary must follow to be an effective servant of the Lord on the mission field:

The Principle of God's Presence

The Principle of God's Presence states that God exists, and He is near to them who call upon Him in truth. This principle can be found in two verses of Scripture. First, Hebrews 11:6 states, "But without faith it is impossible to please him: for he that cometh to God must believe that he is, and that he is a rewarder of them that diligently seek him." Many missionaries have a difficult time believing what God can do, because

ESTABLISHING THE CALL OF A MISSIONARY

they are yet to be convinced of who He is. God will never be pleased with those who will not learn to live by faith. A missionary must have a faith that is certain that God is truly there. Atheists notwithstanding, the Lord has revealed Himself to all mankind. Despite this fact, many do not fully realize the person of God in His fullness.

> *If the missionary can ever grasp who God truly is, having faith in what He can do will be a foregone conclusion.*

If a missionary can ever grasp who God truly is, having faith in what He can do will be a foregone conclusion. The same verse goes on to say that not only does God exist, but He rewards those who diligently seek Him. In the mortal quest to find the one true God, the Biblical promise, "seek and ye shall find" is both veritable and relevant. However, for a missionary, who ought to already be a believer in the Lord, the search is not to find God, but rather to seek to be near God. Living by faith means living in the close presence of the Lord. The second verse is found in Psalm 145:18, which declares that "The LORD is nigh unto all them that call upon him, to all that call upon him in truth." The Lord is only as far as a prayer. Just as He rewards those who seek Him diligently, He is near to those who call upon Him sincerely. God has promised in His Word that He will never leave us nor forsake us. Acts 13:4 speaks of the presence of the Holy Spirit of God who leads and guides as He sends a missionary forth. The promise of Christ in the Great Commission is dear to the heart of every missionary, "and, lo, I am with you alway, even unto the end of the world. Amen" (Matthew 28:20). As a missionary goes, the Lord has promised to go with him. Remember the words of the Lord to Joshua when He said, "the LORD thy God is with thee whithersoever thou goest" (Joshua 1:9).

The Principle of God's Provision

The Principle of God's Provision states that God will supply all that is necessary to accomplish His work. "But my God shall supply all your need according to his riches in glory by Christ Jesus." (Phil.

God will supply all that is necessary to accomplish His work.

4:19). To be effective, a missionary must be convinced that God is able to provide for his every need. Hudson Taylor famously stated that "God's work done in God's way will never lack God's supplies." Yet, the average missionary spends much of his time worrying about the lack of provision, whether it be financial or otherwise. No one should be too quick to judge when a missionary is struggling financially, that he is out of God's will. God sometimes brings His children through trials to increase their faith. Nor can it be said that a missionary who is receiving an abundance of monetary support is necessarily sanctioned by God. There are some who serve their father the devil who have huge followings and large coffers. Nevertheless, the principle of God's provision should bring a calm assurance to a missionary. It is not the place of a missionary to worry about God's responsibility. The Lord Himself has promised that He would supply, and a missionary's job is to simply trust that God will keep His promises.

The Principle of God's Protection

The Principle of God's Protection states that God's hand of protection is upon those He sends to the extent of accomplishing His purpose. The promise of Christ's presence in Matthew 28:20 implies that the Lord will watch over those who are sent out into the world. This promise does not mean that a missionary will face no obstacles, endure no pain, encounter no problems, and bear no burdens. The Scriptures teach quite the opposite. 2 Timothy 3:12 writes, "Yea, and all that will live godly in Christ Jesus shall suffer persecution." Ecclesiastes 9:2 states, "All things come alike to all: there is one event to the righteous, and to the wicked." How can both God's protection and the suffering in the lives of the righteous be reconciled? The difference is that when troubles come (and they will) the righteous have a refuge in which to turn. Psalms 86:7 says, "In the day of my trouble I will call upon thee: for thou wilt answer me." The meaning is clearly explained in Psalm 34:19, "Many are the afflictions of the righteous: but the LORD delivereth him out of them all." A missionary must have faith that the perfect will of God will be accomplished in the life of the man who is willingly and faithfully serving Him. Sometimes His will is accomplished though trials. Nonetheless, the protecting hand of the Lord is on His own. Even Satan himself acknowledged this fact in the book of Job, showing that he has no power over a person without the consent of the Lord. Job 1:10 states, "Hast not thou made an hedge about him, and about his house, and about all that he hath on every side?" The Lord will protect those whom He sends. A missionary is safer on a foreign field inside the will of God than in his home country outside of the will of God. David Livingstone said, "I would rather be in the heart of Africa in the will of God, than on the throne of England, out of the will of God." In the will of the Lord, a missionary is invulnerable. No power on earth or hell below can touch the anointed man of God so long as he is obediently following the will of God to accomplish His purpose. Problems will most definitely come; however, the Lord's protection will be there to guide through those trials. Romans 8:37 states, "Nay, in all these things we are more than conquerors through him that loved us."

> **God's hand of protection is upon those He sends.**

Conversely, the man of God can easily slip from this hedge of protection by turning aside from the will of the Lord into wickedness. It is implied in the New Testament that there is a special realm of spiritual protection upon God's people within a local New Testament church. When someone is turned out of the membership of a church because of sin, they are cast from this special protection into the hands of Satan (1 Corinthians 5). This same principle can be seen in the promise of God to the nation of Israel in Psalm 125. The Lord promised to establish those that trust in the Lord, and furthermore, would not allow the yoke of the wicked to abide upon them so long as they did not turn aside from Him "unto their crooked ways."

They that trust in the LORD shall be as mount Zion, which cannot be removed, but abideth for ever. As the mountains are round about Jerusalem, so the LORD is round about his people from henceforth even for ever. For the rod of the wicked shall not rest upon the lot of the righteous; lest the righteous put forth their hands unto iniquity. Do good, O LORD, unto those that be good, and to them that are upright in their hearts. As for such as turn aside unto their crooked ways, the LORD shall lead them forth with the workers of iniquity: but peace shall be upon Israel (Psalms 125:1-5).

The Principle of God's Power

The Principle of God's Power is this: God is big enough and powerful enough to take care of all the stumbling blocks, obstacles, hindrances, and problems in the life of a missionary. "And what is the exceeding greatness of his power to us-ward who believe, according to the working of his mighty power, which he wrought in Christ, when he raised him from the dead, and set him at his own right hand in the heavenly places, far above all principality, and power, and might, and dominion, and every name that is named, not only in this world, but also in that which is to come" (Ephesians 1:19-21). Worrying about the future shows a lack of faith in God. A missionary that is consumed by worry does not trust that his God is big enough or powerful enough to overcome the problems in his life. God, however, is omnipotent; He is infinite in power. Ephesians 3:20 states that the Lord is "able to do exceeding abundantly above all that we ask or think." A person who tries to fight his battles in the power of his own might, rather

> *God is big enough and powerful enough to take care of all the stumbling blocks, obstacles, hindrances, and problems in the life of a missionary.*

than the power of God, is certainly destined to fail. Through faith, a missionary must come to realize that it is God who fights the battle. "Thus saith the LORD unto you, Be not afraid nor dismayed by reason of this great multitude; for the battle is not yours, but God's" (2 Chron. 20:15).

Chapter Eleven

Deputation and Fund Raising

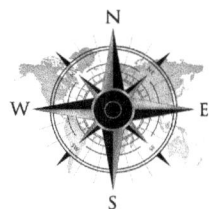

Ministry Presentation and Fund Raising

As a new missionary gets ready to go to the mission field, the question of finances and how to raise them arises. One of the basic premises and theological foundations of this missionary handbook is to demonstrate that mission boards and societies outside the authority of a local New Testament church are not only a historically bad idea, but also a Biblically unscriptural idea. Mission work is the right and responsibility of the local church, and missionaries should be sent out by a local church. They should answer to no other authority but their sending church and God. The nature of local-church-sent missionaries does not, however, preclude the fact that churches may, and by Biblical precedent, ought to help one another in the cause of mission work (Bogard). The most Biblically correct way for churches to help one another is not through a missionary organization, but rather through missionary deputation.

As a missionary prepares to embark on deputation, he must realize that this is truly a part of the ministry. Deputation is not a "necessary evil," as it is called by some missionaries. It is not an evil at all, but rather an opportunity to share Christ among churches of like faith. It is an opportunity to share the burden for the mission field with others. It is an opportunity for other churches to partner with a missionary and take part in the blessings of the Lord in foreign lands.

One of the hardest parts of deputation is scheduling appointments. It is often difficult to contact pastors who are busy in their own ministries and not available when you call. Austin Gardner, in *The Deputation Manual for Missionaries*, states that a missionary must think of scheduling appointments as his job (Gardner 55). He ought to get up early in the morning just as if he were going to any other field of employment, get dressed, and find a quiet spot to call churches, contact pastors, and schedule mission presentations. A missionary should call eight hours a day, every day, until his schedule is filled. Why eight hours? Because scheduling appointments for deputation is a job, just like any other job. He must be persistent, because it may take twenty phone calls to reach one pastor. It may take fifty phone calls to make one appointment. A missionary may have to call the same church or pastor several times before being able to reach him. This should not be a discouragement to a missionary, but rather looked upon as all part of the work. This principle of persistence is taught by Jesus Christ in Scripture.

> *And he said unto them, Which of you shall have a friend, and shall go unto him at midnight, and say unto him, Friend, lend me three loaves; For a friend of mine in his journey is come to me, and I have nothing to set before him? And he from within shall answer and say, Trouble me not: the door is now shut, and my children are with me in bed; I cannot rise and give thee. I say unto you, Though he will not rise and give him, because he is his friend, yet because of his importunity he will rise and give him as many as he needeth. And I say unto you, Ask, and it shall be given you; seek, and ye shall find; knock, and it shall be opened unto you. For every one that asketh receiveth; and he that seeketh findeth; and to him that knocketh it shall be opened (Luke 11:5-10).*

In this passage, Christ teaches that importunity (persistence) will pay off when dealing with men and also in your prayer life. This same persistence will quickly fill the schedule of a missionary who is willing to spend the time contacting churches. Gardner also presents the goal of at least thirteen appointments per month. This means that a missionary should seek an appointment every Sunday morning service, every Sunday night service and every mid-week service. Any unscheduled church service during the period of deputation is a wasted opportunity. It is the job of a missionary on deputation to present his ministry and minister in as many churches as he possibly can. Some missionaries take several years to raise their support. Others raise the necessary funds in a few months. Those who are more successful are the ones who take deputation seriously, and work at it full time.

Missionary Reports and Letter Writing

The missionary report is the singular most important element of contact with supporting churches that a missionary has in his arsenal (B. Barnett 149). A missionary that does not send out regular reports will inevitably lose financial support. Not only is it important to have regular reports, but it is also important to design the report correctly. Missionary reports are often called prayer letters or newsletters. Regardless of the name, the report should be eye-catching, well written, and sent out to supporters on a regular basis. An effective newsletter should be comprised of different complex segments of text and design. These different segments are essential in a newsletter, and without these essentials, the newsletter is incomplete.

The Title

The title of the newsletter should be eye catching and consist of the following elements: the name, the subtitle, the origin and the date. The name is the most important part of a newsletter. It is the main element that should draw attention and interest from the reader. The name should immediately identify the ministry being presented. The subtitle should expound on the name and tell the reader who the missionary is and what the ministry is. Subtitles are explanatory and introductory to those who are viewing the report for the first time. The newsletter should always be clear about who and where the letter is from (i.e. "Missionary Aaron Goodpastor in Argentina is a ministry of the First Baptist Church of Smalltowne, USA"). It should be perfectly clear where the newsletter is coming from. Who is putting it out and what is the address? Address and subscription information can be saved for the masthead, but it should always include who is responsible for the newsletter in the nameplate. The reader needs to identify the latest report so the correct edition can be displayed. Failure to include the date can cause confusion regarding which report is the most current. Churches want to know when they should take down an old report. Including the date will also keep a missionary accountable for writing and sending current reports.

The Masthead

The masthead is the section of the report that includes contact information. It should be prominent on every newsletter. A typical masthead includes content like: field address, phone number, website and email address, sponsoring church with contact information, and any other pertinent information. Without the masthead, churches will not know how to send support to the missionary or contact him for more information. The masthead can be in the header below the title, in a sidebar, or in the footer of a newsletter.

Within the body of the newsletter, several issues need to be addressed:

Grammar and Spelling

The body of your newsletter should be correct in grammar and spelling. Nothing screams incompetence like mistakes in a

Figure 26. *A sample newsletter showing the basic essential design segments in a typical layout.*

Missionary reports should be simple yet eye catching. Layouts should be clean and professional. All pertinent information should be included.

newsletter. Proper writing style, grammar and spelling may not earn any meritorious comments from supporters, but the lack of these elements will most certainly call your competence into question.

> *Nothing screams "Incompetence!" like mistakes in a newsletter.*

Section Breaks

Break up the text into small, readable sections. A long narrative with no breaks will ensure that all but the most devout readers will instantly lose interest and never read a word. Text boxes or paragraphs with title headers are great examples of section breaks.

Font (Type Style)

A clean, readable font should be chosen. Stay away from hard to read fonts. Some fonts may look pretty, but if the text is difficult to read, it will most likely not be read.

Headlines

Each section should be titled with a headline to tell the reader what the text is about. These may represent different areas of the ministry on the mission field, current needs, prayer requests, personal interest reports, etc.

Graphics and Photographs

Newsletters that are all text are dull and boring. Very few, if any, will bother to read them. A missionary should not assume that people want to read a report. He should develop a newsletter that grabs attention and begs to be read. Graphics and photos should complement the text of the newsletter. Random pictures that have nothing to do with the subject matter should be avoided. Pictures related to the text should be placed in that particular section of text. This will draw the reader's interest to learn more about the photo.

Captions

Photographs should be captioned. The names of everyone in a photo should be listed, as well as the circumstances of the picture. Captions should be very brief: one, or at most, two sentences. The font should be small, and the text should fit right under the photograph. The font should also be different than the body text to differentiate the caption from the body. There should be ample margin space around the caption text to avoid confusion with surrounding text.

Design

There is no reason that a missionary today should have to handwrite or type a monotonous report with no forethought, design, or color. Programs such as InDesign, Publisher, Word, or Pages should be used to build a visually interesting report that will draw positive attention and curiosity from the reader. A complimentary color palette should be used. Certain colors clash, others harmonize. This is not subjective, it is science. Certain colors should be used together, while others will create a jarring sense of confusion. The report should be eye-catching. Most missionary reports end up in a pile on a desk or hanging on a bulletin board. The professionally designed, eye-catching report that stands out from the crowd will not only be the one that is read most often, but will also speak volumes about the missionary who wrote it.

Simplicity

A newsletter can easily become cluttered and visually overwhelming. If at first glance, the eyes of the readers are overstimulated, the reaction will be to turn away. This is the opposite result of what you want. Proper margins and space between sections are essential to making the newsletter feel professional and uncluttered. Too many graphics with clashing colors or too much detail is overstimulating. Be careful with including too many words, too many statistics or just too much information. A missionary should not feel that he must tell every detail, but rather a concise summary of events. It should be kept simple, short and to the point. Readers can easily be turned away with information overload and a claustrophobic design.

Readability

The text of the newsletter should be written properly, yet conversationally. Each section should read as if the missionary were speaking directly to the reader. After writing the report, it should be re-read to see if it is understandable. Most people are complimentary of their own writing and read right over their own mistakes. Always have another person proofread the report for errors before it is sent out.

Consistency

Each time the newsletter is sent out, it should be easily recognizable. This requires a consistent format. The title and masthead should be kept the same in every newsletter. If a missionary decides to change the format, it should not be done often. A consistent design and look will ensure that the report will be recognized for its unique appearance in each issue by those who are reading reports on bulletin boards and missionary report areas.

Prayer Cards, Bookmarks, Magnets, etc.

One very important printed element that is required of a missionary is a prayer card. The missionary prayer card should be small enough to fit inside a Bible or a pocket. Some common sizes are 2x3 inches (business card size) 3x5 inches (notecard size), 4x6 inches (postcard size), and bookmark format. Another common item that is often distributed is business card size magnets. There are several online printing services that will print all sizes of cards in full color for a minimal cost. Two of the most inexpensive online printing services are Vistaprint.com and Postcards.com.

All relevant contact information should be given, such as: name, place of ministry, sending church, address, phone number, website and email address, as well as where to send support. The layout should be professional, uncluttered, and visually attractive. On two-sided cards, text should be reserved for the reverse. Some missionaries will include a ministry logo, Bible verse, or even birthday and anniversary dates of the family. Remember to keep it simple. The prayer card is a point of reference for information and contact, and is not the medium for large amounts of information.

> *Prayer cards should be made in great numbers and given out to everyone.*

Prayer cards should be made in great numbers and given out to everyone in attendance at every meeting that a missionary attends. In addition, a stack of prayer cards should be left in a prominent place of every church that is visited. Many church members will keep these prayer cards (if they are well designed and professional looking) in their Bibles, on their refrigerators, or somewhere in their home. They serve as a reminder for others to pray for a missionary on the field. The efficacy and power of prayer cannot be overemphasized. Saints on their knees keep missionaries on their feet.

Public Speaking Techniques of Deputation

The Journal of Personal Selling and Sales Management published an article on the theory of buyer-seller similarity. The generally held theory was that a consumer audience immediately judged a salesperson by their outward appearance and behavior, and that a salesperson who was most similar to themselves in outward appearance and behavior would be looked upon in a more positive light, increasing the effectiveness of the sale. However, according to the findings of the study, this was not true (Lichtenthal 1-14).

> *This synthesis of findings suggests that internal similarity can increase a business buyer's willingness to trust a salesperson and follow the salesperson's guidance and, therefore, increase the industrial salesperson's effectiveness. In contrast, the literature reviewed also indicates that, under most circumstances, observable similarity exerts a negligible influence on a business buyer's perceptions or a salesperson's effectiveness. This, the key finding is that it is more important for buyers and sellers to think alike than to look alike.*

The study implied that there is no substantial benefit from simply matching salespeople and buyers demographically. Salespeople of a different race, different accent, or from a different background were at no less of an advantage just because of their demographics. Salespeople who could identify potential areas of internal similarity and build upon those areas were the most effective.

Even though a missionary is not a *salesperson*, per se, nor are churches *buyers*, the implications of this study can certainly be applied to the deputation experience. It has been suggested that a person who is demographically different than the congregation will have a more challenging time in both gaining the respect of the audience and support from the church. However, according to this study, most people are more affected by the "internal similarities" listed as a persons' "perceptions, attitudes, and values" than by external characteristics such as appearance, ethnicity or even how well the presentation is made. This is a very important fact in that a missionary must connect with a church on a personal, emotional basis. He must effectively express his beliefs and values and connect spiritually with his fellow Christians on the level of the heart to win them over and open their eyes to his burden.

Missionaries will have many opportunities to speak publicly, in church worship services and in other meetings also. The smart missionary will take advantage of every opportunity he can to present his ministry. These opportunities might be meetings such as: youth camps, men or ladies' meetings, national, state, and local association meetings, mission rallies, revival meetings, conferences, retreats, and other church functions.

A missionary on deputation should prepare his presentation in several formats. There will be occasions when a presentation is limited to a specific allotted time. If a missionary is asked to keep to a particular amount of time, it is not only bad form, but rude and disrespectful to go beyond that time. Missionaries should prepare and practice giving a one-minute, two-minute, three-minute, five-

DEPUTATION TIPS

- **Share Your burden**
- **Focus on the ministry, not on money**
- **Use visuals (video, etc.)**
- **Connect with the people**
- **Preach the Word!**
- **Observe time limits**
- **Invite the audience to partner with you in the ministry**
- **Speaking one-on-one is just as important as speaking from the pulpit**
- **Always be courteous and thankful for the opportunity to speak**

Figure 27. *Deputation Tips*

minute and ten-minute presentation, being careful to include all relevant information. Most television commercials are a mere thirty seconds, and contain a vast amount of information about a product or service. When a missionary discards the extraneous and unnecessary, he is able to free up time for pertinent information. If he feels that he is incapable of giving such a short presentation, then he should consider making a short video instead. It may be wise to make two or more ministry presentation videos of varying lengths to be played at the appropriate times. When time is short, a quick personal introduction followed by a brief video may be the best course of action. There will be other times that a missionary will be given an extended period to speak. In these situations, he should be prepared to not only present his ministry, but also preach the Word of God. It is tempting to only have one or two sermons to preach at every meeting, yet a missionary should always be prepared in case he is asked to preach several nights to the same congregation. Though there is nothing sinful about preaching the same sermon more than once, a minister of gospel should be in constant study of the Bible. A man who has only one sermon reveals the fact that he is not being faithful in study and preparation of the Word of God.

The Missionary Display

Along with every other aspect of a missionary's life, ministry, and presentation, the display that is presented in churches and other meetings should be professional, clean and informative. A trifold board akin to those used in an elementary school science fair shows a lack of professionalism and forethought (Gardner 30 ff). However, a well thought, clean, expertly constructed display will reflect not only on the missionary himself, but also upon the work of the ministry in which he is involved. The display should not be cluttered, but have sufficient information about the field of labor and ministry to hold interest in the passerby. A missionary should employ something of interest to catch the eye of the onlooker and draw them to the display. Many missionaries today employ vertical roll-up banners which pack away into small cases and are easy to transport. Others use full-size folding backgrounds. However, depending on the size of these professionally printed backdrops, they may be more at home in an exhibition hall than in a church vestibule. The display table should include photos of the field and ministry. A photobook, such as those that can be printed by Shutterfly, Vista Print or even Walmart will draw interest, look professional, and pack away nicely. Other items could include cultural objects from the field and informational literature such as brochures, prayer cards, and business cards. Whatever the choice in the missionary display, care should be given to make sure the display can be set up and taken down quickly, packed away neatly for travel, and take up as little space and weight as possible for the traveling missionary.

Deputation Logistics

It is extremely expensive to be on full-time deputation. While scheduling appointments, the missionary should try not to backtrack to areas already traveled, scheduling in a consistent pattern one area at a time. This is not always possible, as churches may request that the missionary attend a pre-scheduled conference. However, as much as is possible, the missionary should take care to not waste resources and time traveling back and forth across the country. Another valid deputation technique is to find a central base in each area from which to work, traveling from that base of operation to appointments within a day's drive. Because the cost of hotels is prohibitively expensive, try to find a mission house, church guest room, or family who is willing to provide housing for a period of time. Across the United States, there are many places that are willing to house a missionary and his family free of charge. Taking advantage of these places can save thousands of dollars in housing costs.

Missionary Video Production

A missionary presentation video is a vital tool that should be utilized during deputation and also online. Not every person is skilled in or even has the means of producing a professional video, however certain advances in technology have brought these capabilities within reach of most people. Video production software ranges from user-friendly, drag-and-drop style programs to complex, professional, studio-grade applications. Most smart phones now have rudimentary video editing capabilities that can produce stunning results. For more professional results, there are ministries that specialize in video production. Some will even volunteer to accompany a missionary to the field, shoot the video, and edit the clips all free of charge. However the video is produced, it can be displayed in churches on deputation (many of which now have fixed video projectors in their auditoriums) and also online through websites and social media.

Not all venues will have the capability or equipment to show a video, so a missionary should invest in display equipment while on deputation. Some video projectors are quite inexpensive, but a missionary will require a very bright projector to display his video in a church auditorium. Projector brightness is measured in lumens. For instance, a 60-watt incandescent light bulb will emit approximately 800 lumens. In dark rooms with little to no ambient light, a cheap, low lumen projector might work. However, most church auditoriums have windows, and during daylight hours, this ambient light cannot be blocked out, even when the lights are turned off. For these situations, a minimum of 3000 lumens is recommended. The resolution of the projector is also a factor in the overall cost. Projectors can range from VGA (640x480 pixels) to widescreen HD format (1920x1080 pixels), and even 4K (3840x2160 or 4096x2160 pixels) Technology is constantly evolving and improving. A missionary should purchase a cost-effective solution which meets his personal needs.

Missionary Website Production

The twenty-first century is an age of information technology. There are few businesses, churches or ministries who do not have a website. The majority of the world, even in third-world countries, is connected to the internet. Apart from those who are working in closed countries, there is no excuse for a missionary not to have a website. A website will inform visitors about the ministry, direct them to churches, and even provide a platform for receiving donations. A few years ago, it was necessary for a person who wanted to build a website to either be educated in HTML coding or pay someone else a hefty sum to build it for them. Today, there are user-friendly, drag-and-drop systems that make it easy for anyone to create a website. Some of the most popular online website builders are Wix, Weebly, and Squarespace. There are also many ministries that will build and host a website for a missionary free of charge. A simple web search will bring up dozens of hosting sites that will build and host a website for missionaries.

Online Media Strategies

In this age of social media, sites such as Facebook, Twitter and Pinterest provide an opportunity for missionaries to reach a worldwide audience that they would otherwise never be able to contact. Mailing hard copies of printed reports and prayer cards may still be necessary, but today's missionary is missing a tremendous opportunity by not using these online media tools at his disposal. Facebook, for instance, had over 2 billion active users as of their earnings report published in June 2017. Missionaries can instantly post updates to thousands of followers though text messages, photos, videos, live feeds, and more. Website blogs and online bulletin boards are another great resource to reach the masses online.

Missionaries and churches may also want to avail themselves of the powerful tool of online targeted advertising. Modern websites use tracking "cookies" to follow user activity online. For instance, if a user was looking at purchasing *The Baptist Missionary Handbook* on Amazon.com, he might find that when he clicked on a different website, there would be an advertisement for the book. Internet companies easily track the interests of individuals online. Most people gladly give their personal information. For example, each Facebook user has published almost every personal fact of their lives such as likes, employment, education, relationships, friends, and other preferences. These details are compiled by Facebook to categorize people into targeted advertising groups. This may sound frightening to the average person, yet for someone who is seeking to reach a particular audience such as those who are interested in "Baptist foreign missionaries," it is a tremendous opportunity. Search engines such as Google compile web search data for marketing information in a similar way. For a very small cost, anyone can take advantage of targeted online advertisements to reach out to a global audience.

Chapter Twelve

THE CROSS-CULTURAL MISSIONARY

Culture and Worldview

An effective cross-cultural missionary must be familiar with both the culture and worldview of the people group to whom he is ministering. (Winter, 401). Culture can be defined as the collective body of customs, behaviors, values, and material characteristics that make up a unique, shared identity of a people group. The system of behaviors that differentiate one group, society, or nation from the next is what makes up a cultural identity. A person's culture is based upon their worldview. Worldview is the system of core beliefs and assumptions that make up a person's concept of the world. Both culture and worldview are heavily intertwined. Culture is how a person behaves and worldview is the system of

> *To be an effective cross-cultural missionary, you must be familiar with the culture and worldview of the people group to whom you minister.*

thought that controls that behavior. To the outsider, a foreign culture may seem strange, their behavior completely irrational. However, after learning the worldview of a people group, the customs and actions of the people become understandable, even if not approved by the outsider. David Burnett explains the two in this manner,

> *Culture may be likened to a game of chess. To a person who has no knowledge of the game the players seem at first to be moving the strangely shaped pieces at random. With time the observer begins to see that there is an order and pattern for every piece, and then finally they see that there is an overall strategy employed by the players. Culture may be likened to the total game, while the worldview is the unseen set of rules that determine how the game is played. (Burnett, Clash of Worlds 12 f)*

Cultural Bias and Acculturation

When a missionary crosses into a new and different cultural environment in which he is unfamiliar, he has no experience of the new culture to draw upon when making judgments calls or behavioral decisions. A person will naturally interpret this new context, make assumptions, and draw conclusions based on his own culture and worldview. This concept of behavior is called "cultural bias." For instance, certain gestures may be considered positive in one culture but have a negative connotation in another. Many western cultures might interpret the "thumbs up" gesture to mean "OK" or "thanks." However, in countries such as Greece, Sardinia, and Iran, as well as some Southeast Asian and South American cultures, giving a "thumbs up" is an insult equivalent to showing your middle finger in the US. There are many types of cultural bias, but they all stem from making false assumptions or uninformed judgments and decisions based upon a person's own cultural experience. Cultural bias often leads to social mishaps and various other problems.

For missionaries who plan on ministering in a foreign cultural environment for an extended period of time, cultural bias must be overcome through the process of acculturation. Acculturation is the process of learning to understand and correctly navigate the context of a foreign culture. As a person becomes increasingly familiar with the environment, behavioral cues, roles, and the underlying worldview of a culture, he can more easily relate and minister to the people of that culture. Acculturation is unfortunately far from a simple process. Many missionaries find it difficult to ever learn to understand the native culture in which they work.

The Fourfold Model of Acculturation states that four scenarios may play out in the life of a cross-cultural worker: assimilation, separation, integration, and marginalization.

Assimilation

Assimilation is a type of acculturation in which a person fully adopts the foreign culture as their own and discards the cultural behaviors, norms, and values of the society of which they are from. Many immigrants are pressured to assimilate and adopt the host culture in order to fit in. Many, if not most countries and societies in the world are nationalistic, proud of their cultural identity, and xenophobic. Immigrants, cross-cultural workers, and foreign missionaries may feel compelled to suppress their own cultural distinctiveness to espouse the ideas and behaviors of their new environment. The problem with assimilation is two-fold: first, by suppressing their own cultural identity, they lose a part of themselves. Secondly, assimilation can never be one-hundred percent successful. No matter how well a missionary learns the language, understands the culture, and behaves like the locals, he will at least partially be looked upon as an outsider. Even the most fully assimilated missionary is still a foreigner. The job of a missionary is not to assimilate into their culture, but to bring Christ to the people of that culture.

Separation

Separation is the polar opposite of assimilation. When a missionary, through a personal cultural bias, feels that his own cultural identity is superior to that of the host culture, he separates himself from that culture. Separation often occurs during the process of navigating cultural stress. It is often temporary, yet some missionaries make it their lifestyle. For example, some missionaries live in compounds with other foreigners. These communities result in ethnic enclaves in which their culture can flourish apart from the surrounding environment. It is not a bad thing for a missionary to practice his own culture in a foreign country. However, a missionary bent on forcing his cultural behaviors and ideas onto a foreign culture is bound to face problems. To a certain extent, every person living in a foreign country will practice some form of separation, whether it be within the repose of his own home or by choosing to speak to a person in his own language over a native speaker. A missionary must remain keenly aware of how any separation will affect his testimony and rapport with the people of the host culture.

Marginalization

Marginalization occurs when a long-term, cross-cultural missionary realizes that has neither fully assimilated into his host culture, nor can he fully associate himself with his own culture because of the changes that have occurred in himself from living in a foreign culture. Marginalization is a social dysphoria that results from the process of acculturation. A Canadian missionary to Nigeria realizes one day that no matter how hard he has tried, he will always be considered an outsider to the native population. However, as he returns home on furlough, he realizes that his years on the mission field have changed him. He no longer thinks or behaves like his Canadian friends and family. In his mind, he has become marginalized – a social misfit who does not fully "fit in" in any culture. The good news is that even though a missionary may not fully assimilate nor return to his pre-missionary life, he has learned to "become all things to all men," and can learn to be comfortable no matter where he is. How? It is only through the grace of God that a missionary can say, "I have learned, in whatsoever state I am, therewith to be content" (Philippians 4:11).

Integration

In the process of acculturation, integration is the ultimate goal. Integration is process whereby a cross-cultural missionary is intertwined into the host culture while maintaining his own culture. Integration occurs when a missionary, though not fully becoming a native, is accepted as a part of the community. Integration can only occur when a missionary is conversant in the culture and comfortable enough to reach out to those in the host culture. Integration takes time, yet does not happen without considerable effort. Proverbs 18:24 is applicable in this context, "A man that hath friends must shew himself friendly." Integration is not for "fitting in," but rather for reaching out. A missionary must integrate into a culture to the extent that is necessary for reaching people for Christ, yet without compromising Biblical truth. If a missionary wants to reach people for Christ, he must be willing to reach people where they are. This includes reaching out into the host culture. He must be willing to learn their language. He must be willing to learn why they think and behave the way they do. He must be willing to sit down with them in an unfamiliar context until it becomes second nature to him. He must be willing to learn their customs, manners, and social mores. He must learn to accept their way of life to the extent that it does not violate scripture. At the same time, he is comfortable with his own cultural identity and becomes acclimated to the fact that he will never feel fully at home upon this earth in any context because his true home waits for him in the future.

Hot Climate Versus Cold Climate Cultures

World cultures can generally be divided into two distinct categories. Cultures are either task-oriented or relationship oriented. Though some cultures may hold to these traits on a greater scale than others, a basic understanding of this categorization of cultures will help missionaries navigate the hurdles of cross-cultural ministry.

Cultural types are typically defined by the climate in which they are commonly found. In the seminal work on cultural acquisition, *Foreign to Familiar*, Sarah Lanier uses the term *cold-climate culture* to define a task-oriented society and *hot-climate culture* to define a relationship-oriented society (S. A. Lanier 15 ff). Though task-oriented cultures are typically found in colder climates and relationship based cultures are normally found in warmer climates, there are some exceptions. Rural communities tend to be more relationship oriented, while urban areas tend to be more task oriented. People in cold climates living in a rural area may exhibit the characteristics of a relationship-oriented person. Those living in high-population urban areas, though they may be in a relationship-oriented culture, will most likely exhibit some of the characteristics of a task-oriented culture. However, "hot-climate cultures" and "cold-climate cultures" have become commonly accepted terminology in cross-cultural anthropology. Hot-climate (relationship-oriented) cultures are those that are based upon relationship building in which the society is concerned with hospitality and the feelings of others. Relationship-oriented cultures are driven by community, connection, and interaction rather than schedules or tasks. In contrast, cold-climate (task-oriented) cultures give priority to schedule, time and efficiency in completing the task at hand (Elmer, Cross-Cultural Connections 117). A task-oriented person may seem rude and indifferent to someone from a relationship-oriented culture. In contrast, a relationship-oriented person may seem unproductive to a cold-climate person, focusing too much on "unnecessary" conversation.

Lanier lists the following areas as task-oriented cultures: Canada, Northern United States, Northern European countries, the Jewish population of Israel, Southern Brazil, and the white populations of the following countries: New Zealand, Australia, Argentina, and South Africa. The populations of most large cities also tend to be more task-oriented. The following areas are typically populated by relationship-based cultures: Southern United States, most Asian countries, the Middle East, Africa, Latin-American cultures (except for Southern Brazil and Argentina), and the Mediterranean.

Direct vs Indirect Communication

The way that people communicate in hot-climate cultures is different that cold-climate cultures. (S. A. Lanier 31-39). A missionary crossing from a hot-climate to a task-oriented culture must learn these differences in order to communicate effectively. Hot-climate cultures tend to communicate in an indirect fashion. Their concern is more about preserving the feelings of the other person than bluntly stating the facts. The relationship between two individuals will always be more important than straight talk. Confrontation may still occur, but hurtful information is usually conveyed in a roundabout way. For instance, if a missionary schedules a meeting with a person from a hot-climate culture, and that person can't make it, he may still agree and say something to the effect of, "Okay, I'll meet you at 5:00 tomorrow. I just have some business to attend to first." Of course, he doesn't show up. In his mind, he didn't lie – he believes he did a good thing by telling you what you wanted to hear rather than making the uncomfortable statement that he couldn't actually come to the meeting. His answer leaves open the possibility that his business might not be finished, thus saving face for not coming.

When discussing business, small talk will always occur first. To the person in a hot-climate culture, the small talk is important for the sake of building the relationship. Trust must be established before the parties are comfortable enough to move on to conducting business. A task-oriented person would see it as a waste of time, preferring to get right to business. In the task-oriented culture, efficiency is key - even in communication. Relationships and the feelings of the other party are not a consideration when conveying information, just the cold, hard facts. Since time is important to the task-oriented person, any activity that deviates from accomplishing the task at hand is seen as wastefully inefficient (Elmer, Cross-Cultural Connections 150 ff). The small talk of the hot-climate person would most likely do nothing more than aggravate the task-oriented person. A hot-climate missionary going to a task-oriented culture must learn that efficiency and direct communication are important values there. He should not take it personally that they do not communicate in the same manner, nor share his hot-climate values. A task-oriented missionary moving to a hot-climate culture must learn the indirect form of communication and realize that relationship building is the more important value there.

> ## POLITELY REFUSE BEFORE ACCEPTING
>
> An example of indirect communication is taken directly from the Southern United States, which is considered a hot-climate culture. When teaching this lesson to students from the North in a cross-cultural acquisition class, I pointed out a peculiar thing that Southerners do. Having been raised in the South, it seems it's an unwritten rule in the South that you politely refuse something that is offered you the first couple of times, even if you want it. Only on the third offer would you accept. In the hot-climate culture of the South, this serves two purposes. Primarily, it would be impolite to take advantage of the host's generosity by accepting it right away. Secondly, to ensure that the offer is genuine and the host isn't offering something that might be an inconvenience to them if you were to accept, you would only agree to take it after the host repeatedly insisted. Lanier makes this same observation about accepting a cup of coffee from a hot-climate person, "If you were to say 'yes' the first time to the coffee, you would appear too forward, too eager, and the coffee would become the focus, not the hospitality."

Figure 28. *Missionary Insights: Politely Refuse Before Accepting*

Individualism vs. Collectivism

Cold-climate cultures tend to be more individualistic. That is, they value self-actualization and independence from the group. In a task-oriented culture, it is important for a person to "find himself" or "be his own man" (S. A. Lanier 42). It is acceptable to have an individual opinion that is different from others, and initiative is encouraged. Hot-climate cultures, on the other hand, are group-oriented. The identity of the individual is inexorably linked to the group as a whole (Elmer, Cross-Cultural Connections 135 ff). The opinion of one will reflect the opinion of the group. The hot-climate culture will hold to a group mentality of belonging. The community and needs of the group far outweigh the needs of the individual. In the group-oriented culture, every action reflects not just on the individual, but on the entire group. The group-oriented person will usually suffer an imposition or personal inconvenience as long as there is benefit to the group or to the relationship. While working with a group of English teachers on the mission field, I found it appalling that most of them could not speak English. Their lack of fluency translated into poor performance by their students. In the classroom, students were allowed to exchange answers during exams so that everyone would be ensured of a passing grade. In a collective-minded culture, the performance of the group was paramount, even if it meant that no one learned anything. However, singling out a person for poor performance (or anything else, for that matter) is a cultural faux pas. If a person in a hot-climate, collective culture is singled out of a group for their opinion on a certain subject, he or she will inevitably turn to the group for a consensus before answering.

Inclusive vs Exclusive Cultures

Hot climate cultures are considered "inclusive" cultures, because inclusive nature of the group-oriented society. In an inclusive culture, everyone in the group is considered and included in all activities. To them, it is considered rude to exclude anyone present from plans that are being made. There are no private conversations when others are around. There is no private snack or meal. Everything is shared with the group. Meals in many hot-climate cultures are served in large dishes in which everyone eats together, rather than being served in separate plates. "The Maoris of New Zealand have a proverb: 'You bring your basket, I'll bring mine, and together we'll feed everyone.' The important thing is that it is shared (S. A. Lanier 59)." In an inclusive culture, everything

INCLUSIVE MEANS NEVER ALONE

In an exclusive culture, privacy is valued and highly prized. Many people in exclusive cultures tend to enjoy time alone. To the hot-climate person, there is hardly a worse fate than being alone. Take, for example, this story that a missionary in Southeast Asia once told me: (Names have been left out for his protection since he works in a closed country.) It was Chinese New Year, and there were great festivities taking place, especially in the southern part of a neighboring country, where they would travel for the holiday. After a long drive, the missionary and his family arrived at the border. The small border town was empty. There wasn't a soul to be found anywhere, as most of the population had left to enjoy the festivities. As the immigration officials checked their travel documents, his wife and children passed through with no problem. He was the last in line, and there was a problem with his visa. He couldn't cross the border. "That's perfectly fine with me!" he said to his wife. "You go on with the kids and enjoy yourself. I'll just stay here and enjoy some peace a quiet for a few days." As a person from a cold-climate, exclusive culture, he really meant it. He would stay at a small hotel, kick back in a hammock, and read a book. There would be no loud music, no throngs of party-goers, no fireworks exploding all night. Just quiet solitude, rest, and repose. With the government offices all closed for the holiday, there was nothing more he could do anyway. So, his family crossed the border and left without him. What he didn't know, was that this scenario haunted the minds of the immigration officials. They were a hot-climate, inclusive society. In their minds, nothing could possibly be worse than for this man to be stuck all alone at the border, separated from his family, and unable to enjoy the festivities. While he relaxed in his bungalow, the officers decided to pay him a visit. They asked him to get on the back of a motorcycle and then drove him through trails in the jungle across the border to rejoin his family. Though he was perfectly content to stay, they would have none of it. They couldn't possibly allow a person to be alone.

Figure 29. *Missionary Insights: Inclusive Means Never Alone*

is shared and free to be used by whoever has need of it. When a person in an inclusive culture acquires something, it is shared with, and by right, the property of the group. Cold-climate cultures are considered "exclusive" cultures. The rights of the individual are exclusive to the individual. The idea of individual property rights is a concept of a cold-climate, exclusive culture. When Europeans first colonized the Americas, owning land was a foreign concept to the Native Americans. They believed that land was a commodity to be shared by all. In many inclusive cultures around the world, food is a commodity to be shared by all, so that no one will ever go hungry. In Thailand, if strangers show up at a home, local custom demands that the host provide them a meal.

Cultural Concepts of Hospitality

The concept of hospitality, or how a guest is treated, is different in hot and cold-climate cultures (S. A. Lanier 71 ff). For the task-oriented person, entertaining guests is usually a scheduled activity that is pre-planned and by invitation only. In hot-climate cultures, most everything is spontaneous and relaxed. Food is often at the center of having company, and is perfectly fine without any advanced notice. In many hot-climate cultures, one significant custom is that the host is expected to take care of all the needs of the guest. This means that whoever gives the invitation pays the tab for everyone. In American society, it is not unusual for guests to split a bill at a restaurant and pay for their own meals. In a hot-climate culture, it would not only be rude, but absolutely unheard of for the host not to pay the entire bill.

Sarah Lanier gives the example of cold-climate individuals visiting a hot-climate culture. In America, food "has gone from primarily being a source of nourishment to being a source of entertainment... When Americans travel to a country where food is still primarily a source of nourishment, they may not realize how offensive it is if they refuse food offered them just because they don't like it" (S. A. Lanier 46). Eating food in the group-oriented culture is about accepting the hospitality of the host rather than the likes or dislikes of the individual. It is about being nourished, and not about the tastes or opinion of the guest.

> ### DON'T SPLIT THE CHECK
>
> One day while teaching at a local school overseas, a fellow missionary's wife mentioned that we would be eating at a certain restaurant that evening and invited all the teachers to join us. I informed her that local custom meant that she would be paying for everyone that came. She was floored. She couldn't possibly pay for everyone that had been invited, so she immediately went to each teacher to tell them that they could still come, but would need to pay for themselves. She went home, and I stayed to teach two more classes. I overheard several of them talking about how rude the Americans were. That evening, we went to the restaurant with the other missionary family. No teachers showed up. The missionary wife called two of the teachers and asked if they were coming. In their hot-climate cultural way, they both said, "We're on our way." An hour later, she called again. The answer was the same, "We're on our way." The teachers never showed up. In a hot-climate culture, an invitation means that the host takes full responsibility for the guests. To ask a guest to take that responsibility or even share in it is unthinkable.

Figure 30. *Missionary Insights: Don't Split the Check*

Monochronic vs. Polychronic Cultures

Cultures can be further divided into either monochronic and polychronic. Monochronic simply means doing one thing at a time and polychronic means doing multiple things at the same time. When speaking of cultures, however, these terms define how a society views the nature of time itself. A monochronic culture views time as a linear concept where time is a controlling factor of life. Schedules and punctuality are important values in a monochromatic culture. The calendar and clock are ruling forces that determine behavior. Time is considered a valuable commodity that must be "well spent." The concepts of "wasting time" and "losing time" are essential beliefs in the monochronic worldview. Monochronic cultures are task oriented, individualistic, cold-climate cultures. In contrast, a polychronic culture views time as cyclical or recurring without boundaries. To a polychronic person, a moment is never lost because it will happen again in the next cycle (i.e. day, week, month, year). In polychronic cultures, time is not measured by productivity and schedule, but by events and relationships. They are not governed by the clock. Polychronic cultures are relationship-oriented, communalistic, hot-climate cultures. If there is an event being held, the event itself is important, not the time in which it is occurs. For instance, if a party is being held in a polychronic culture and you are told that it will be at 6:00pm, the time holds a different meaning than in a monochronic culture. At 6:00pm, guests may not be arriving at the party. For some, the party is the only event of the day, so they have arrived at the venue early – some have possibly been there all day. For the majority of guests, they realize that it's 6:00pm, so it's time to start preparing for the party. The event and the people there are the important parts, not the time that it begins. Polychronic cultures are spontaneous rather than time conscious.

Past, Present or Future Oriented Cultures

Cultures can also be driven by the concepts of past, present, or future orientation. Past-oriented cultures are guided by their history, heritage, and customs. They are resistant to change and place a high value on established traditions. In past-oriented cultures, historical precedent guides decision making and policies. China, Britain, and Japan are examples of past-oriented cultures. Present-oriented cultures are focused on the here and now. They are neither guided by the past nor concerned about the future. Living from day to day with little thought of future planning, present-oriented cultures are driven by a *carpe diem* attitude of short-term goals and instant gratification. Many Latin American and African cultures, as well as many modern subcultures are present-oriented. Future-oriented cultures are innovative societies who are constantly looking to change the future by their work in the present. They are willing to sacrifice in the present to achieve their goals for the future. Future oriented cultures are open to change and willing to explore new ideas. Cross-cultural missionaries who cross the divide of a cultural time context must understand the differences in a person's concept of time.

Dr. Douglas Wiersema relates the story of constructing a church building in Romania. Working alongside of the Romanians, he had brought his power tools: circular saw, drill, pneumatic nail gun. Yet, the workers refused to even touch the "American" inventions, preferring to use their old hand tools. When he approached a man using an old hand-cranked drill, he said, "Just use the power drill! It will do in seconds what will take you a half-hour." An American wouldn't give a second thought to using a new tool that he had never seen before if it meant better efficiency. That's because America is a future-oriented culture. Romania, on the other hand is a past-oriented culture, and Doug's actions elicited a past-oriented response. "We've been using these hand tools for centuries, and they've always worked just fine. You Americans think that your new-fangled inventions are better? Our ways are tried and true, and we will never change our ways."

High vs Low Context Cultures

Cultures that have lasted for many centuries have had time to develop more rules of decorum than that of younger societies (S. A. Lanier 79 ff). These cultures are known as "high-context cultures." In these rigid cultures, a missionary must be very careful to abide by the formal guidelines of society. This may or may not take place in formal settings. In rural villages of older societies which have a high-context culture, there are many rules that must be followed of things that must be done and things that should not be done. There may be actions and behaviors that are considered taboo in a high-context culture. To understand the thoughts, behaviors, and colloquialisms in a high-context society, a person must have a high amount of contextual knowledge of the culture. For instance, in Thailand, which has over one-thousand years of national history, everything matters. It is impolite to point a finger at someone, and extremely rude to point with the foot. Another person's head should never be touched. Shoes should be removed before entering a home. It is impolite for a person to cross their legs or arms. The mouth should be covered by the opposing hand when using a toothpick. A visitor is expected to bring a gift to the host when visiting a home. A greeting is always initiated by the person of lower status. Even the language itself is dictated by custom. Different levels of vocabulary are used to show varying degrees of respect. *Kawp koon* is the word for "thank you" used by a person of lower status to the person of higher status. *Kawp jai* also means "thank you," but used by the person of higher status to a person of lower status. Another example would be the five levels of eating depending upon the situation and respect given to those who are partaking. *Gin Khow* means to "eat rice;" the word "rice" being used commonly in place of the word "food." *Tahn Khow* also means to "eat rice;" the word *gin* being replaced by a more proper word for "eat." *Tahn Aahaan* means to "eat food;" the word for "rice" now being replaced with the more proper word for "food." *Ruprataan Aahaan* is the next level of respect; the word for "eat" now being substituted with a higher form of dining. Finally, there is a word used only for royalty also meaning "to eat:" *sa-weri pak-grayahan*. There are also no less than eight other words for eat on the more common to vulgar scale.

A casual culture, also known as a low context society, will be more casual in every way. There are few formalities to bother with or rules to abide by. Low context societies are often found in newer cultures and also in island nations, were the environment seems to be more conducive to a casual lifestyle. A person coming from a low context to a high context society may find it difficult to juggle all the rules with which they are bombarded. A missionary in this situation might feel overwhelmed by the expectation to abide by rules in which he is not even aware. The person going from a high to a low context society may however be offended at the lack of protocol and not realize that the offending culture has no concept of the system of guidelines that regulate his behavior. To be effective in a cross-cultural situation, a missionary must be aware of these differences and behave accordingly.

Cultural Contextualization vs Religious Syncretism

Cultural contextualization is the process in mission work whereby the Scripture is communicated in a way that is relatable and understandable in the context of the cultural environment. There are many examples in scripture which teach the concept of cultural contextualization. The incarnation of Christ in human form is an example of how God reached out to mankind in a way that was relatable, approachable, and understandable. A missionary must first learn the culture to effectively communicate in that culture. He must preach the Word and conduct himself in such a way that the message of the gospel is clearly understood in the context of that culture. The principle of contextualization is based on the fact that religious conversation is intimate conversation, and individuals must connect on a personal level before an intimate, religious dialogue can begin. The Apostle Paul taught the principle of contextualization in the following passage:

> *For though I be free from all men, yet have I made myself servant unto all, that I might gain the more. And unto the Jews I became as a Jew, that I might gain the Jews; to them that are under the law, as under the law, that I might gain them that are under the law; To them that are without law, as without law, (being not without law to God, but under the law to Christ,) that I might gain them that are without law. To the weak became I as weak, that I might gain the weak: I am made all things to all men, that I might by all means save some. And this I do for the gospel's sake, that I might be partaker thereof with you (1 Corinthians 9:19-23).*

In contrast, religious syncretism is the fusion or blending of two belief systems. Syncretism occurs when pagan beliefs or traditions are added or substituted into Christianity. The most common example of religious syncretism is in the adoption of pagan gods and spirits into Catholicism. The worship of these gods continues, yet the names are changed to that of Catholic saints. While contextualization is necessary to an extent, there is a well-defined line between contextualization and syncretism. One is the incorporation of culture for personal connection and relatability. The other is a blatant compromise of Biblical truth in favor of pagan belief. Christians are free to incorporate their culture and traditions into their practices and mode of worship if they do not contradict the teachings of the Word of God. If a cultural belief or tradition is sinful or causes another to stumble, it must be discarded.

Many modern theologians and missionaries talk about indigenous church planting and incarnational ministry in which a missionary must be careful to not try to change the culture of the host society, but rather let them develop their own form of Christianity within the context of their culture and society.

> *As a person's worldview changes, so too will their attitudes, presuppositions and behavior.*

There is an inherent theological error to this line of thinking that has resulted in syncretism rather than conversion. The Lord commanded in His Word not to follow the customs of the heathen in their superstitious idolatry. "Thus saith the LORD, Learn not the way of the heathen, and be not dismayed at the signs of heaven; for the heathen are dismayed at them. For the customs of the people are vain" (Jeremiah 10:2-3). An American missionary's goal is not to export an American brand of Christianity with all the nuances of American culture. Neither is it the goal of a missionary to create a new system of Christian religion which is nothing more than pagan syncretism in the guise of cultural contextualization. A missionary's goal is to export the Christian worldview, in light of a Christ-like, bibliocentric cultural attitude which is both transcendent of all culture and universal in application. Once Christ is accepted into the heart of a new believer, the very fabric of their pagan or secular worldview begins to come unwound. As their worldview changes, so too will their attitudes, presuppositions and behavior. Cultural norms that do not line up with the Christian worldview are thrown into conflict, and new believers are forced to choose between cultural familiarity and Christian principle. This is true of every believer.

Culture shock and Cultural Stress

Culture shock is both a psychological and physiological response to the effects of exposure to a wildly different environment as a person is thrust into a foreign culture. Ronald Koteskey speaks of culture shock as a crisis stage involving confusion, disorientation, and lack of control (Koteskey). As a missionary first encounters a foreign culture, the sights, sounds, and smells are unfamiliar and strange. Communication is difficult or impossible, and the comfort zone of familiar experience is completely absent. He may not know or even understand what is going on around him and confusion sets in. He becomes disoriented as he becomes aware that he is the foreigner, and is disconnected with the society and environment that he is in. The effects are physical as well as mental. If a missionary has traveled over several times zones, he may experience jet lag, insomnia and drowsiness, creating physical exhaustion which can affect the immune system and overall mood. Differences in hygiene, as well as a lack of resistance to local bacteria may lead to further health complications. This all culminates into a feeling of helplessness and lack of control as a missionary realizes that he is ill equipped (because of unfamiliarity) to face these challenges (Elmer, Cross-Cultural Connections 43 ff).

Cultural stress is a different issue which is faced by a missionary on a long-term basis. Unlike the singular trauma of culture chock, cultural stress is the culmination of the effects of the constant bombardment of cultural dynamics in the everyday life of the foreign worker. Koteskey defines cultural stress as the "daily stress and anxiety of negotiating life in an environment that will always be somewhat foreign" (Koteskey). Some of the problems that result in cultural stress are language and communication issues, misunderstanding of customs and behavior, navigation of the foreign environment, and even homesickness. A missionary who fails to deal with cultural stress in a positive way may begin to feel anger, anxiety, and disappointment. He may withdraw to

THE CROSS-CULTURAL MISSIONARY 249

become less involved with the foreign surroundings and have less interaction with the people there.

Though culture shock is a temporary issue, there is no easy way to combat and cultural stress, and to an extent, the stress of living in a foreign culture will always be a present factor in the life of a missionary (Koteskey). There are, however, ways to lessen the effects of cultural stress. First and foremost, a missionary must have an active prayer life and close relationship with the Lord. Without this outlet, a missionary will never survive the field. The Lord is able to take the burdens of the missionary and is powerful enough to overcome all obstacles in his life. On the part of the missionary, there are other things that he can do to minimize cultural stress. The main factor that creates anxiety in the heart of a missionary is the fear of the unknown. As the culture and environment become more familiar, the less anxiety is felt. Involvement and education of the culture and worldview of the mission field will aid in reducing cultural stress. Having knowledge and experience of your surroundings will diminish the anxiety of the unknown. Many missionaries feel overwhelmed and decide to withdraw, locking themselves away in their homes to escape the pressure of the world outside. This may be one of the most counterproductive behaviors in dealing with cultural stress. When the missionary eventually emerges back into the environment from which he is hiding, he will feel even more overwhelmed.

> ***Cultural stress is the culmination of the effects of the constant bombardment of cultural dynamics in the everyday life of the foreign worker.***

As the communication barrier is broken with language learning, one of the largest stress factors is reduced. A missionary that never learns the language and speaks only through a translator not only does the people he is ministering to a disservice, but also does a disservice to himself. He will be in constant cultural conflict and confusion because of the language barrier.

It is important for a missionary to make friends of the nationals, and establish himself as having a new life on the mission field. A missionary is not only there to work, but to live. He and his family should find recreational activities that they enjoy. Eventually, he must settle his own personal differences with his new home and learn to live, work, play, and feel comfortable there.

Over time, a missionary will begin to change from the person that he used to be. His new experiences will begin to shape him in a way that neither others from his country, nor those native to the field will ever understand. He will become a hybrid of both worlds, never fully fitting into either, but learning to be comfortable in both. He will come to realize that no matter how long he stays or how hard he tries, he will never be fully accepted on the field of labor, and when he returns home, he will have changed so much that he is no longer fully accepted there either. The life of a missionary is the quintessential story of the pilgrim and stranger traveling through a world where he has no home, yet seeking his home above. He joins in chorus, understanding the true meaning if the words, "this world is not my home. I'm just a-passin' through."

Chapter Thirteen

MISSIONARY PRACTICALITIES

The Missionary Field Survey

Before moving to the mission field, a missionary should take the time to conduct a field survey. The survey trip should be long enough to experience the culture and get a small taste of what it is like to live on the mission field. At least one month is recommended, however a survey of several months would give the prospective missionary a better picture of what lies ahead. While on the field survey, some of the things to look for would include: a person, family, or group interested in the gospel; opportunities that could be God's open door for ministry; housing costs, availability of utilities, appliances and furnishings; access to healthcare; schooling, including language learning and schooling for the missionary's children; postal services, costs and fees; access to a phone, whether cell phones, satellite phones, or land lines; internet access; and radio and television access. Compile a list of needed supplies and try to find access to those supplies while on the survey trip. The supplies on this list should include: groceries, medicine, tools, building supplies and equipment, personal care items, electronics, books, clothing and shoes. Some Americans or Europeans may be surprised to find that even though clothing and shoes may be available for purchase, they may not be offered in the appropriate size. In many developing countries, the average person is much smaller than the average American. American and European missionaries may find it hard to obtain anything that will fit them on the foreign field.

Financial considerations on the field survey should answer the following questions: What is the cheapest way to receive money from the States? (wire transfer, ATM withdrawals, international banking, checks through mail) Can a bank account in that country be opened and maintained? What are the foreign transactions fees that will be incurred? How much is travel at different times of the year? What is the cost of living on the field? (food, gas, utilities, housing, etc.) What specific ministry expenses will there be? What is the cost of a vehicle? Is it more cost effective for a church building to be purchased, rented, or constructed? What are the governmental costs of living, such as visas, permits, and even graft?

Cultural, religious and demographic considerations on the field survey should answer the following questions: What is the socio-economic status of the target population, such as salaries, minimum wages, and living conditions? What are the cultural norms and taboos of the host culture? What are the religious beliefs of the host culture specific to the region and target population? What are the demographics of the area? The *Culture Shock* series is a great resource for finding answers to cultural questions in seventy-seven countries of the world. Joshuaproject.net gives a great insight into target demographics and provides an invaluable resource to prospective missionaries on the status of evangelization of the 10,112 people groups of the world (joshuaproject.net).

Shipping and Shopping Overseas

Goods that cannot be found on the mission field will have to be shipped or mailed. Some fields may require that a missionary bring large amounts of supplies, possibly in a shipping container. On

Field Survey Checklist	
Things to Research:	**Items to look for:**
☐ Personal Contacts	☐ Groceries
☐ Opportunities for Ministry	☐ Medicine
☐ Housing Costs	☐ Tools
☐ Utility Costs	☐ Building Supplies
☐ Banking	☐ Personal Care Items
☐ Money Transfer	☐ Electronics
☐ Hospitals	☐ Books in Your Language
☐ Language Schools	☐ Clothing & Shoes in Your Size
☐ Schools for Children	
☐ Postal Services	☐ Appliances
☐ Phone Service	☐ Furniture
☐ Internet Access	☐ Office Supplies
☐ Visa Costs and Requirements	☐ Bibles and Christian Literature in the Native Language
☐ Recreational Activities for the Family	

Figure 31. *Field Survey Checklist*

other fields, a missionary may find that very little will need to be shipped, and most everything can be bought there. It should be noted that there are thousands, if not millions of people that already live quite comfortably in foreign countries. If they are able to find all the supplies and needs for their lives, a missionary should also be able to find most of his needs there also.

It may cost several thousand dollars to ship a container of personal effects to another country. Many countries will hold containers for several months in customs before allowing it to pass, and import taxes may be in excess of 75-100% of the combined cost of all items being shipped. Because of the prohibitive cost and hassle of shipping crates and containers overseas, missionaries ought to consider purchasing as much of their supplies as possible on the field, rather than shipping.

Another option is airline cargo or excess luggage. Purchasing excess luggage is expensive, but there are benefits. The luggage will arrive with the missionary, and dealing with customs in the airport is usually much easier than at a shipping port. If there are other travelers who visit the missionary on the field, luggage can be sent with them to save money.

Housing and Living Conditions

There are two schools of thought when it comes to missionary housing on the foreign mission field, "go native" position and the "missionary compound" position. These two schools of thought should be considered as two opposing poles on a continuum in which a missionary must place himself.

The first school of thought is that the missionary should "go native." This position holds that a missionary should live in housing that is equivalent to that of the native population. If the people live in grass huts in a village, the missionary should move into a grass hut to live amongst the people in the village. This position recognizes the importance of being relatable to the people to whom a missionary must minister. It does not, however, take into consideration the needs and comfort of the missionary and his family.

The second school of thought is that of a missionary compound, in which the missionary lives in a confined and secluded retreat which is cordoned off from the foreign environment. Often, a missionary compound may be inclusive

> ## THE IMPORTANCE OF A SURVEY TRIP
>
> **2 Corinthians 4:18 "While we look not at the things which are seen, but at the things which are not seen: for the things which are seen are temporal; but the things which are not seen are eternal."**
>
> Rachel and I packed our bags and set out on our field survey of Thailand, not knowing what might be in store for us. It was my second trip to Thailand. It was Rachel's first time traveling out of the country, and her first time on a plane. We had our plane tickets in hand, but not much else. We had no idea where we would go, where we would stay, or what we were going to be doing. Some people might call that walking by faith, while others would just call it ignorance. We spent a month surveying the country and seeking God's will for our lives. Regardless, the Lord watched out over us and His hand guided us all along the way. When we returned to the field a few months later, we had a much clearer vision as to where we were headed. The Lord laid several goals upon our hearts of things we needed to strive for – things like evangelism, church planting, a Bible school, and reaching the hearts of the Thai people for the service of God. After the survey trip, moving to the mission field seemed a little less scary.

Figure 32. *Missionary Insights: The Importance of a Survey Trip*

of, or adjacent to homes of other foreigners or missionaries, creating a community where the home culture of the missionary may be practiced and enjoyed. A missionary compound creates a comfortable "home away from home," where missionaries and their families can escape the cultural stress of the foreign environment. The downside to the missionary compound is that a missionary builds a wall (literally) around himself, separating him from the people, culture, and surroundings of the field. The people may look at him as unapproachable and distant, and may hold him in contempt if the compound is thought of as too luxurious.

There may be situations in which the living conditions are not a matter of choice. A missionary may be called to a remote village where all that is available is a small wooden house or grass hut. There may be other fields which are so extremely dangerous that not only is a walled compound necessary, armed guards may be needed for protection.

For the vast majority of missionaries, the housing situation will lie somewhere in between these two extremes. A missionary must take care not to be distant, however, he should also provide for the comfort and wellbeing of his family when it is possible. As he makes a home on the mission field, it should be a place of rest a repose for him, not in opulence, but rather in simple comfort. Each mission field is different, and a missionary must prayerfully consider the ramifications of how his lifestyle will affect his testimony and ministry.

Teaching English as a Second Language

Teaching English as a second language is such a helpful tool for the English-speaking missionary that it deserves special mention. As the international language of commerce and travel, the ability to speak English is highly sought after. Teaching English to foreign nationals can open many doors of opportunity for ministry (Moreau 197). In countries where missionary visas are not easily obtained, a teaching visa may be an alternative option. English classes are an effective way of reaching out into the community with a skill that most every English speaker already possesses. There may be areas in which not everyone is allowed to teach English. Some countries may require a teaching certificate or a certification in TESOL (Teaching English to Speakers of Other Languages). Though a teaching certificate would require a four-year degree in education, the TESOL certification can be obtained in six weeks or less. Many missionaries use the Bible in their English lessons, using this tool to spread the Word of God.

Missionary Kids on the Foreign Field

Missionaries with children who will be living with them on the field must take into consideration the physical and emotional needs of their families. The culture shock and cultural stress of moving to a foreign field will affect children as well as adults. Children seem to be more resilient to change, but parents must be aware of the issues that will inevitably arise from this extreme life change. They will be leaving their friends, extended family, church, and school behind. Missionary kids should be encouraged to participate in the mission work and get involved with the people immediately, making new friends and finding new interests on the field.

Schooling is another major factor to consider. In some places, international schools are available where a child may complete their schooling in their native tongue. In other areas, a missionary might be encouraged to enroll their children into the local school system. Despite the obstacles (such as language barriers) this will thrust missionary kids into the thick of the culture, and will help them integrate into society much more quickly than most adults. Other missionaries may choose to homeschool. Homeschooling is the favored choice of most missionaries because of its flexibility of schedule. The missionary life is often unpredictable and filled with constant travel. Homeschooling offers the flexibility to pick up and move at any time, and teach a parent-selected Christian curriculum. Plus, when it comes time for deputation and furlough, missionary kids can homeschool on the road. Nonetheless, homeschooling requires commitment and discipline to maintain the standards of a proper education for missionary kids.

Hospitals, Medication and Diseases

Healthcare is always a major concern, especially with missionaries or their family members who have special medical needs. To that end, a survey trip should include a visit to local hospitals and medical facilities to see what is available and what is not. Most hospitals and doctor's offices in third-world countries are sub-standard in sanitation and equipment. An unsanitary medical facility should be used only under extreme caution. Insurance coverage overseas should also be researched. Many companies who provide excellent coverage in America do not provide coverage for someone while they are in a different country.

Most countries outside of the United States do not regulate pharmaceuticals in the same rigid manner as America, and pharmacies will gladly sell any item. Because of this, a missionary should have access to a *Physician's Desk Reference* manual or similar reference to help self-diagnose and medicate in the absence of a doctor or adequate medical facility. First aid and CPR techniques should be in every missionary's arsenal of knowledge.

Mental and Emotional Health

Because of the high rate of missionary attrition and the negative effects of cultural stress, sending churches may find it useful to evaluate a prospective missionary for not only spiritual knowledge and skills, but also mental health. Many people with past emotional and mental health issues find that problems will resurface and become much more intense when faced with the stress and anxiety of a foreign field. Though most missionary sending agencies test their candidates for mental health issues, local churches are ill equipped for this type of evaluation. There are however, several self-guided personal inventories that can be used as rudimentary evaluations of personality and mental health to assess the need for a more professional level of help and counsel. Some of these tests include:

A wonderful resource for a variety of missionary issues are the brochures and books of Dr. Ron Koteskey available for free online at *missionarycare.com*. Dr. Koteskey addresses dozens of topics ranging from interpersonal relationships to mental health.

Another issue that can affect the success of a missionary is marital problems. If a couple is suffering from marriage issues before moving

> **PERSONALITY ASSESSMENTS:**
>
> The Minnesota Multiphasic Personality Inventory
>
> The Sixteen Personality Factor Questionnaire
>
> The Myers-Briggs Type Indicator
>
> The Four Temperaments Test

Figure 33. *Personality Assessment Tests*

> **MENTAL HEALTH SCREENING ASSESSMENTS**
>
> - Depression
> - Anxiety
> - Bipolar disorder
> - Post-traumatic stress disorder
> - Psychosis
> - Eating disorders
> - Substance abuse

Figure 34. *Disorders assessed in mental health screening*

to the field, this could be an indicator of more serious problems that may arise once on the foreign field. Though no marriage is without its occasional problems, any serious marital issues should be resolved before moving to the field. A good place to start would be the administration of the "Marital Satisfaction Inventory" or "MSI," to evaluate any issues a couple may be having. Whatever the problem, whether it be marital, psychological, or even physical, the adverse effects of the transition to a foreign environment will take its toll, and the problems are often magnified exponentially.

Compassion Fatigue

Most missionaries, given enough time on the mission field, will experience a type of burnout termed "compassion fatigue" (Koteskey). Compassion fatigue is "a deep physical, emotional and spiritual exhaustion accompanied by acute emotional pain." Mission work is a very demanding enterprise, and a missionary is often required to give of himself to the point of personal emptiness. A missionary may be physically exhausted from labor, and yet rest does little to refresh him. He may be emotionally exhausted as he is constantly giving to others and never receiving anything in return. He may also be spiritually exhausted as he pours his soul out to others yet feels empty even when there are spiritual successes. Compassion fatigue is a common problem in almost all service industries. Workers are driven to the point of exhaustion until they feel they have nothing left to give. Unfortunately, in the case of a missionary, the demands are unceasing. As Christ pointed out to His disciples, "ye have the poor with you always" (Mark 14:7), there will always be those in need that come to a missionary with demands and wants. Compassion fatigue can also result from a lack of time to accomplish all that is demanded from a missionary. When this occurs, the exhaustion felt by a missionary can often turn into apathy, resentment, bitterness, and even hatred towards the people to whom he is ministering. Numbers 11:14-15 is a prime Biblical example of compassion fatigue as felt by Moses.

> *"I am not able to bear all this people alone, because it is too heavy for me. And if thou deal thus with me, kill me, I pray thee, out of hand, if I have found favour in thy sight; and let me not see my wretchedness."*

The following two verses speak of God's answer to the issue that Moses faced. As Moses was overwhelmed with responsibility,

> *"the LORD said unto Moses, Gather unto me seventy men of the elders of Israel, whom thou knowest to be the elders of the people, and officers over them; and*

bring them unto the tabernacle of the congregation, that they may stand there with thee. And I will come down and talk with thee there: and I will take of the spirit which is upon thee, and will put it upon them; and they shall bear the burden of the people with thee, that thou bear it not thyself alone" (Num. 11:16-17).

Though asking for God to kill him was not the correct response, Moses did the right thing in coming to the Lord for help. A missionary facing compassion fatigue would be wise to go to the Lord with this problem (and every other issue). The Lord told Moses to gather other responsible men and delegate the burden

---

FINDING A LOVE FOR SOULS

John 4:35 "Say not ye, There are yet four months, and then cometh harvest? Behold, I say unto you, Lift up your eyes, and look on the fields; for they are white already to harvest."

One of the hardest tasks I've had to face in the ministry, one that frankly I'm ashamed of, was finding love in my heart for other people in the world. Enough love, that is, to get up and try to do something to help those people. Sometimes we may feel like Jonah when he didn't want to share the gospel with the Ninevites because he felt they didn't deserve it. The fact of the matter is that no matter what our feelings may be towards others, God still loves them. Truthfully, it is because of God's love that we are sent, not because of our own. In our hearts, there is no true love... not without God. You must let your life be saturated and controlled by the love of God. Then, as you go, you will find that God's love for people will become your love for people.

Figure 35. *Missionary Insights: Finding a Love for Souls*

to them, so that they could help him bear the load. A missionary is not an island unto himself. He is merely a small part of the overall plan of God. If he comes to this realization, he will not be overwhelmed in trying to do everything, all the time.

Intervention Strategies

There are several intervention strategies in emotional and psychological issues dealing with grief, depression, loneliness, anxiety, stress, anger, guilt, etc. Every missionary will at some time deal with each of these, however, if they persist, it could be an indicator of a more fundamental problem. A constant struggle with multiple emotional issues on the mission field could be a sign that there is a spiritual problem in the relationship of the missionary and the Lord. This is easily remedied by a penitent heart, time in the Word, and prayer. However, not all mental and emotional issues are caused by spiritual problems, and a missionary with this mindset may hurt himself or others by denying the proper care that he needs.

Depression, anxiety, and many other psychological problems can be caused by chemical or physiological factors. A hormonal imbalance, illness, medicines, and many other factors can be to blame. Treatment can be as simple as changing sleep habits or taking medication. The Word of God also has much to say about these types of problems. Second Timothy 1:7 states, "For God hath not given us the spirit of fear; but of power, and of love, and of a sound mind." One thing that the child of God must not do is to blame the Lord for unsoundness in the mind. These emotional and psychological issues do not come from the Lord. When someone is faced with unsound thoughts or feelings, it is good to remember the advice of the apostle Paul who admonished the Philippians to think upon good things,

> *"Finally, brethren, whatsoever things are true, whatsoever things are honest, whatsoever things are just, whatsoever things are pure, whatsoever things*

are lovely, whatsoever things are of good report; if there be any virtue, and if there be any praise, think on these things" (Phil. 4:8).

Furlough and Reverse Culture Shock

Furlough, or returning temporarily to the home country of the missionary, is a necessary part of mission work for several reasons. First, there is a Biblical precedent to give account of the mission work to the sending church (Acts 14:26-28), and also to other churches (Acts 15:3-4). Secondly, missionaries need a time of physical, emotional, and spiritual refreshing. If the mission field can be compared to the front lines of battle, no commander would constantly keep his soldiers at the battle front without reinforcement and relief. Even Christ Himself instructed His disciples to come apart from the coming and going of the ministry to rest in Mark 6:31. "And he said unto them, Come ye yourselves apart into a desert place, and rest a while: for there were many coming and going, and they had no leisure so much as to eat." With the aforementioned issues of cultural stress, compassion fatigue and so many other obstacles on the field that seem almost insurmountable, furlough is more than a privilege to enjoy, it is a necessity.

When a missionary reenters his home country, he may experience what is called "reverse culture shock." Though it sounds strange, he is really experiencing culture shock, except directed toward his home country (Elmer, Cross-Cultural Connections 194). Spending years on the mission field, a missionary experiences many changes in his attitudes, behavior and though processes. He is a different person than when he left. This change is inevitable, and must occur for a missionary to cope with and navigate a foreign culture. However, when returning to his native culture, he expects that everything has continued just as he left it. The truth is much different. Life in that country has continued without him. Not only has he changed, but the people that he left have changed also. Relationships are sometimes harder to pick back up where they left off because of these changes. Missionaries come back excited to share stories of their life on the field. Yet, he soon finds that his experiences aren't met with the same excitement. People "back home" can't understand or relate to his life in a foreign culture that they have never experienced. A missionary may feel as if he is in a "time warp," having missed out on years of experiences and changes in the land that he has left. He can instantly see changes that, to the people there, have been gradual, yet to him seem drastic. Most commonly, missionaries are shocked at the change in values in society at large, opulence and waste in American society after being abroad, and the pace of life which is much different than that which they have become accustomed. Both mental and spiritual preparation for these challenges can help alleviate the intensity of the effects of reverse culture shock.

Evangelistic Strategies in Mission Work

As a missionary enters a new field, he must consider how to reach people for Christ. A basic knowledge of how to simply share the gospel is essential. Anyone who has professed their trust in Christ should be able to lead another person to the Lord. A commonly used method is sharing the Roman Road of salvation, using verses from the book of Romans to lead a person to the knowledge of the gospel, or simply quoting a passage such as John 3:16 or Ephesians 2:8,9. In non-Christian cultures, the presentation of the gospel may need to be prefaced with a preliminary education of God, the Bible, and the person of Jesus Christ. There are many regions which have never been exposed to even the name of Christ, or, if they have heard, have a distorted idea of who Jesus is. In parts of Buddhist controlled Asia for instance, villagers confessed that they have heard the name "Jesus" mentioned, but thought that it was the name foreigners gave to Buddha. In the Buddhist religion, as well as others, there is no concept of a Creator or an all-powerful God. In these areas, the message of the gospel cannot be fully

Methods of Evangelism

- **House to House Evangelism**
- **Public Preaching Evangelism**
- **Media Distribution**
- **Relationship Evangelism**
- **Meeting or Group Evangelism**
- **Intercessory Evangelism**

Figure 36. *Six Methods of Missionary Evangelism*

understood until the fundamental concepts of the existence of God, creation, and the fall of man are explained. The knowledge of the Buddhist worldview helps a missionary avoid the mistake of where to begin. Following the leading of the Spirit will help in discerning who to speak to and what to say. In this particular case, a missionary must begin in the first chapter of Genesis.

There are many different methods of evangelism that a missionary may employ, based upon his situation and the opportunities afforded him. For instance, he may practice **house to house evangelism** in which he goes from door to door speaking directly to people in their homes. This is an effective form of evangelism if it is permitted. In some fields, it is dangerous or even illegal to solicit door to door. Another method is **public preaching evangelism**. If it is permitted, missionaries may draw great crowds of curious onlookers to hear what the foreigner has to say. **Media distribution** is a form of non-confrontational evangelism in which gospel tracts, leaflets, brochures, and other printed material is distributed. The positive side of media distribution is that very large audiences can be contacted. Statistically, however, very few converts are made though printed media alone. Jews for Jesus reported statistics showing that responses indicating more interest in gospel tracts ranged between 0.25% and 0.6%. There must be follow up with personal contact. The Bible states that "Faith cometh by hearing, and hearing by

A Lesson Learned

Luke 14:23 And the lord said unto the servant, Go out into the highways and hedges, and compel them to come in, that my house may be filled.

I felt like kicking myself. You see... it rained. It rained hard. I ran a route to pick up kids for church in our pickup truck. A few could sit up front, but most had to sit in the back. I would average 25-30 kids, and once I had 55 in my truck at once! Not many wanted to get wet that day, but for those who were in the back of the truck ready to come to church, I wanted to hurry back so they wouldn't get too wet. Most of the kids lived in the communities and villages close to the church, but there was one girl who lived 16 kilometers away. Her house was down a rough dirt road that I knew would be a muddy mess from the rain. As I drove along, I thought to myself, "She doesn't even come all the time... and I need to think about the other kids. They're getting soaked back there. I'll go out to her village this evening, but not now. Not during this storm." So, I did go... that evening. When she got into the truck she said, "Bro. Danny, where were you this morning? I had invited lots of people from my village to come to church, and there was a big crowd waiting for hours for you to come pick us up, but you never came. We waited in the rain for you." The other villagers never came back. We can always find excuses for not doing what we ought to, but in the battle for souls, unfaithfulness comes with a price.

Figure 37. *Missionary Insights: A Lesson Learned*

the word of God" (Romans 10:17). Yet, three verses prior it also proclaims, "How shall they hear without a preacher?" Another form of evangelism is known as **relationship evangelism**. In many closed countries where the gospel cannot be preached freely and openly, it may be necessary for a missionary to form strong bonds of relationships with individuals before they will be allowed to speak (often behind closed doors) of the gospel message of Jesus Christ. The next form of evangelism that a missionary can employ is that of **meeting or group evangelism**. This is often the standard method of sharing the gospel on the mission field as a missionary gathers a small group for a Bible study or church meeting, whether in a home or at a church facility. Many churches will begin in this manner. The last form of evangelism is known as **intercessory evangelism**, or simply, prayer for souls. There will always be instances where a missionary is incapable of reaching out to an individual on a personal basis. Fortunately, there is no soul that is out of the reach of God. A missionary must bathe all his efforts in prayer, and remember that it is the Lord who saves; it is the Spirit that convicts; it is Christ who promised to draw all men unto Him. There is power in prayer, and a faithful, praying missionary is an effective missionary.

Autonomous, Reproducible Churches

The goal of a missionary is to plant autonomous churches on the field with reproducible methods. "And the things that thou hast heard of me among many witnesses, the same commit thou to faithful men, who shall be able to teach others also" (2 Timothy 2:2). The struggle for most missionaries is the balance between helping the nationals and allowing them to grow on their own. After much research, Bible study, years of practical experience, and discussions with other cross-cultural missionaries, I have personally concluded that the most Biblically based, reproducible, and practically reliable method of autonomous church planting is this: *a missionary must remain an itinerant discipler of new church leaders.* He should not get involved in pastoring the local church plants personally, but rather ordain local leaders to hold that position. Though in some circumstances it is necessary to hold that position temporarily, there is a significant difference in a pastor and the Biblical role of the missionary. When a missionary assumes a long-term role of the pastorate, he does himself and the church a disservice. The local congregation will learn to rely on the missionary rather than assert themselves to serve the Lord personally. A missionary must also take care not to employ nationals in church work for monetary gain. If he gives a salary to the nationals, they will learn to rely upon foreign dollars rather than give to the Lord personally.

> ## Depend on the Lord, Not the Missionary
>
> Here is a personal story of how easy it is for people to become dependent on the missionary: Each Sunday, I would visit several villages and pick up people for church, which was built in a central location. Each person had their own transportation, but they became used to me coming by and giving them a ride to church. Sometimes, over fifty people would pile into my small Ford Ranger pickup truck, hanging onto bars attached to the sides and back, and even some climbing on top of the cab. On the Sundays that I was out of town, no one would come to church. Even though they had personal and public transportation available, they wouldn't come on their own. They came to rely on something that I did for them that they could easily do themselves. I'm not saying to never pick people up for church. The point here is that every aspect of ministry on the mission field should be to direct the local population to continue serving the Lord in the absence of the missionary. In other words, a missionary's job is not to pastor and perform church work on the field, but to disciple others to pastor and perform church work on the field. He must balance a watchful eye over the ministry as he leads in spiritual things with the autonomy of the local congregations. A missionary's job is to teach others to depend upon the Lord, not on the missionary.

Figure 38. *Missionary Insights: Depend on the Lord, Not the Missionary*

A missionary should develop a personal strategy for church planting and evangelism in his target culture by utilizing reproducible church planting strategies and methodology. The role of the missionary is a diminishing one in a church plant; he should work himself out of the job (Hodges 41). Any strategy that is employed should seek to achieve the goal of self-supporting, self-governing, and self-propagating local churches (Terry and Payne 104).

It is my prayer that men seeking to serve the Lord on the mission field will take these Biblical principles and historical examples of faith to serve the Lord by propagating the gospel of Jesus Christ to all the world, and to every creature!

> *"The grace of the Lord Jesus Christ, and the love of God, and the communion of the Holy Ghost, be with you all. Amen" (2 Corinthians 13:14).*

Danny S. Jones
Missionary to Thailand

Bibliography

"Mission." Merriam-Webster.com. April 2017.

.ed, Saint Jude. "About Saint Jude, Shrine of St. Jude Thaddeus, San Francisco, Ca." Stjude-shrine.org (2016).

"A Brief Memoir of the Rev. Adoniram Judson." Baptist Magazine 1830.

Abrams III, Cooper P. The Translation of the Greek Word "Ekklesia" as "church" in the English Bible, and the use of the Term "the church" and its Ramifications. 2017. 5 April 2017.

Adeney, W.F. The Greek and Eastern Churches. Edinburgh: T & T Clark, 1908.

Adlam, S. The First Baptist Church in America. Memphis: Southern Baptist Book House, 1890.

AggressiveChristianity.net. The Correct Meaning of "Church" and "Ecclesia". 2017. 5 April 2017.

Allen, Roland. Missionary Methods: St. Paul's or Ours. Dallas: Gideon House Books, 2016.

Anderson, Courtney. To the Golden Shore: The Life of Adoniram Judson. Valley Forge: Judson Press, 1956.

Ashcraft, Robert. "Educational Perspective." Missionary Baptist Perspectives. Texarkana: Bogard Press, 1984.

Ashford, Bruce Riley. Theology and Practice of Mission. Nashville: B&H Publishing Group, 2011.

Barnes, Albert. Barnes Notes on the New Testament: Hebrews. Grand Rapids: Baker Books, 2005.

Barnes, Timothy D. Constantine and Eusebius. Cambridge: Harvard University Press, 1981.

—. "Legislation Against the Christians." Journal of Roman Studies, Vol. 58 (1968).

Barnett, Betty. Friend Raising. Seattle: YWAM Publishing, 1991.

Barnett, Mike. Discovering the Mission of God. Downers Grove: Intervarsity Press, 2012.

Barrett, David. World Christian Encyclopedia. Oxford: Oxford University Press, 1982.

Bazar, Kenneth. The Biblical Basis of the American Baptist Association Fellowship. Texarkana: Bogard Press, 1985.

Bechtel, Florentine. "The Brethren of the Lord." The Catholic Encyclopedia. Vol. 2. (1907).

Belcher, Joseph. The Religious Denominations in the United States: Their History, Doctrine, Government and Statistics. Indianapolis: Spicer & Roll, 1857.

Binns, John. An Introduction to the Christian Orthodox Churches. Cambridge: Cambridge University Press, 2002.

Bogard, Ben M. Associations Are Scriptural. Texarkana: Bogard Press, 1971.

—. Pillars of Orthodoxy. Louisville: Baptist Book Concern, 1900.
—. The Baptist Way Book. Texarkana: Bogard Press, 1946.

Bosch, David J. Transforming Mission. Maryknoll: Orbis Books, 1991.

Bounds, E.M. E.M. Bounds on Prayer. Peabody: Hendrickson Publishers, Inc., 2006.

Bowman, Alan K. The Cambridge Ancient History, Vol. XII. Cambridge: Cambridge University Press, 2005.

Brackney, William H. Baptists in North America. Hoboken: Blackwell Publishing, 2006.

Britannica, ed. Encyclopædia. "Nestorius." Encyclopædia Britannica (2006).

—. "Saint Judas." Encyclopædia Britannica (2008).

Brock, Sebastian. "Bardaisan." Gorgias Encyclopedic Dictionary of Syriac Heritage (2011).

Bromiley, Geoffrey. The International Standard Bible Encyclopedia. Vol. 1. Grand Rapids: Eerdmans Publishing Co., 1979.

Brooks, Dr. Ray O. "Scriptural Church Association." A.J. Kirkland Memorial Lectures. 6-9 December 1983.

Brown, Colin. The New International Dictionary of New Testament Theology. 3 vols. Grand Rapids: Zondervan, 1979.

Brownlee, William Craig. Saint Patrick and the Western Apostolic Churches: Or, The Religion of the Ancient Britains and Irish Not Roman Catholic, and the Antiquity, Tenets and Sufferings of the Albigenses and Waldenses. New York: American and Foreign Christian Union, 1857.

Burnett, David. Clash of Worlds: What Christians Can Do in a World of Cultures in Conflict. London: Monarch Publishers, 2002.

Byrnes IV, William H. "Ancient Roman Munificence: The Development of the Practice and Law of Charity." Rutgers Law Review vol. 57, issue 3 (2005): 1043-1110.

Camden, William. "Romans in Britaine." Britannia (1605).

Canfield, Leon H. "The Early Persecutions of the Christians." The Lawbook Exchange (2005): 86-99.

Cantor, Norman F. The Civilization of the Middle Ages: A Completely Revised and Expanded Edition of Medieval History. New York: Harper Perennial, 1994.

Cardoza-Orlandi, Carlos F. Mission: an Essential Guide. Nashville: Abingdon Press, 2002.

Carey, William. An Enquiry into the Obligations of Christians to Use Means for the Conversion of the Heathens. Leicester: Ann Ireland, 1792.

Carpenter, John. "New England Puritans: The Grandparents of Modern Protestant Missions." Fides et Historia (2002).

Carroll, J.M. The Trail of Blood. Lexington: Ashland Avenue Baptist Church, 1931.

Chapman, John. "Doctrine of Addai." The Catholic Encyclopedia. Vol. 5 (1909).

Christian, John T. A History of the Baptists Vol. I & II. Texarkana: Bogard Press, 1922.

Clarke, Adam. Adam Clarke's Commentary on the Bible. Nashville: Abingdon Press, 1966.

Clark, Henry B. Freedom of Religion in America: Historical Roots, Philosophical Concepts, Contemporary Problems. Piscataway: Transaction Publishers, 1982.

Coleman, Lyman. The Antiquities of the Christian Church. New York: Baker and Scribner, 1846.

Cooper, Robert. Culture Shock! Thailand. Marshall Cavendish: Singapore, 2005.

Crawford, T.P. Churches to the Front. Benton: Landmark Media Production, 1892.

Cross, I.K. Landmarkism: An Update. Texarkana: Bogard Press, 1984.

—. The Commission: Its Authority and Responsibility. Texarkana: Bogard Press, 1974.

—. The Truth About Conventionism. Little Rock: Seminary Press, 1955.

Culbertson, Howard. Nothing Left but the Covers. 21 January 2013. <http://engagemagazine.com/content/nothing-left-covers>.

Dearmore, Roy F. Biblical Missions. Garland: Rodgers Baptist Church, 1997.

Dewey, Bill. Why I Left the Southern Baptist Convention. n. p., 1979.

Dickens, Mark. Church of the East Timeline. 2010. 5 April 2017.

Dictionary, Merriam Webster. "Catholic." n.d. Merriam Webster. 5 April 2017.

Dvornik, Francis. The Idea of Apostolicity in Byzantium and the Legend of the Apostle Andrew. Cambridge: Harvard University Press, 1958. Dumbarton Oaks Studies, IV.

Ehler, Sidney Zdeneck. Church and State Through the Centuries: A Collection of Historic Documents with Commentaries. New York: Biblo & Tannen Publishers, 1967.

Elmer, Duane. Cross-Cultural Conflict. Downers Grove: Intervarsity Press, 1993.

—. Cross-Cultural Connections. Downers Grove: Intervarsity Press, 2002.

—. Cross-Cultural Servanthood. Downers Grove: Intervarsity Press, 2006.

Encyclopedia, World Heritage. "Timeline of Christian missions." World Heritage Encyclopedia (2002).

Eusebius, of Pamphilius. "The Life of Constantine." Shaff, Philip. Post Nicene Fathers. New York: Cosimo Classics, 2007.

Fahlbusch, Erwin. The Encyclopedia of Christianity, Volume 5. Grand Rapids: Wm. B. Eerdmans Publishing, 2008.

Fann, Ann-Geri'. How to Get Ready for Short-Term Missions. Nashville: Nelson Publishers, 2006.

Farmer, David Hugh. The Oxford Dictionary of Saints (5 rev. ed.). Oxford: Oxford University Press, 2011.

Fenlon, J.F. "St. Bartholomew." The Catholic Encyclopedia (1907).

Ferrar, W.J. The Proof of the Gospel: Being the Demonstratio Evangelica of Eusebius of Caesarea. New York: The Macmillan Company, 1920.

Ford, S.H. The Origin of the Baptists. Texarkana: Bogard Press, 1950.

Foreman, L.D. and Payne, Alta. The Life and Works of Benjamin Marcus Bogard Vol. I. Little Rock: Seminary Press, 1965.

Foreman, L.D. Credenda. Little Rock: Seminary Press, 1950.

Frend, W.H.C. The Early Church. London: Hodder And Stoughton, 1982.

—. The Rise of Christianity. Philadelphia: Fortress Press, 1984.

Frend, William H.C. Martyrdom and Persecution in the Early Church. 2008: James Clarke & Co, Cambridge.

Galli, Mark. 131 Christians Everyone Should Know. Nashville: Holman , 2000.

Gardner, Austin and Howeth, Tony. The Deputation Manual for Missionaries. Alpharetta: Our Generation, 2006.

Gavila, Philip. "Biblical Basis of Missions in the New Testament." Winter Haven: Westwood School of Missions, 25 October 2016. Class Lecture.

Glover, Conrad N. and Powers, Austin T. The American Baptist Association 1924-1974. Texarkana: Bogard Press, 1979.

Glover, Robert H. The Progress of World-Wide Missions. New York: Harper and Row, 1960.

Gonzalez, Justo L. The Story of Christianity Vol. 2: The Reformation to the Present Day. Grand Rapids: Zondervan, 2010.

Goodsell, Fred Field. You Shall be my Witnesses. Boston : American Board of Commissioners for Foreign Missions, 1959.

GotQuestions.org. What is Landmarkism? What is "Baptist Bride" theology? 2017. 5 April 2017.

Graves, J.R. Old Landmarkism: What is It? . Texarkana: Baptist Sunday School Committee, 1880.

Greene, H. Leon. A Guide to Short Term Missions. Waynesboro: Gabriel Publishing, 2003.

Gregory, John Milton. The Seven Laws of Teaching. Grand Rapids: Baker Books, 1884.

Harbus, Antonia. Helena of Britain in Medieval Legend. Rochester: D.S. Brewer, 2002.

Harper, Douglas. "Church" etymonline.com. 2017. 5 April 2017.

Herbermann, Charles George. The Catholic Encyclopedia. New York: The Encyclopedia Press, 1913.

Herbermann, Charles, ed. "St. Matthew." The Catholic Encyclopedia (1913).

Hervey, George Winfred. The Story of Baptist Missions in Foreign Lands. St. Louis: Chancy R. Barns, 1884.

Hesselgrave, David J. Planting Churches Cross Culturally: North America and Beyond. Grand Rapids: Baker Books, 2000.

Hildinger, Erik. Warriors of the Steppe: A Military History of Central Asia, 500 B.C. to 1700 A.D. Cambridge: Da Capo Press, 1997.

Hiscox, Edward. The Baptist Church Directory. New York: Sheldon & Company, 1859.

Hisel, Berlin. "Baptist History Notebook." Winter Haven: Baptist Training Center Publications, 2017.

Hodges, Melvin L. The Indigenous Church. Springfield: Gospel Publishing House, 2009.

Hoke, Steve and Taylor, Bill. Global Missions Handbook. Downers Grove, IL: Intervarsity Press, 2009.

Hovey, Alvah. An American commentary on the New Testament: Issues 13-18. n. c.: n. p., 1890.

Ingram, James. The Saxon Chronicle. London: Longman, Hurst, Rees, Orme, and Brown, 1823.

Iverson, Dick. Team Ministry. Portland: City Bible Publishing, 1984.

Jackson, D.N., Bogard, B.M., Ballard, L.S., Matheny, M.P. Conventionism Refuted: An Appeal to Baptist Orthodoxy in Faith and Practice. Texarkana: Baptist Sunday School Committee, 1927.

Jerome. The Perpetual Virginity of Blessed Mary Fragment 15. n.d. 5 April 2017.

JewsforJesus.com. Summer Campaign Statistics. 1 September 1993. 5 April 2017.

Johnstone, Patrick and Jason Mandryk. Operation World. Tyrone, GA: Authentic Media, 2006.

Jones, Danny S. "Westwood School of Missions Catalog 2015-2016." College Catalog. Winter Haven: Westwood Missionary Baptist Church, 2015.

Joseph Jr, Ken. 十字架の国-日本 [*Jujika no kuni - Nihon*]. Tokyo: Tokuma Shoten, 2000.

Josephus, Flavius. Josephus: The Complete Works. Nashville: Thomas Nelson Publishers, 1998.

joshuaproject.net. April 2017. Frontier Ventures.

Kaiser Jr. , Walter C. Mission in the Old Testament. Grand Rapids: Baker Academic, 2012.

Kline, A. S. Suetonius: The Twelve Caesars. Poetry In Translation, 2010.

Koteskey, Ronald L. What Missionaries Ought to Know... A Handbook for Life and Service . Wilmore: New Hope International Ministries, 2015.

Lambert, Malcolm. Medieval Heresy: Popular Movements from Bogomil to Hus. London: Edward Arnold Publishers Ltd., 1977.

Lanier, Sarah, A. Foreign to Familiar. Hagerstown, MD: MacDougal Publishing, 2000.

Lanier, Walter Clyde. "Lectures in Biblical Theology." Brandon, 1997.

Latourette, Kenneth Scott. A History of the Expansion of Christianity. New York: Harper and Brothers Publishers, 1938.

Lederleitner, Mary T. Cross-Cultural Partnerships. Downers Grove: Intervarsity Press, 2010.

Levy, David M. The Tabernacle: Shadows of the Messiah. Bellmawr: The Friends of Israel Gospel Ministry, Inc. , 1993.

—. The Tabernacle: Shadows of the Messiah. Bellmawr: The Friends of Israel Gospel Ministry, Inc., 1993.

Lichtenthal, J. David and Tellefsen, Tomas. "Toward a Theory of Buyer-Seller Similarity." The Journal of Personal Selling and Sales Management 21.1 (2001): 1-14. <http://www.jstor.org/stable/40471807>.

Liddell, H.G. and Scott, Robert. Greek-English Lexicon. Oxford: Oxford University Press, 1935.

Lightfoot, J.B. "The Brethren of the Lord:" Galatians. London. 1865

Lindberg, Carter. A Brief History of Christianity. Somerset: John Wiley & Sons, 2009.

Livermore, David A. Serving With Eyes Wide Open. Grand Rapids: Baker Books, 2006.

Livingstone, F. L. Cross and E. A. The Oxford Dictionary of the Christian Church, 3rd edition. Oxford: Oxford University Press, 1997.

Lyall, Leslie T. A Passion for the Impossible: The Continuing Story of the Mission Hudson Taylor Began. London: OMF Books, 1965.

Maier, Paul L. Eusebius: The Church History. Grand Rapids: Kregel Publications, 1999.

Mason, Roy M. The Church That Jesus Built. Clarksville: Bible Baptist, 1986.

Medlycott, A. E. India and the Apostle St. Thomas. London: Gorgias Press, 1905.

Melton, J. Gordon. "American Baptist Association" The Association of Religious Data Archives. 2009. 5 April 2017.

Moffett, Samuel Hugh. Biographical Dictionary of Christian Missions: "Alopen". Grand Rapids: Eerdmans Publishing Company, 1999.

Moltmann, Jurgen. The Church in the Power of the Spirit: A Contribution to Messianic Ecclesiology. London: SCM Press, 1977.

Moreau, A. Scott. Introducing World Missions: A Biblical, Historical and Practical Survey. Grand Rapids: Baker Academic, 2004.

Morland, Samuel. The History of the Evangelical Churches of the Valleys of Piedmont. London: Henry Hills, 1658.

Mosheim, John Laurence. Mosheim's Ecclesiastical History Ancient and Modern. n. p.: Repressed Publishing LLC, 1849.

Moule, Arthur Christopher. Christians in China Before the Year 1550. London: Society for Promoting Christian Knowledge, 1930.

Nasranis. Mission of Saint Bartholomew, the Apostle in India. April 2017.

Natumewicz, C. F. Freculphus of Lisieux, His Chronicle and a Mont Saint-Michel Manuscript. St. Petersburg: Steenbrugge, 1966.

Neill, Stephen. A History of Christian Missions. London: Penguin Books, 1986.

Nevins, William Manlius. Alien Baptism and the Baptists. Emmaus: Challenge Press, 1977.

of Hierapolis, Papias. Exposition of the Sayings of the Lord. Fragment X. n.d. 5 April 2017.

Olson, C. Gordon. What in the World is God Doing? The Essentials of Global Missions. Cedar Knolls: Global Gospel Publishers, 2003.

Ott, Craig and Gene Wilson. Global Church Planting: Biblical Principles and Best Practices for Multiplication. Grand Rapids: Baker Academic, 2011.

Owen, John E. "Biblical Association." Credenda II. Little Rock: Seminary Publications, 1984.

Pal, Krishna. The First Hindoo Convert: A Memoir of Krishna Pal, a Preacher of the Gospel to His Countrymen More Than Twenty Years. Philadelphia: American Baptist Publication Society, 1852.

Pendleton, J. M. Baptist Church Manual, Revised. Nashville: Broadman Press, 1966.

—. Landmarkism. Carlisle: Landmark Media Productions, 1899.

Pendleton, J.M. Three Reasons why I Am a Baptist. Cincinnati: Moore, Anderson & Company, 1853.

Presler, Titus. Horizon of Mission. Cambridge: Cowley Publications, 2001.

Ray, D.B. Baptist Succession: A Handbook of Baptist History. Cincinnati: Geo. E. Stevens & Co., 1871.

Reed, Roy M. The Glorious Church: Nine Positive Ways to Identify the New Testament Church. Texarkana: Bogard Press, 1955.

Roberts, Alexander. Ante-Nicene Fathers. Vols. 1-10. Peabody: Hendrickson Publishers, 1885. 10 vols.

Robinson. Robinson's Morphological Analysis Codes. n. d. e-Sword Electronic Bible Study Software.

Robinson, Robert. Ecclesiastical Researches. Cambridge: Francis Hodson, 1792.

Rodgers, Alice June. If You're Going on the Mission Field. n. c.: n. p., 2001.

Rogers, James A. Richard Furman: Life and Legacy. Macon: Mercer University Press, 2001.

Ryrie, Charles C. The Ryrie KJV Study Bible. Chicago: Moody Publishers, 2008.

Scarboro, J.A. The Bible, The Baptists, and The Board System. Fulton: J.A. Scarboro, Publisher, 1904.

Schaff, Philip. Ante-Nicene Fathers, Volume 8. Peabody: Hendrickson Publishers, 1885.

Schnabel, Eckhard J. Paul the Missionary: Realities, Strategies and Methods. Downers Grove: IVP Academic, 2008.

Sills, M. David. The Missionary Call. Chicago: Moody Publishers, 2008.

Sire, James. The Universe Next Door. Downers Grove: InterVarsity Press, 2009.

Slapak, Orpa. The Jews of India: A Story of Three Communities. Jerusalem: The Israel Museum, 2003.

Slick, Matt. Christian Apologetics and Research Ministry. April 2017.

Smallwood, E. Mary. "Domitian's Attitude toward the Jews and Judaism." Classical Philology (1956): 1-13.

Smith, George. The Life of William Carey, D.D: Shoemaker and Missionary. Cambridge : Cambridge University Press, 2011.

Spurgeon, C. H. Metropolitan Tabernacle Pulpit. London: The Banner Of Truth Trust, 1888.

Spurgeon, C.H. Lectures to My Students. Grand Rapids: Zondervan Publishers, 1954.

Spurgeon, Charles Haddon. The New Park Street Pulpit, Vol. VII. London: Banner of Truth Trust, 1964.

"St. Cleophas." Catholic Online (2017).

Stokes, G. T. "Novatianus and Novatianism." A Dictionary of Early Christian Biography (1911).

Stravinskas, Peter M. J. The Catholic Answer Book, Volume 1. Huntington: Our Sunday School Publishing Division, 1990.

Strong, James. Strong's Exhaustive Concordance of the Bible. Nashville: Abingdon Press, 1890.

Taylor, William. Too Valuable to Lose: Exploring the Causes and Cures of Missionary Attrition . Singapore: World Evangelical Fellowship, 1997.

Telford, Tom. Missions in the 21st Century. Wheaton: United World Missions, 1998.

Terry, John Mark and J. D. Payne. Developing a Strategy for Missions: A Biblical, Historical, and Cultural Introduction. Grand Rapids: Baker Academic, 2013.

Terry, John Mark; Smith, Ebbie; Anderson, Justice;. Missiology: In Introduction to the Foundations, History and Strategies of World Missions. Nashville: Broadman and Holman Publishers, 1998.

Thayer, J.H. Thayer's Greek Definitions. n. p., 1896. e-Sword Bible study software program.

Towns, Elmer. http://elmertowns.com. 2017. 5 April 2017.

Tozer, A.W. The Pursuit of God. Dallas: Gideon House Books, 2017.

Trimingham, J. Spencer. Christianity among the Arabs in Pre-Islamic Times. London: Longman, 1979.

Tucker, Ruth A. From Jerusalem to Irian Jaya. Grand Rapids: Zondervan, 2004.

Tylor, E.B. Primitive Culture: Researches into the Development of Mythology, Philosophy, Religion, Art, and Custom. New York: Gordon Press, 1871.

Van Rheenen, Gailyn. Missions: Biblical Foundations & Contemporary Strategies. Grand Rapids: Zondervan, 1996.

Vedder, Henry C. A Short History of the Baptists. Valley Forge: Judson Press, 1907.

Vincent, Marvin R. Word Studies in the New Testament. Peabody: Hendrickson, 1887.

Wardin, Albert W. Baptists Around the World: A Comprehensive Handbook. Nashville: Broadman & Holman, 1995.

Webster, Noah. "An American Dictionary of the English Language." "Death". New York: S. Converse, 1828.

Wellman, Sam. William Carey: First Modern Missionary. n. c.: Wild Centuries Press, 2013.

Wesley, John. John Wesley's Explanatory Notes on the Whole Bible. New York: Carlton & Porter, 1754.

Wiio, Osmo. Wiio's Laws - and Some Others. Espoo: Welin-Goos, 1978.

Winter, Ralph D.; Hawthorne, Steven C. Perspectives of the World Christian Movement. Pasadena: William Carey Library, 1981.

Wright, Randal A. Achieving Your Life Mission. Springville: Cedar Fort, Inc., 2009.

Yohannan, K.P. Revolution in World Missions. Carrollton: GFA Books, 2004.

Zahn, T. "John the Apostle." The New Schaff-Herzog Encyclopedia of Religious Knowledge, Vol. VI (1908).

INDEX

A

Abgar 141
ability 31, 100, 190, 201
Abraham 85, 87, 88, 92
adaptability 199
Africa 139, 144, 148, 154, 211
Albie 158
Albigenses 157, 158, 160
Algeria 139
altar of incense 90
American Baptist Association 175
American Board of Commissioners for Foreign Missions 166
Amish 161
Anabaptists 156, 160, 161, 162
Ananias of Damascus 40
Andrew 145
Andronicus 40
anēr 38
antilēmpseis 45
Antioch 40, 41, 43, 44, 62, 64, 144
apoluō 37, 44
apostellō 37, 40
apostle 37, 38, 40, 147
apostolos 37, 40
Arabia 40, 151
ark 84, 85, 91
Arkansas Baptist State Association 175
Armenia 142, 155
Arnoldists 157
Arnold of Brescia 157
Asia 142, 152
assembly 27, 28, 55, 56, 57, 59, 89, 149, 160, 173, 174
Association of Baptists for World Evangelism 178
Assuristan 140
atonement 91
attrition 31, 196
Austria 140
authority 37, 41, 44, 46, 57, 59, 60, 61, 62, 63, 64, 65, 66, 67, 97, 101, 144, 154, 172, 173, 174, 181

B

Bactria 140
baptidzontes 101
baptism 35, 38, 62, 102, 154, 155, 156, 162, 167, 173, 174
Baptist Bible Fellowship International 177, 178
Baptist Evangelistic Missions Association 178
Baptist Faith Missions 178
Baptist International Missions Incorporated 178
Baptist Mid-Missions 178
Baptist Missionary Association of America 176
Baptist Missionary Association of Texas 175
Baptist Missions to Forgotten Peoples 178
Baptist World Mission 178

Barnabas 40, 41, 43, 44, 67, 183
Bartholomew 145
Battle of Milvian Bridge 150
Beza, Theodore 55
Bible study 35, 164, 167
Bishops Bible 56
Bithynia 147
Bob Jones University 178
Bogamils 156
Bogard, Benjamin Marcus 175
Brainerd, David 165
brazen altar 90
brazen laver 90
Britain 140, 141, 166
British-Burmese War 168
Britons 140, 143
Brittany 140
Buddhist 152, 168
Bythinia 139

C

Canaan 85, 87
Carey, Dorothy 165, 197
Carey, Felix 167
Carey, William 164, 166, 197
Catholic 64, 142, 145, 154, 155, 156, 157, 158, 160
Central Missionary Clearinghouse 178
Chaignards 158
Character 191
China 139, 144, 151, 175
Chi-Rho 150
Chlorus 149
church planting 31, 152
Church succession 173
Clarke, John 163
commission 27, 28, 35, 37, 42, 44, 57, 101, 166, 174, 181
communication 193, 204, 205
compassion 32, 99, 200
Confirmation 189
Congregationalist 166
Constantine the Great 143, 150

Constantius 143, 149
Crawford, T. P. 171, 172, 175, 275
Creator 84
cross-cultural 31, 85, 203
cultural 28, 85, 95, 201, 203, 206
Cunctos Populos 142
customs 203

D

Dauphine 158
David 34, 88, 89, 91, 92, 165, 187, 211
death 28, 33, 35, 85, 98, 102, 142, 145, 148, 149, 154, 165, 167, 185, 197
Decius 148, 154
Denys 141
deputation 169, 198
Deruvian 140
didaskō 102
didaskontes 101
Diocletianic persecution 149
Dionysius 141
discipleship 28, 201
doctrine 29, 56, 58, 102, 154, 155, 156, 160, 161, 164, 167, 169, 173, 186, 192
Domitian 146
Donatists 148, 154, 160
Donatus 154
Duvianus 140

E

Ebenezer 208
Edessa 141
Edict of Milan 143
Edict of Thessalonica 142
Edict of Toleration 150
Edwards, Jennie 175
Edwards, Johnathan 165
Egypt 87, 94
eido 99

ekklesia 56
ekklēsiā 55, 56, 57, 59
ekpempō 44
Epaphroditus 40
Ephesus 64
Episcopalians 169
episkopē 38
Esau 87
Ethiopia 145, 152
Eusebius 144, 147, 148, 149, 150
Evangelical Baptist Missions 178
evangelization 28, 102
evangelize 29, 46, 57, 67, 84, 144, 181, 191
executor 63, 101
Exodus 87, 94, 186
exousia 60

F

Fairfax Baptist Temple Missions 178
faith 15, 28, 29, 46, 62, 87, 90, 141, 143, 149, 150, 156, 157, 158, 162, 173, 174, 185, 193, 198, 207, 208, 211, 212
Faithway Baptists 177
Father 61, 83, 96, 97, 98, 99, 101, 103, 164
Firth of Forth 141
Flavia Domitilla 147
Flavius Clemens 147
France 140, 147, 156
Fuganus 140

G

Galerius 149
Gaul 139
Gazares 160
General Association of Baptist Churches 175
General Missionary Convention of the Baptist Denomination 169
Gentile 90, 94, 95
Gnosticism 156
golden lampstand 90
Gospel Mission movement 172, 177
Graves, J.R. 171
Great Bible 56
Great Commission 16, 28, 36, 41, 42, 59, 61, 65, 66, 84, 93, 101, 139, 165, 181, 209
Gregory Thaumaturgus 142

H

Hadrian 141, 147
Hadrians Wall 141
Hall, Gordon 166
Hardshell Baptists 171
Helena 143
hell 60, 85, 99, 161, 195, 211
Henricians 157
Henry of Lausanne 157
Hephthalite Huns 151
Hesselgrave 29, 46
Hibernia 141
hierarchy 43, 59, 64, 66, 142, 156, 174
hilastērion 91
Himyarites 152
Holy Spirit 29, 41, 43, 44, 45, 61, 91, 97, 98, 182, 183, 184, 191, 209
humanity 28, 95, 99
Hyles-Anderson College 178
Hyppolytus 148

I

Independent Baptist Fellowship International 178
India 140, 144, 151, 165, 166

International Baptist Missions 178
International Mission Board 171
Interstate and Foreign Missionary Baptist Associational Assembly of America 176
Ireland 141
Israel 87, 88, 89, 90, 92, 94, 95, 186
Italy 142

J

Jackson, Doss Nathan 175
Jacob 87, 95
James 29, 33, 36, 40, 56, 145, 165, 199, 200
Japan 151, 154
Jerusalem 87, 88, 89, 103, 143, 146, 161
Jewish 140, 146, 151, 175
Jewish Himyarites 151
Jews 146, 175
John Mark 196
John the Baptist 38, 40, 145
Jonah 94
Jonah syndrome 95
Joshua 32, 85, 87, 209
Joshua Project 32
Judas 38, 61
judgment 57, 83, 84, 97
Judson, Adoniram 166, 169
Junia 40
Jureidini, S.M. 175
Justin Martyr 147

K

knowledge 15, 16, 17, 31, 55, 85, 89, 186, 191, 199, 203, 205, 207
Korea 154
Kublai Khan 152
Kungyueh 141

kyriakon 56

L

Landmark Baptists 172, 175
Landmarkism 42, 171, 172
language learning 199, 201
leadership 42, 67
Liberty University 178
local New Testament church 28, 38, 42
Lollards 158
London Missionary Society 166
love 34, 95, 96, 186, 188, 200
Lucius 140
Lyon 140

M

Macedonia 42
Macedonia World Baptist Missions 178
Mandalay 168
Manichean 156
Maranatha Baptist Missions 178
Marco Polo 152
Marcus Aurelius 147
mathayteusatay 101
Matthew 28, 32, 56, 61, 64, 91, 97, 101, 145, 184, 200, 209, 210
Matthews Bible 56
Maximinus the Thracian 148
Mediterranean 95
Melchezidek 87
Mennonites 161
mercy-seat 91
Messianic 92
Methodists 169
methodology 27, 29, 31
Ming dynasty 152
missio Dei 35, 97
Missiology 27, 47, 57
Missionary Baptist 171, 192
mission board 42, 166, 174

Mongolia 144, 151
Morocco 140
Moses 87, 94, 186
Munger, M.M. 175

N

Najranian Arabs 151
Nero 146
Nestorians 144
Newell, Samuel 166
Nicolaitans 142
Nineveh 94
Noah 84, 85
North American Mission Board 171
Northern Baptist Convention 177
Nott, Samuel 166
Novatians 154, 160
Novatianus 154

O

obedience 85, 186
Old Line Baptists 171

P

Pandateria 147
para-church 42, 44, 62
Paris 141
Parisii 141
Parthia 140
Particular Baptist 164
Pataenus of Alexandria 140
Paul 28, 40, 41, 43, 44, 62, 67, 145, 155, 185, 186, 192, 197
Paulicians 155, 156, 157, 160
pedobaptism 156, 157, 167, 171, 173
pempō 37
Pendleton, J.M. 63
Pensacola Christian College 178
Pentecost 61
Persia 144, 175
Peter 60, 84, 85, 145, 156, 157, 158, 165
Peter de Bruys 157
Petrobrussians 156, 157
Phagan 140
Philip 145
Pictland 141
Pontian 148
Pontus 142
poreuthentes 101
Powell, C.R. 175
preach 36, 38, 42, 83, 94, 102, 158, 195, 200, 206
preaching 35, 44, 85, 95, 169, 173, 201
Premillennial Missionary Baptist Fellowship 177
Presbyterians 169
Primitive Baptists 171
Principle of Gods Power 212
Principle of Gods Presence 208
Principle of Gods Protection 210
Principle of Gods Provision 209
Principle of the Faithful Servant 182
Principle of the Sacrificial Servant 184
Principle of the Seeking Servant 183
Principle of the Willing Servant 186
prophetic 92, 93
propitiation 91
propitiatory 91
Protestant 59, 156, 162
Puritans 163

Q

qualifications 39, 189, 190, 196, 206

R

redemption 35, 94, 97
ReMAP 31
Rice, Luther 166, 169
Richard Furman 169
righteousness 84, 85, 89, 94, 97, 186, 203
ripto 100
Roger Williams 163
Roman Empire 142, 148, 150
Rome 140, 141, 142, 145, 147, 148, 149, 154, 155, 161

S

salvation 35, 62, 83, 88, 89, 90, 94, 95, 99, 102, 156, 157, 164, 167, 173, 187, 206
Samaria 95, 103
Sardinia 148
Savior 35, 39, 44, 62, 96, 145
Scarboro, J.A. 175
Scotland 141
Second Great Awakening 172
Senones 141
separation 98
servanthood 206
servants attitude 198
Shepherd of Hermas 139
Siccars 160
Silas 40
sin 28, 32, 34, 83, 90, 97, 99, 100, 186, 196
Solomon 89, 187
Son 61, 66, 83, 96, 97, 98, 99, 101, 139, 155
Southern Baptist 171, 172, 271, 275
Southern Baptist Convention 171, 172, 275
Sovereign Grace Baptists 171
spelling 204

spiritual gifts 201
Switzerland 141
symbolism 87, 90, 94
syncretism 31
Syria 144, 175

T

tabernacle 90, 98
table of shewbread 90
Tarshish 95
Taylor, Hudson 29, 210
Tennessee Temple University 178
tent making 29
Terminalia 149
Tertullian 141
testimony 45, 85, 196, 207
Tetrarchy 149
Textus Receptus 56
Thayer 38, 100, 101
Theodosius 142
Theotokos 145
Thomas 140, 145
Tigris River 95
Timothy 28, 34, 40, 43, 60, 188, 195, 196, 197, 203, 205
title 145, 163, 199
Tozer, A.W. 193
Trajan 147
Tramontani 160
Tunisia 139
Turlepins 160

U

Uighurs 152

V

Valerian 148
veil 91
Vienne 140

W

Waldenses 157, 158, 160
Ward, William 167
Welsh Baptists 164
West Coast Baptist College 178
Westwood Missionary Baptist
    Church 192
World Baptist Fellowship 177,
    178

Y

Yemen 151
Yohannon, I.N. 175

Z

Zoroastrianism 156

The Baptist Missionary Handbook

and other Christian Education resources are available for order online at:

www.baptisttrainingcenter.org

BAPTIST TRAINING CENTER PUBLICATIONS
WINTER HAVEN, FLORIDA

Also available from Amazon.com
and other retail outlets

www.ingramcontent.com/pod-product-compliance
Lightning Source LLC
Chambersburg PA
CBHW071304110426
42743CB00042B/1164